George W. Carleton, Radical Freelance

The Philosophers of Foufouville

George W. Carleton, Radical Freelance

The Philosophers of Foufouville

ISBN/EAN: 9783337239169

Printed in Europe, USA, Canada, Australia, Japan

Cover: Foto ©Thomas Meinert / pixelio.de

More available books at **www.hansebooks.com**

THE

PHILOSOPHERS OF FOUFOUVILLE.

BY RADICAL FREELANCE, ESQ.

" La philosophie, dont on a quelquefois passé les bornes, les recherches de l'antiquité, l'esprit de discussion et de critique, ont été poussés si loin, qu' enfin plusieurs savans ont douté," etc. — VOLTAIRE.

NEW YORK:

G. W. CARLETON, PUBLISHER.

LONDON: S. LOW, SON, & CO.

MDCCCLXVIII.

CONTENTS.

THE

PHILOSOPHERS OF FOUFOUVILLE.

—◦o;◦{◦◦—

CHAPTER I.

*The Inauguration at Harmony Hall, with an Account
of the New Utopians.*

THE building now used for the celebrated Water-cure
Establishment at Foufouville, New Jersey, was built
for a very different purpose. It was erected by the
late learned Dr. Goodenough, in the latter years of his
life, in order to give a practical demonstration of those
theories of social reform that he had long inculcated in
his writings, and to which he now resolved to devote, not
only his time, but his fortune.

The doctor, with his habitually liberal views, in-
structed his architect, Palladio Styles, Esq., N. A. A.,
to design the building in such a manner that, by
simply extending the wings, it could be made to contain accommodation for one thousand inmates, — this
being as many as he thought it advisable to collect in
one institution at the beginning of his enterprise; but
he contemplated making ample preparations for the
great increase that he anticipated in the numbers of
the Harmonians (or New Utopians, as they were called
by the public); and on the square mile of land he had

7

purchased, selected the eleven most eligible sites, for the erection of the first eleven additional phalansteries that should follow the success of the one with which he initiated his grand scheme. Of course, more land would be required for agricultural purposes when the community should become so greatly increased; but he trusted, that in the meantime, the six hundred and forty acres already purchased would afford sufficient food for the members of the society during the first few months.

It was in the spring of the year 185– that the doctor removed to the new building at Foufouville, accompanied by his first five proselytes, or " disciples," as he was accustomed to call them.

Assembling them, on the day of their arrival, in the great music-hall (now used as the refectory of the Water-cure Establishment), he thus addressed them, —

" Beloved brothers and sisters : St. Augustin tells us that ' we are all seekers after happiness ; but that how to obtain it, is a question that has excited numerous and lively disputations among the learned.' We are about to solve this great problem. A new light has dawned upon mankind, — a light which, rising over Foufouville, is destined to shed its refulgence throughout the whole world. Foufouville is to be the Mecca of untold generations of Harmonians. We have this day inaugurated a new era, and henceforth, in our written communications to each other, will date from this memorable epoch, the first day of the first month of the first year of the Harmonian era.

" I regret that there are some among you who do not as yet fully concur in all my doctrines, but do not doubt that those who are still more or less affected by long contact with the gentiles, will in time be brought to recognize the value of the Harmonian philosophy, by the cogency of my arguments, and the triumphant demonstration that is about to be made of its practical utility; and it is a matter of congratulation that all are so far agreed as to have cheerfully subscribed to the rules of the establishment.

"I will enumerate the following, as being among the most important ones:

"Our food shall consist of fruits and vegetables, with such animal products as are not obtained by a sacrifice of life.

"The flesh of creatures into whom the Almighty has breathed the breath of life is strictly prohibited.

"My mind is not yet clear on the subject of eggs. It is known that some of them contain the vital principle, while some do not. We will reserve the determination of this delicate question for future discussion.

"Of the advantages of a vegetable diet, I am a living example, for, although not above the average height, I weigh nearly three hundred pounds.

"The deleterious juice of the grape is tabooed.

"Likewise that vile weed, tobacco.

"Also those highly injurious drugs, tea and coffee.

"Perfect equality shall exist between us.

"All property shall be in common; and we shall depend for our subsistence on the labor of our hands.

"In regard to the marriage state, while I am not absolutely opposed to it, I believe that it should not be entered into without long deliberation, and then solely for the purpose of carrying out that sublime, that holy instinct of our nature, to increase and multiply; and not, as I fear is too often the case, merely from a desire to gratify the whims of the flesh. For this reason, husbands and wives will be kept rigidly separated from each other, excepting at such times as the laws of physiology teach us may be favorable to the attainment of the great end in view.

" St. Augustin informs us that ' philosophers hold two different opinions in regard to those movements of the soul which the Greeks call, πάθη, the Latins, with Cicero, *perturbationes,* others, *affections,* or, as more in accordance with the Greek expression, *passions.* Some maintain that they exist even in the soul of the sage, but moderated, and under the control of reason, which imposes its laws upon them, and restrains them within proper bounds. Such was the opinion of the Platonicians and Peripatetics. Others, like the Stoics, held that the soul of the sage is unmoved by them.'

" This, beloved brothers and sisters, is the whole secret. You have merely to let your passions be subordinate to your reason. And here in Harmony Hall we will demonstrate to an admiring world how easily this desirable consummation is to be attained.

" In this calm retreat — like St. Simon Stygites on top of his pillar — we shall be secure from the raging passions and numberless temptations that beset less fortunate mortals. Separated from the outer world, from its lusts, its hatreds, its avarice, its contentions, we will tranquilly glide down the vale of years in perpetual harmony, peace, and good-will."

The doctor's peculiar views on the institution of marriage may be partially accounted for from the fact that his union with the late Mrs. Goodenough (Xantippe, daughter of Timothy Bangs, Esq., President of Salem

College) had been extremely infelicitous ; owing, it was
said, to the lady's hasty temper, and her entire want of
sympathy with the benevolent projects of her husband to
ameliorate the condition of mankind. The only living
issue of this union, a daughter named after her father's
favorite virtue, Charity, was sixteen years of age when
the doctor disposed of his property, much of it at a sacrifice, in order to give effect to his theories by the foundation of Harmony Hall, — for such was the name of the new
institution at Foufouville.

Miss Charity Goodenough, who, of course, accompanied
her father, gave a passive assent to his teachings, though
it may be doubted whether or not she fully comprehended
the purport of all of them.

But the doctor's most enthusiastic disciple, and his
right-hand man in the realization of his scheme, was Professor Nicholas Malpest. This gentleman was supposed
to be of foreign birth, but the fact was not certain, as he
was extremely reticent in regard to his origin. Little
was known of him, excepting that previous to his acquaintance with Dr. Goodenough, he had eked out a precarious
livelihood by delivering lectures on social reform in different parts of the country.

He was soon taken into the doctor's intimacy, on account of the singular accordance of their philanthropical
views, and had been of great assistance to the old gentleman — at least, so he said — in the management of his
affairs, particularly in the investment of his money ; for
the good doctor was totally unacquainted with business
(except as it was conducted among the Greeks and Romans), and it was Professor Malpest who had counselled,

and finally negotiated the purchase of the property at Foufouville.

He was at this time about forty-five years of age, tall and thin in person, with long, dark hair, dyed and artificially frizzled like that of a mulatto, and piercing black eyes, which squinted in a manner that would have given him an exceedingly sinister expression, had he not always worn spectacles to conceal the defect. It was also known that he had false teeth.

Miss Serena Minerva Griffin — a lady of an uncertain age, but which was certainly more than thirty — was another member of the society. She was an earnest and sincere admirer of the doctor, although she did not give an entire assent to all his doctrines. On the subject of marriage, in particular, she quite differed from him. Notwithstanding his own disagreeable experience, he ever maintained that that union should be permanent. " Whom God hath joined," he would say, " let no man put asunder."

" Dear, good man ! " Miss Minerva would rejoin. " He is so inexperienced. He does not know the fundamental difference between the sexes. Why should woman be bound for life to one whom she loathes ? Freedom, indeed ! Talk not to me of freedom while such slavery exists. Look at Nature ; behold the birds of the air and the beasts of the field ! Let us take Nature for our guide. She will not lead us astray."

The name of Miss Griffin had been long before the public, as an eloquent expounder of the rights and wrongs of her sex.

But the most prominent female member of the society was Mrs. Elizabeth Strongitharm. This lady was about forty-four years of age, hard in features and in disposition, and always dressed in what is known as the Bloomer costume. She was, in short, what might be denominated a strong-minded woman, and had been a leading oracle at the meetings of the Female Rights Association, over which she had occasionally presided.

She did not concur with the doctor in all his views, nor with Miss Griffin in anything, except in regard to the superiority of woman over man, and the long catalogue of wrongs to which he had subjected her. "Man," she would say, " by the false laws of a debased state of society is enabled to impose upon feeble woman ; but no man ever took advantage of me, nor ever shall."

The last of the doctor's five proselytes, whom it remains for us to describe, was Joseph Peewit, Esq. This gentleman had been taken in marriage by Mrs. Strongitharm some years before, notwithstanding he was much younger than she. They had not been united according to the forms of any religious denomination, but by the insertion of the following announcement in the newspapers : —

" Know all men and women by these presents, that I, Elizabeth Strongitharm, and Joseph Peewit, being free from the grovelling superstitions of this degenerate age, untrammelled by the impositions of hireling priests, and unterrified by the oppressive, unequal, and tyrannical laws of a sycophantic society, do hereby take each other for husband and wife, until death do us part, or until this copartnership shall be dissolved by mutual consent.
" ELIZABETH STRONGITHARM.
"J. PEEWIT."

She had not taken Mr. Peewit's name ; for, " Why,"
2

said she, "should woman sacrifice her name, rather than man his? Peewit may assume *my* name if he choose, but I take that of no man — not I."

Their union was unblessed with issue.

As absolute equality was one of the cardinal principles of the organization; there could be no such personage as a president, or presiding elder. "Nevertheless," said the doctor, who was still on the rostrum, "as I have lived longer in the world, and am more experienced in its ways than any of you, I trust, dear brethren, that you will be guided in a great measure by my advice in the settlement of the important questions that will arise in relation to the moral, intellectual, and social welfare of mankind in general, and of the society of Harmonians in particular."

Mrs. Strongitharm objected decidedly to be guided by the advice of any one, and especially of a man. She had always followed her own judgment, and always intended to do so. "It might, however, be well," she observed, "to form a sort of Council for the transaction of the daily business of the society. It should consist of about half a dozen members."

"A sort of committee of the whole," suggested Mr. Peewit.

"Sir?" said Mrs. Strongitharm, with a frown.

"Nothing," answered her — we were about to write "lord and master," but that would be a misnomer, as the pantaloons were both figuratively and literally worn by the lady.

"The suggestion of a Council meets my approbation," said Miss Griffin; "although it does emanate from Mrs. Strongitharm; and as there will doubtless be a greater number of females than males in the community, — women

in the present state of society being so much more progressive than men, — it is just that the voice of the former
should preponderate ; I would therefore recommend for
the rapid despatch of business, a Grand Council consisting
of twenty women and four men."

Professor Malpest rose and stated that he agreed with
the doctor, and he also agreed with the ladies. The doctor was the Nestor, the Mentor, the Moses of the society,
and he for one would ever listen to his counsels with the
most profound respect and veneration, as to the voice of
wisdom and virtue. Who (with the exception of himself) had sacrificed more for the furtherance of the great
work of human regeneration? Both were co-laborers in
the same humane field. The doctor had very properly
contributed the lucre he would no longer need ; while he
(carried away by his feelings of benevolence, and the admirable logic of the doctor) had not hesitated to sacrifice
the brilliant, though worldly career that was opening before him, in order to devote his time, his wealth (what
little he had), and he might add, his life itself, should it
become necessary, to this noble cause. The advice of the
ladies was also good, he would even say, most excellent,
and was a convincing proof of that penetration, that deep
insight, that intuitive reason, peculiar to the sex. He
would venture to observe, however, that just at present,
while their numbers were somewhat limited, the selection
of the persons to compose the Grand Council might perhaps be deferred for a few days without serious disadvan-
tage, as there were questions of more pressing necessity
that awaited decision. He therefore took the liberty of
reminding his assembled brothers and sisters that it was
growing late, and they had not yet chosen a cook.

This proposition of the professor seemed to dampen the spirits of the whole party, and was followed by a silence of several minutes.

The gentleman himself was the first to break it by stating that, as to himself, he had assumed (much against his will) the arduous duties connected with the financial department, and must therefore decline being a candidate for culinary honors; but he did not doubt that an adept would be found among some of the accomplished ladies present.

"Of course," said Mrs. Strongitharm, "since we have resolved that all the work shall be done by members of the society, in order to protect ourselves from contaminating contact with those who do not conform to our peculiar views, it is not only advisable, but necessary, to distribute amongst us impartially the various duties of the establishment. As I am unfortunately ignorant of the culinary art, I have decided to take the responsible office of housekeeper, and therefore propose that Miss Griffin undertake the more easy work of the kitchen."

"I shall do·no such thing," answered Miss Griffin. "It may, perhaps, be proper that the oldest female in the community should act as duenna to us younger ones. I do not object; and, as I feel myself peculiarly fitted for the position of secretary, it seems to me eminently just that the youngest lady should do the cooking."

"I will gladly do my part in the household labors," said Miss Goodenough; "but am really quite ignorant of kitchen work; still I will cheerfully try to cook, if some one will be so kind as to direct me."

After a protracted discussion, Miss Griffin consented to instruct Miss Goodenough until such time as she should be able to perform her work unaided.

The two ladies then descended to the kitchen, where with the assistance of Mr. Peewit a fire was started in the immense range. This was a complicated structure, built on the model of that in the hotel of the Metropolis, and contained all the appurtenances requisite for providing meals for upwards of five hundred persons.

Raw materials for the supper had already been provided by the forethought of Professor Malpest, who, in addition to the duties of treasurer, had hitherto performed those of general manager of the society. It had been observed that although everything he did was done by the advice of Dr. Goodenough, yet that this advice was invariably given in accordance with suggestions that had emanated from the professor himself. Flesh of course there was none; but there were flour, corn-meal, rice, macaroni, sugar, potatoes, beans of many kinds, — in short, a small grocery store complete. The ingredients were there but the question was how to put them together. Miss Griffin, who had undertaken to direct, was as ignorant as Miss Goodenough, who was the executive. Some information vouchsafed by the doctor in regard to the Grecian method of making a bread called μάδδα was of no assistance to them whatever. The result was that they concocted a number of pasty messes which were deposited, some in the oven, and some in a frying-pan; the former it being hoped would turn into bread, while the latter was an attempt at flapjacks. While the messes were baking and frying, Miss Goodenough thought it would be an excellent opportunity to put her room in order, — Miss Griffin having kindly offered to keep watch over the cooking, and see that all went right during her absence; but hardly had Miss Goodenough left the kitchen, when Miss Griffin was

2*

seized with an idea for her hitherto unpublished lecture
on the "Co-relation of the Sexes," and, in the inspiration
of the moment, bread and flapjacks were forgotten, as,
with paper and pencil in hand, the mental faculties of the
young lady became completely absorbed in making notes.
The consequence was, that when Mr. Peewit, who had
been dubbed waiter, came in with his tray, the flapjacks,
which had been frying for nearly an hour, presented an
appearance similar to that of the ancient parchments that
are dug up at Herculaneum, being burnt to cinders, while
the bread had a black crust an inch thick.   The milk now
boiled over, and Mr. Peewit, Miss Griffin, and Miss
Goodenough in making a simultaneous effort to seize the
skillet, upset it, spilling its contents to the last drop.   As
the butter, cheese, preserves, and other small delicacies
had not yet been received, the Harmonians were obliged
to content themselves with a frugal repast of burnt un-
leavened bread and water.

"We must expect trials and tribulations, my dear
friends, at the beginning of our enterprise," said Dr.
Goodenough.   "What great work was ever achieved without privations and sacrifices?   Let us be thankful to
Divine Providence that he has given us these crusts, with
this pure water, the wine of Nature."

Professor Malpost said "Amen;" but the expression of
his face did not indicate a feeling of thankfulness.

"When *I* undertake to do a thing, I *do* it," said Mrs.
Strongitharm.

"It was the fault of the milk," said Miss Griffin.   "If
that had not boiled over, I should not have overlooked the
bread; but since my incapacity for such low work is
manifest, I hereby decline any further responsibility."

As Miss Goodenough had burned her fingers in extricating the bread from the oven, and would consequently be unable to resume the work, there was but one resource, Mr. Peewit was installed cook for the following day. He ventured upon a few words of remonstrance, but was easily silenced by a look from Mrs. Strongitharm, and the words, " Sir, would you have *me* do it?"

After the simple, and—to all save Dr. Goodenough— unsatisfactory supper, the company assembled in the large reception room (now the packing apartment of the Water-cure Establishment).

" Papa," said Miss Goodenough, " this great unfurnished room is dismal."

" My child," answered the doctor, " nothing should appear dismal to us, now that we have entered on our glorious work. As to me, I am joyous, I am hilarious in anticipation of the future. It is true that at present, in consequence of the paucity of our numbers, the rooms have a deserted appearance ; but soon you will see pilgrims arriving from every land, and these vast halls will be filled with a peaceful, contented, and loving multitude, who will fly to this haven of refuge from the storms of the outer world."

" This is the new ark," said Professor Malpest, " and Dr. Goodenough is its Noah."

" And are we the beasts?" inquired Mr. Peewit.

The professor muttered something about " asses," but it was not distinctly heard.

" My friends," said the doctor, " since music, as Aristotle tells us in the eighth book of his treatise on Government, acts upon the soul as gymnastics do upon the body, and tends to lull the evil passions of our nature, let us pass the remaining hours of the evening with vocal and instrumental harmony. We will adjourn to the music hall where brother Nicholas has already placed the instruments. Charity will play on the harp, while Miss Griffin, — Sister Minerva, — like a new Cecilia, transports our souls to heaven on the melodeon."

" I will play the jews-harp," said Mr. Peewit.

" No, sir," answered Mrs. Strongitharm, sharply ; " you will take your flageolet, on which you have already had same practice, and accompany me on the trombone."

" We will all bear our part," said the doctor. " Brother Nicholas we know is accomplished with his fiddle, and as, in my wild and thoughtless youth, while still dazzled by the tinsel and glitter of mundane shows, I acted as drummer-boy to the 777th Reg. N. Y. S. M., — being perhaps an inspiration of Providence to prepare me for present usefulness, — I will play the kettle-drum."

The amateur musicians placed themselves before their respective instruments ; but we will not attempt to describe the performance. Miss Charity, indeed, played well on the harp, while the professor and Miss Minerva were not unskilled on the violin and melodeon ; but there was no one to mark the time, it being considered contrary to the principles of the society for any one to be a leader in anything. Hence discord dire and unexampled was the result. In the midst of the softest strains of the harp and melodeon, the flageolet would give a squeak, or the trombone resound through the vacant halls with a boom like the last trump, while the doctor without cessation pounded vigorously on his kettle-drum. The good old gentleman was insensible to the dreadful discord. He saw in his mind's eye the hall thronged with a happy band of rejoicing and regenerated Harmonians, and, in fancy, heard their thousand voices raised in a chorus of praise and thanksgiving.

Jack, the pet poodle of Mrs. Strongitharm, and, according to the whispers of the malicious, the chief object of her affections (for women, even the strong-minded, must have somebody or something to love), was frightened almost into fits by the direful clamor and cowered for safety beside his mistress; but a blast of the trombone drove him thence, and he fled with his tail between his legs, and trembling with terror, into the farthest corner of the room.

A ring was heard at the door-bell, and the dog set up a loud barking.

"Peewit," said Mrs. Strongitharm, pointing to the door, which her obedient husband proceeded to open, hitting the dog a rap over the head with his flageolet as he passed. The beast howled.

"Wretch!" screamed Mrs. Strongitharm, springing forward and snatching up the poodle in her arms.

The howl and the scream so startled the musicians that, with the exception of the doctor, they all stopped playing; the professor giving a sigh of relief as he laid down his bow. As to the doctor he kept on beating his drum, heedless of the interruption, and in fact quite unconscious that he was playing solo. He perceived his error just as Mr. Peewit re-entered the room accompanied by a well-dressed young gentleman about twenty-four years of age, with a carpet-bag in one hand and a flute in the other.

"Leander Lovell!" exclaimed the doctor, jumping up, knocking over the kettle-drum, which rolled in a great circle around the room, and giving the visitor a vigorous shake of the hand. "So you, too, have become converted. This is really encouraging."

"I have come, sir," answered Mr. Lovell, "in the hope of being received into the Society of New Utopians, — I beg pardon, — I mean Harmonians."

All eyes were directed towards the new-comer; those of Professor Malpest with an indescribable expression, but which certainly was not one of pleasure. Miss Goodenough colored visibly.

"This is truly a triumph for the cause," said the doctor, turning towards the company, and holding Lovell by the hand. "Only a week ago my young friend was still devoted to worldly pursuits, and my most convincing arguments seemed lost upon him. He and brother Nicholas had a dispute in my presence, — I may even say, an acrimonious dispute, — about the utility and practicability of our enterprise. But, behold! he is here. Such is the power of reason. Did I not tell you it would be so? Soon you will see them come streaming in by hundreds and by thousands. We must set about building a new phalanstery at once. Brethren, welcome our new brother."

The initiatory ceremonies of Mr. Lovell's reception into the society consisted of a bow from Professor Malpest, a nod and a grin from Mr. Peewit, a stiff courtesy from Mrs. Strongitharm, a courtesy and a simper from Miss Griffin, a furtive glance and a slight pressure of the hand from Miss Goodenough.

"Brother Joseph," said the doctor to Mr. Peewit, "Leander would doubtless like to partake of some refreshment after his journey."

" Let me give no trouble," answered Lovell ; " a bit of cold meat will suffice, with a cigar afterwards."

" Meat ! Tobacco ! " exclaimed the doctor.

"Ah ! excuse me, I forgot," answered Lovell.

Mr. Peewit went out to cut some bread, there being nothing else, accompanied by Mrs. Strongitharm, as if to show him how to do it.

Miss Griffin left the apartment to prepare Mr. Lovell's room for him.

" This is a glorious beginning," said the doctor, catch- ·ing Professor Malpest by the button-hole ; " I feel posi- tively hilarious."

" It is the happiest day of my life," answered the pro- fessor, with a scowl as he observed Lovell conversing in an undertone with Miss Goodenough, who was still seated by her harp.

"Leander, this is a delightful surprise," said she ; " are you in earnest in joining us? "

" I shall remain as long as you do, Cherry," said he. " When I called on your father a week ago, intending to ask his consent to our marriage, Professor Malpest unfor- tunately happened to be with him."

" The odious man ! " said Miss Charity.

" And as if the fellow divined the object of my com- ing," continued Lovell, " he immediately drew me into a discussion about this Quixotic scheme of your father's, and, as I abhor dissimulation, I expressed my opinion in rather stronger language than was becoming or prudent. Fool that I was, not to perceive that in ridiculing the New Utopians I was injuring my own prospects. Your father became exceedingly indignant, and almost ordered me out of the house. Malpest smiled, and I saw, when

too late, that he had outwitted me ; but when I heard that
you had actually removed to Harmony Hall, I determined
on a *coup de guerre*, and have come here with the deliberate intention of acting the hypocrite."

"How good of you, Lenny!" said Miss Charity.

"I fancy our new brother's supper must be ready," said
Professor Malpost, taking advantage of a pause in the
doctor's self-congratulations. "He will not find it quite
equal to those to which he has been accustomed in the
metropolis ; but then, of course, he has not come amongst
us in search of pleasure."

"Of course," retorted Lovell, in a tone that was intended to be significantly sarcastic; "no one could be
base enough to join in Dr. Goodenough's philanthropical
projects from interested motives."

Mr. Peewit now looked in and nodded his head.

"Your bread and water await you, sir, in the banquet
hall," said the professor.

"A crust of bread, sir," answered Lovell, with a lofty
air, " will taste better to me here than fried oysters elsewhere."

"Ha!" cried the doctor, slapping him on the back,
"you are a true Harmonian. Does not Marcus Aurelius
tell us that to be happy we have only to regard with
indifference that which is of itself indifferent? And do
we not all know that the pleasures of this world are of
little account?"

The evening concluded with a simple prayer by Dr.
Goodenough. He thanked his Creator for his numberless
blessings, and invoked his aid in the prosecution of the
great work so auspiciously commenced that day.

Professor Malpost responded with a loud "Amen."

When the parties separated for the night, Peewit, from sheer force of habit, was about to follow his wife, but she almost petrified him with an indignant look and the words, "Sir, you forget where you are. Your apartment is at the other end of the house."

3

CHAPTER II.

*In which Matters and Things at Harmony Hall are ar-
ranged to the Satisfaction of Everybody.*

It was Dr. Goodenough's intention to so regulate the
internal economy of his household that the community
should be entirely self-supporting, and the phalanstery
contain within its bounds all that could be needed for the
corporeal or spiritual wants of its inhabitants, so that
they might dwell perpetually in a world of their own, free
from the contaminating influence of those whose ways
were not their ways. In pursuance of this plan it was
intended that all the work should be done by the Harmonians themselves, and a division of labor was agreed
upon, by which the gentlemen were to attend to the out-
of-doors work, while the ladies took charge of the household duties. This arrangement was not only assented to,
but was actually recommended, by the ladies themselves,
notwithstanding it was the method that prevailed outside
of the precincts of Harmony Hall, and notwithstanding
Mrs. Strongitharm's oft-repeated assertion, that " woman
was capable of doing whatever man could do." But the
first day's experience of this system demonstrated the
impossibility of carrying it out to the letter until some
more useful proselytes should arrive.

The brothers and sisters had assembled in the banquet
hall for breakfast, the set hour for which had long passed,
when a loud cry for aid was heard from the kitchen. Mr.

Peewit, the cook, had rashly undertaken to provide boiled rice for the morning meal, and had accordingly filled a large pot with the cereal, and then poured in water up to the brim. As the mixture became warm the rice began to swell, and Peewit to skim it off. But, as the mess grew hotter and hotter, the rice swelled faster and faster; and by the time the water boiled, the bewildered Peewit, who had filled every plate, dish, and other utensil at hand with rice, and beheld it still rising over the pot, and dropping and hissing on the hot stove, as lava pours from Vesuvius, became apprehensive that the stuff was bewitched, and yelled for assistance. The ludicrous sight that met the eyes of the company, when they rushed into the kitchen, convinced them that Peewit had not yet found his vocation.

The attempt of the Harmonians to carry on the agricultural operations of the phalanstery, by their own unaided labor, began as unsuccessfully as their abortive experiments in cooking. As it was quite time to commence ploughing, the implement was got ready (for the foresight of Professor Malpest had provided for everything), and the doctor marshalled his forces for the work. As none of the gentlemen had any practical knowledge of the use of the plough, Mr. Lovell proposed that Mrs. Strongitharm should turn a few furrows, as women were so much superior to men; but the lady indignantly rejected the proposition, and, giving Lovell a withering glance, delegated the duty to Peewit, saying, " We are both one."

Mr. Peewit accordingly grasped the reins in one hand, and the handle of the plough in the other, and rather hesitatingly ordered the horse to " get up." The docile animal obeyed the figurative order, but, in starting, jerked

the reins out of Peewit's hands. The gentleman ran for
ward to catch them, and, in doing so, inadvertently put
his foot in front of the plough, the consequence being that
a furrow was made in his flesh instead of in the ground,
which made him feelingly aware that though flesh and
dust may be chemically and theologically similar, there
is, nevertheless, some occult difference between them. A
stone that fortunately stood in the way of the share partly
protected the foot, so that the injury was slight, but it
obliged Peewit (not much against his will) to give up
work for the rest of the day.

Lovell now took the reins, but, never having ploughed
through anything harder or deeper than the mud in the
streets of New York, his efforts to turn the sod were
quite unsuccessful.

Peewit and Lovell having failed, the doctor tried his
hand. He made a pretty good start, and looked around
with a somewhat triumphant expression at his crestfallen
competitors, but the plough catching in a root, the old gentleman was thrown violently on the ground, where he sat
gazing in bewildered amazement as the horse trotted off
by himself.

Professor Malpest now undertook the work; but he
made a furrow only about two and a half inches deep,
which was pronounced by all present, and by none more
loudly than himself, to be a lamentable failure.

The necessity of extraneous aid was now apparent,
even the doctor acknowledging the fact, though with a
heavy heart; so the professor posted to the city, where
he engaged the services of a red-haired Irish woman,
named Bridget O'Brien, as cook, and of Mary Short, a
neat, tidy girl, as chambermaid and waitress, while a

Welchman, one John Long, was hired as gardener, or rather man-of-all-work.

Our limited time and space will not permit us to give a detailed account of the daily doings at Harmony Hall, nor perhaps are the events themselves of sufficient interest to the public to warrant our doing so, nor is it necessary to our purpose that we should state more than a few of the most important occurrences that took place, leaving in oblivion those trivial incidents on which an inferior writer would expatiate; our object in this narrative being simply to present to the reader a succinct and impartial account of the causes of the decline and fall of the Society of Harmonians (popularly known as the New Utopians), and the consequent unfortunate failure of Dr. Goodenough's philanthropical projects for the amelioration of the condition of mankind, — projects that have been much misrepresented by a prejudiced and conservative press, which, not content with occasional abuse, has actually been known to ridicule them, and even to speak of the doctor himself with levity; but such was ever the fate of those who were in advance of their age, and have sought to benefit their ungrateful species. Socrates and Joe Smith are familiar examples.

John Long, fortunately for the community, proved to be a faithful and efficient man, and at once began ploughing and planting in earnest. He grumbled a good deal at first at the necessity of a vegetable diet, declaring that he could not work without meat, and would have to leave unless it was provided for him. It was in vain that the doctor argued with him for more than an hour, quoting freely from Galen and Hippocrates, and holding up the example of the Pythagoreans; the Welshman was obdu-

3*

rate. But where the doctor had not succeeded the professor prevailed, and, after a five minutes' discussion, so completely satisfied Long with his lot, that he cheerfully consented to remain.

The professor could not be induced to reveal the arguments by which he had wrought so sudden a conversion.

"The modesty of Brother Nicholas is equal to his merit," said the doctor.

It was not until the final breaking up at Harmony Hall that Bridget, the cook, divulged the secret, that the professor, in consideration of the fact that Long was not an actual member of the society, allowed him a weekly ration of one rump of beef, and stewed kidneys *ad libitum*, all of which was cooked surreptitiously at night.

The domestics being installed, everybody appeared to be contented. The doctor withdrew into his study, where, surrounded by a pile of huge volumes, he busied himself in preparing (against the advice of his publisher) a new edition of his three immortal works, " The New Utopia," " The Regeneration of Man," and " Physiological Studies on the Development of Healthy Offspring." He kept up a voluminous correspondence with reformers and enthusiasts, male and female, in different parts of the world, and also devoted much time to the consideration of various plans, projects, and designs connected with the carrying out of his benevolent scheme (none of which, unhappily, were realized). From time to time he would emerge from his seclusion, in order to see what was going on, and to give advice to everybody.

" Should the sexes be evenly divided," he said, one day, " there will be five hundred brothers and as many sisters in each phalanstery. Four hundred and twenty-five of

the men will be obliged to devote themselves to agriculture, so as to provide subsistence for themselves and the
rest of the community ; fifty of them will be engaged in
manufacturing the clothing and numberless miscellaneous
articles needed, while the bakers, carpenters, blacksmiths,
etc., will comprise the rest ; but what to do with all the
women I cannot determine. This is a problem that has
caused me much anxious thought and serious disquietude."

Miss Griffin suggested that they be married to the five
hundred men.

Mr. Peewit said they would have enough to do as
nurses to all the children ; whereupon Mrs. Strongitharm
requested him to be so good as to keep his advice to
himself until it was asked. *She* could keep the women at
work.

Miss Goodenough and Mr. Lovell declined to express
an opinion, as they had not thought of the matter at all.

Professor Malpest said that he had considered this embarrassing subject profoundly ; and, after long meditation
upon it, had come to the conclusion that it would perhaps
be advisable to wait until the parties had actually arrived,
before endeavoring to decide it.

The professor, as financier and general manager, was
the most busy man in the establishment, with the exception of the doctor. Mr. Lovell offered his services as
book-keeper, but with singular self-abnegation the professor declined them, saying, "he could find time, between
the intervals of his other labors, to keep the accounts
himself."

The doctor, however, occasionally had work for Lovell
in the office.

Mrs. Strongitharm was an exacting, if not tyrannical and overbearing house-keeper.

Miss Griffin continued making notes on "the co-relation of the sexes."

Miss Goodenough passed her time in worsted work and embroidery.

As to Messrs. Lovell and Peewit, they undertook to assist John Long on the farm, — he to do the ploughing, the harrowing, the digging, the heavy work in short; while they did the hoeing, planting, trimming, etc.; but, although he kept a sharp eye on them, they made so many mistakes, planting the peas in hills, sowing the melon-seed and corn broadcast, pulling up his early spring radishes, which they mistook for weeds, and committing such other enormities, that he finally begged them, as a favor, to bestow their services on some one else.

"Vegetables," said Miss Griffin, "are merely coarse food for the body; but flowers, beautiful flowers, speak the voice of nature to the mind, and feed the soul with inspiration."

"Oh, how I doat on flowers!" said Miss Charity.

So the two gentlemen — to the relief of Long — set themselves to work to lay out a garden in rear of the building. The ground plan was not unlike that of a church; for there was a broad walk down the middle, and one on each side, like the three aisles, while at the lower end, a grove of trees, between which they constructed some rustic seats, would do for the chancel.

Mr. Peewit proposed to put a fountain in the centre; but the water supply proved an insuperable difficulty. Lovell thought it might be accomplished by the aid of a ram; but as Peewit did not think a ram could be equal to a single horse-power, and the horse was needed in the field operations, the project was abandoned.

Thus, for a week or two, everything went on serenely at Harmony Hall. Compared with the New Utopians, the Happy Family at the museum was merely a collection of discontented prisoners. But this felicity was apparent rather than real. Clouds were gathering, as will be narrated in the next chapter.

CHAPTER III.

Symptoms of Discord appear in Harmony Hall.

ONE afternoon Miss Griffin, pencil and tablets in hand as usual, seated herself under the trees at the end of the garden, as if with literary intentions. Miss Goodenough was planting some rosebushes, while Messrs. Lovell and Peewit were exceedingly busy sowing seeds along the borders near the side walls. And we will mention here that when the young plants came up a week or so afterwards, the two ladies were quite surprised to find that they formed the words, " Charity," and " Minerva," apparently written on the earth in the softest green. Mr. Peewit said that the latter was a token of gratitude for the bread poultice with which Miss Griffin had dressed his injured foot; for this young lady, having attended some lectures at the Female Medical College, had constituted herself the physician and surgeon of Harmony Hall. The secretaryship had been appropriated by Professor Malpest.

She was soon joined by Miss Goodenough, who sat down by her side to rest a while, as she said, although the true reason was that she had been annoyed by the professor staring at her from his office window.

" My dear," said Miss Griffin, — for such was the affectionate epithet with which she usually addressed Miss Goodenough, — " my dear, have you not observed something peculiar of late in the manner of Professor Malpest towards a certain lady in this establishment?"

Now here it may be well to observe that the professor was always obsequiously polite to the sex in general without regard to age or beauty; and this extreme courtesy being something to which Miss Griffin was not accustomed, she had taken it in the vanity of her heart, as a tribute of admiration to herself. We will furthermore state that Miss Goodenough had noticed that while the gentleman was polite to all, he was particularly deferential and attentive to her. In the music hall the violin ⁀and harp were placed side by side, while the flute was posted on the opposite side of the orchestra. Whenever she and Mr. Lovell commenced working in the garden together, the professor was almost certain to make his appearance, and bore them with a dissertation on horticulture, or some other subject, apparently forgetful of the old adage that three spoil company. If they persisted in continuing their work together, he would leave them after a while, but his exit was invariably followed by a message from her father asking her to come and recite her Greek .lesson, or to practise some new piece on the harp, which not unfrequently was a duet with the violin.

All this Miss Charity had remarked, and she therefore naturally supposed that Miss Griffin's question had reference to herself. And were we writing a romance, and were she our heroine, it would be our duty to make her answer in the affirmative; but, as we are merely giving a faithful and impartial account of some of the events that took place at Harmony Hall, we feel constrained to acknowledge that, with a most reprehensible disregard for strict veracity, she replied that she had not observed anything peculiar in the professor's manner towards anybody. Why she answered thus, we do not know. Being of the male sex, we cannot pretend to fathom the motives of woman. Could it have been an affectation of modesty, or that love of dissimulation which is said to be inborn in the sex? Truly, as Miss Griffin asserted, there is a fundamental difference between the sexes. Were one man to insinuate to another that he had made a favorable impression on a lady's heart, how few would deny the soft impeachment!

Miss Griffin seemed somewhat taken aback at Miss Goodenough's answer, and replied, —

"Then all I have to say is, that some folks can't see with their eyes open."

"Listen to me, Minerva Griffin," said Miss Charity; "that odious man may, or may not be serious in his attentions to me, but of this you can rest assured, I never, never will have him."

"Why, my dear, foolish child," cried the elder lady, "do you suppose he is thinking of *you!* A man of his years and attainments wants a woman of corresponding qualifications."

"Then all I have to say is, that I hope he may get what he deserves," answered Miss Charity, with perhaps a slight touch of malice.

"And what does he not deserve," replied Miss Griffin, enthusiastically; "a man of such elevated sentiments, so accomplished, so delicate, is worthy of any woman's esteem. But how true is the old saying, that only mind can appreciate mind! You are as yet too young and thoughtless, my dear, to comprehend that sweet inter-

communion of soul with soul, that *je ne sais quoi*, that —
Why, look! here he comes through the garden."

"Then I shall escape this way," said Miss Charity;
and, suiting the action to the word, she hastily passed out
of the grove, and directed her steps to the melon-patch
where Mr. Lovell was trying to remedy his error of having sown the seeds broadcast.

The elder lady took up her pencil and tablets and began writing. She at once became so absorbed in her
occupation that she seemed quite startled and looked up
with an air of surprise when Professor Malpost stood before her a moment afterwards. He appeared somewhat
flustered at finding himself in the presence of Miss
Griffin, who observed the change in his countenance, and
assumed a responsive appearance of embarrassment.

"Pardon me, madam," stammered the gentleman, "I
was not aware that you were here — that is to say —
alone. I will not interrupt your meditations; I will
withdraw."

"It is no interruption I assure you," cried the lady,
as the professor was backing out. "I was merely jotting
down a few ideas according to the inspiration of the
moment. Woman's equality with man will one day be
recognized."

"She is superior, madam, superior," answered the
professor, with a bow.

"That is too much to claim for all women," said Miss
Griffin.

"But some are," replied the gentleman, looking significantly at the lady, who modestly cast down her eyes,
not knowing that he would have said and done the same
thing had any other of the sex been in her place.

4

"Woman was not created to exist alone," said the lady, after a pause.

"Nor man either," answered the professor.

"I believe," said Miss Minerva, "it was a Greek philosopher who gave utterance to that beautiful idea of the duality of the soul,— that each man and woman possesses but the half of one, and hence each is constantly seeking its mate."

"I am afraid," said the professor, "that the right halves don't often come together."

"Alas! it is too true," replied the lady; "and the reason is because, in obedience to the requirements of puritanical laws, —

> " 'Woman still must veil the shrine
> Where feeling hides Love's fire divine.'

But I scorn to be shackled by public opinion; I am above the petty prejudices of the age. Nature is my guide. Do you not agree with me that society requires a radical change?"

"Oh, yes, madam,— certainly," answered the professor, somewhat abstractedly, as he caught sight of two figures in the distant melon-patch.

"I knew that your sentiments accorded with mine," said Miss Minerva; "such is the power of sympathy. And may I ask if you have never experienced that yearning of the soul, that longing of the heart for one congenial spirit to minister to your happiness?"

"Well, madam," answered the gentleman, "since you put the question to me directly, I will confess that I have sometimes thought it might be advisable for me to get a wife."

"One," said Miss Minerva, "of an affectionate, confiding, artless disposition, whose intellectual and physical powers are in full bloom."

"All that is desirable, of course," said Professor Malpest.

"I have already divined your thoughts," said the lady, laying her hand on the professor's arm. He started slightly as he fixed his keen black eyes upon her. "You have been seen watching her as she moved about; and I have noticed the almost imperceptible confusion in your manner when addressing her; your apparent endeavor to avoid her at times when she has sought to converse with you, as if you feared the effect of the interview. And now, sir, know that the lady has not been insensible to your attentions; know that your feelings are reciprocated."

"Are you sure of what you say?" said the professor, with unfeigned surprise.

"I ought to be sure of it," answered Miss Griffin, "for no one knows her heart better than I do."

"True," muttered the professor to himself, "they have been much together of late; and then these women can't keep anything to themselves."

"And has not the passional attraction of Nature already whispered it to you?" continued Miss Minerva, casting down her eyes.

"Can't say it has," replied the gentleman; "in fact, she has always acted as if her preference — was rather — given to another; and I was induced to think that such was the case."

"How easily you men are deceived!" said Miss Griffin.

" You have not that intuitive perception of motives possessed by us."

" I must confess," answered Professor Malpest, " I did not suppose that any one had penetrated my design."

" Now that you are discovered,", said the lady, archly, " I presume you will not hesitate to speak openly."

" I do not think it best to be precipitate," answered the gentleman, " because I fear Dr. Goodenough might not be willing to consent as yet on account of her age."

Miss Griffin was completely thunderstruck (metaphorically) by this observation of the professor's, and not knowing exactly how to take it, but feeling considerably nettled, she replied, in a somewhat indignant tone, as follows, —

" I know not, sir, why Dr. Goodenough need be consulted. Were the lady as old as yourself, it might be inferred that you coincided in his peculiar views, as to the object of matrimony."

" I should not trouble myself about his cranks, if I once possessed her," said Malpest ; " but before marrying her there are certain preliminary financial arrangements that I wish to make."

" Men are ever calculating and worldly," replied Miss Griffin ; " even love cannot make them lose sight of their dollars and cents. How different is woman ! — the creature of impulse. But I shall say no more, sir. Perhaps I have erred in saying so much ; but woman was ever artless and open. Speak to the doctor, if you think it necessary." And with a half angry, half reproachful glance at the professor, the still irate maiden stalked majestically out of the grove, and passed through the garden into the house.

"What the devil can be the matter with the woman?" said Professor Malpest to himself. "Because she fancies Charity has a *penchant* for me (it is not impossible that the girl has been imposing upon her for some ulterior object), she gets into a huff because I propose asking the consent of the child's father. Queer creatures—women! I did not think the fruit was ripe; but there may possibly be some truth in what she says, after all; and, if not, why what the girl fancies, or don't fancy, is of little consequence. Delays are dangerous. I will hesitate no longer." And so soliloquizing, the professor directed his steps towards the little room that the doctor called his study.

Now it so happened that there was a stove-pipe hole through the ceiling of the doctor's study into the room above it, on the second story, which was used by Miss Griffin as a dressing-room. The lady was walking up and down the floor, really somewhat agitated after her interview with the professor, but in her own mind greatly exaggerating what in her journal she calls "those sufferings caused by conflicting emotions in a sensitive bosom, which almost overpowered me," when she distinctly heard the voice of the professor, in conversation with the doctor, in the room below. The conflicting emotions would seem about this time to have been too much for Miss Griffin, for she sank down upon the floor directly alongside of the stove-pipe hole, thus unavoidably overhearing the conversation between the two gentlemen. It is said that listeners never hear any good of themselves, and Miss Griffin was destined to be no exception to the rule.

"The propagation of our species," said Professor Malpest, "is one of the primal laws of our being, and mar-

4*

riage is the means whereby we are enabled to carry out
that law. My conscience tells me that I have been dere-
lict to my duty, in having so long delayed the fulfilment
of that sacred obligation."

"My dear brother," answered the doctor, "to those
who, like myself, have once complied with the divine
injunction, and been released from their bonds by the
severance of these mortal ties, I should not advise a repe-
tition; but with those who, like yourself, have never
entered into the connubial state, I regard the intention
of doing so as eminently wise and meritorious. May I
ask if you have selected any one for the purpose of joining
you in the accomplishment of your desires?"

"I have thought of no one as yet," answered the professor. ("What dissimulation!" said Miss Minerva to
herself; "but such is man.") "My strong sense of duty,
however, will not allow me to delay longer, and I have
come to you to ask counsel of your wisdom and experience in the choice of a suitable partner for the work."

"It appears to me," said the doctor, after meditating
for some time, "that sister Minerva possesses the requisite qualifications."   .

The professor made an exceedingly wry face, which,
however, was not perceived by the lady who sat smiling
and blushing by the stove-pipe hole.

"Miss Griffin is doubtless an estimable person," answered the professor; "but surely, sir, you would not
have this solemn engagement entered into where no affection existed between the parties?"

("No affection!" murmured Miss Minerva. "What
can the man mean?")

"Affection," replied the doctor, "is not absolutely

essential to the successful fulfilment of the divine command, to increase and multiply. Mutual respect, of course, there should be ; but more than this, my dear brother, leads to the seeking of mere carnal gratification, in which the great end to be obtained is lost sight of."

"It is certain," said the professor, "that there would be no danger of any gratification of the senses with Miss Griffin." ("Oh, the slanderous wretch!" muttered the incensed young woman.) "But I fear it would be difficult to have the requisite respect for a lady who wears false hair."

("The monster!" exclaimed Miss Griffin, "to speak thus of my water-fall! To traduce a virtuous woman behind her back! But I'll be revenged for this.")

"I respect your scruples," said the doctor, "but know of no other to recommend until our numbers are increased by the thousands now doubtless on the way to join us."

There was a long pause, and then Professor Malpest tried a change of base.

"We must be careful that no black sheep find their way into the fold," said he ; "in truth, I am fearful that there are some such here now ; persons who have joined our society from worldly motives."

"I am astonished," said the doctor. "Can such a· thing be possible? Whom do you suspect?"

"Youth is the age of frivolity and unruly passions," answered the professor. "It is only with the calmness of mature years that a man can properly comprehend, and truly live up to, the sublime doctrines of the New Utopia. The entry of a young man amongst us looks suspicious. We should be on our guard against all such."

"There are none with us at present," replied the doctor, "excepting the son of my deceased friend, Lovell. He long seemed insensible to the irrefutable logic of my arguments; but reason finally prevailed, and I regard his conversion as one of the most remarkable triumphs of my life."

"Such sudden conversions are not to be relied on."

"Brother," said the doctor, "I fear that your long intercourse with the world has rendered you too mistrustful. What possible inducement of a worldly nature could that youth have for joining us?"

"Perhaps, sir, sister Charity could give you some information on that point."

"Charity is a mere child. What do you mean?"

"Parents," answered the professor, "are very apt to regard children as children, until they are such no longer. Miss Charity is young, it is true, but still she is verging on that age — that age — when the feelings of the girl are deepened into the passions of the woman."

"Really, brother Nicholas, you alarm me," said the doctor. "If this is unfortunately true, what is best to be done?"

"I would advise," said the professor, "that she be united to one who, through the holy ceremony of marriage, can enable her chastely to fulfil her woman's mission, — to one whose stormy youth is over, and who adds to the calmness of middle age a profound veneration for yourself and the noble precepts you have inculcated."

(No more of this conversation, we regret to say, has come down to us.)

"A light breaks in upon me," exclaimed Miss Minerva. "Oh, how that villain has deceived me!"

"Who has been deceiving you?" said Mrs. Strongitharm,

entering the room. "You ought to be ashamed of yourself, to let a man take advantage of you. I've no patience with people who can't protect themselves. No man ever yet got the upper hand of *me.*"

"Nor ever tried to, I presume," answered Miss Griffin, who had no love for the house-keeper, notwithstanding she was a masculine personage.

"You are an ungrateful, weak-spirited hussy," replied Mrs. Strongitharm, "and I shall have no more to say to you."

"I can survive the loss, madam," answered Miss Griffin.

"A pretty scandal you are bringing on the community," said Mrs. Strongitharm. "And who is your paramour, pray? Is it the young man, Lovell? If so, I shall have you both discharged."

"Leave my apartment, madam," cried Miss Griffin, vehemently.

"I am the superior of this establishment," replied the house-keeper, haughtily, "and go when and where I will."

"I recognize no superior, here or elsewhere."

"Minx!"

"Minx! Do you presume to call me 'minx,' — vile man-woman."

"Saucy jade! you shall suffer for this impertinence," said Mrs. Strongitharm, leaving the room and slamming the door as a parting shot.

The tiff with the other lady had kept up Miss Griffin's spirits, but now that she found herself alone, the discomfited young woman felt the full force of the shock which both her pride and her feelings had received through the stove-pipe hole, and, throwing herself on the sofa, she wept with rage and mortification.

She heard a slight tap on the door, and in response to her summons to enter, Peewit, who was still lame, hopped in hesitatingly, and looking furtively behind him. In one hand he had a hot bread poultice, and in the other a bouquet, consisting of a great red dahlia surrounded by buttercups, dandelions, johnny-jumpers, and piny flowers.

"You don't look well, miss," said the gentleman. "Has Mrs. Strongitharm made you sick? Is there anything I can do for you?"

"You are a good kind soul, Peewit," answered the lady, "and I am grateful for the sympathy expressed in your face; but a woman's deep nature is beyond your ken. Accept my thanks for these beautiful children of the wildwood. Such delicate attentions speak to the heart. How's your foot?"

"Ah! Miss Minerva; how I wish Mrs. Strongitharm was like you. *She* don't make tender inquiries about my hurt. She only calls me an awkward booby, and says I got just what I deserved. It is getting well; thanks to you."

Peewit putting his foot on a chair, Miss Griffin skilfully undid the bandages, and dressed it with the poultice.

In the mean while, Lovell, getting tired of unearthing the scattered melon-seeds, — a work that seemed interminable, for every morning he would find a dozen young sprouts where he had pulled up one the day before, — left the patch, and walked hand in hand with Charity to the grove, in order to rest a while after his labor.

"I will go to your father this very day," said he, "and ask his consent to our immediate marriage."

" Oh, how happy we will be ! " said she.

" In our own cottage," said he.

" I am afraid, Lenny, that my father will not consent to my going away from him, and I should really regret to leave him."

" I hope," answered Lovell, " that he will in time see the impracticability of his present scheme, and the folly of sacrificing his own interests and yours for the sake of those who have no claim upon him, and some of whom are perhaps taking advantage of his kindness of heart for their own selfish ends ; but do you suppose that, when you are my wife, I could abide by the absurd rules of this establishment? You know that husbands and wives are not allowed to — are kept apart, except " —

Cherry put her hand over her lover's mouth. He pressed it to his lips, and, holding it in his, they held a long and earnest conversation, the purport of which we have been unable to discover.

Their tender colloquy was interrupted by the approach of Professor Malpost, whom they saw coming through the garden. When that gentleman reached the grove, he found Miss Charity quietly engaged in embroidering the initials L. L. in the corner of a cambric handkerchief, while Mr. Lovell was exceedingly busy trimming the trees.

" Miss Goodenough," said the professor, " I regret to disturb you when engaged in such agreeable occupation ; but your father has desired me to bid you go to him immediately as he wishes to speak to you."

Charity rose and went towards the house. The professor started to accompany her, when Lovell called him back to ask his opinion as to the best way of trimming the trees. Malpest, who understood the object of this questioning, advised him to lop them off an inch above the ground; adding that it would indirectly benefit the melon-patch.

" *Brother* Nicholas is facetious," said Lovell.

" It is better to be merry than sad," said Malpest, " and I feel happy to see brother Leander exerting his talents to such good purpose."

" I am glad you appreciate my efforts, sir," answered Lovell, " and doubt not that you will congratulate me when you hear that they have met with their reward."

" I presume my young friend has heard of the individual who counted his chickens before the eggs were hatched ? "

" Yes, sir ; and also of the fox that was caught in his own trap."

The two gentlemen continued to bandy words together for some time ; the dialogue being politely sarcastic on the part of the professor, and cuttingly ironical (or at least he thought so), on the part of Lovell. Both were becoming animated, if not heated, by the verbal skirmish, when it was interrupted by the arrival of Mrs. Strongitharm, who came into the garden, and beckoned to the professor in a mysterious manner to come to her, casting at the same time sinister glances at Lovell.

This gentleman went on with his work of spoiling the trees, while the others held a whispered conference. The lady soon seemed to become somewhat excited and he distinctly heard Malpest say, —

" It is too good to be true."

" Good, sir !" exclaimed Mrs. Strongitharm, aloud. " Do you call it good? It is a scandal, — an abomination."

Oh, yes! certainly, of course," answered the other. " It is a crime, a sin."

A stain on Harmonianism," continued Mrs. Strong-itharm ; and they must be turned out of the establishment before they corrupt the whole community."

"By Jove! the suggestion is good," replied Malpest ; " an example should be made of them. Let us go at once and consult the doctor."

The parties then entered the house, while Lovell sat down on a bench and amused himself by cutting thereon the following cabalistic figure.

When Charity entered her father's presence, in obedience to his summons, the old gentleman took her by the hand, and led her to a chair. The young girl knew, by his solemn deportment, that something important was coming.

"My daughter," said he, seating himself before her, " you are now verging on womanhood, — on that time when the pleasures and pains of the girl give place to others of a more serious nature. The age of youthful frivolity is passing away, and it will soon be time for you to begin your woman's mission on earth. There are objections to deferring this momentous epoch too long. Have you ever thought upon the subject of marriage ?"

" *I*, papa ! "

" Of course you have not. Pardon me for asking the question ; but I have thought of it for you."

Miss Charity blushed (or tried to do so), and looked very hard at an ink spot on the floor.

"I have selected as your partner for life, a man eminently worthy of your esteem, and my most trusty disciple, — brother Nicholas Malpest. I presume my choice is satisfactory to you."

There was a pause.

"Why do you not speak, my child?" said the doctor. "You seem strangely agitated; but this is natural."

"Papa," said Charity, hesitatingly, "I do not love Professor Malpest."

"Love!" exclaimed the doctor; "what can you expect to know about love? I do not ask you to love him."

"O father, would you have me united to a man for whom I had no attachment?"

"Who can have put such mischievous ideas into your head? The passion you speak of is the cause of much sin and misery. I do not intend that it shall exist in Harmony Hall. A general affection for our fellow-creatures is all that I wish. This carnal love is a different feeling. The first, 'intellectus amor,' is proper in the eyes of God and man; but as to the second, ' ut castis auribus vox amoris suspecta est.' But I will not enlarge on the subject, for it is better that you should remain in ignorance of it."

"I do not wish to take this important step," said Charity, "without due meditation and preparation. If you intend to force me to marry that man, give me at least a month for reflection."

"I intend to use no other force than the voice of reason," answered the doctor. "Your request is eminently proper. It is granted, and in a month I shall expect to receive your assent. Now, my child, go to your room and ponder over the coming change in your condition."

Miss Charity withdrew from the study, but did not go directly to her own room. She went first to that of Miss Griffin, in order to seek counsel and consolation from her older friend, not knowing that the latter was by far the most in need of relief to her wounded feelings.

The two damsels unbosomed their sorrows to each other; Miss Charity telling hers *in extenso;* but Miss Minerva only making a partial revelation; for hers, she said, was a silent grief. When told of the doctor's design, she expressed the most unbounded astonishment and indignation that he should think of throwing his daughter away on " such an unprincipled, deceitful villain."

" But nothing shall ever induce me to have him," said Charity.

' " You are a sensible girl," answered Miss Griffin. " I cannot conceive how any woman could look at such a man."

" It grieves me to disobey my father, or to thwart him in any way," said Charity; " but I cannot believe that filial duty makes it obligatory on me to sacrifice the happiness of my life to his peculiar views, and I regret that I did not acknowledge to him that my heart was given to Mr. Lovell; but you know, Minerva, how a woman shrinks from confessing such things, even to a parent."

" Why should woman conceal her feelings, and pine in solitude?" replied Miss Griffin; " man does not. My advice to you, as a sincere friend, and one who has a thorough knowledge of human nature, is, that you tell Mr. Malpost frankly that you detest him, and that your young affections are centred on Leander. That will of course, allay the passion with which he pretends you have inspired him, and he will immediately cease his importunities."

" But I cannot truly say that I actually *detest* him," answered Charity. " I acknowledge that in his presence I feel a sort of instinctive aversion; but I do not detest anybody."

" That is a distinction without a difference, my dear," replied Miss Griffin. " You have an aversion to him. I sympathize with you. Tell him you loathe him, you abhor him."

" I will be guided partially by your counsel," said Miss Charity, " and will go to him and tell him candidly that I am indifferent to him."

" I will accompany you when you do so, dear. My presence will enable you better to undergo the trying scene."

" I don't think it will be very trying."

" Then Charity, you know not your weakness," said Miss Griffin, judging her friend by herself.

Miss Goodenough now went to her own room, while Miss Griffin relieved her overburdened mind by writing a philippic against the male sex in general, and Professor Malpest in particular, although she did not mention him by name.

In the mean while, Lovell, having satisfactorily finished his wood-cut of the two hearts united by a true lover's knot, went up to his room, polished his boots, put about a quarter of a pound of pomatum on his hair, dressed himself with unusual spruceness, and then proceeded in search of the doctor. Mr. Lovell was in an exceedingly happy frame of mind, for he did not doubt that the probation he had undergone, at Harmony Hall, had thrown the veil of oblivion over his unfortunate *fiasco* in the doctor's office in town, and he was consequently sanguine that the old gentleman would at once consent to the consummation of his happiness.

He had prepared (a month before) a speech for the occasion, in which he set forth his social standing, his prospects in life, and his unalterable devotion to Charity, all of which, excepting the last, was already known to the doctor. But now, when he entered the actual presence of his prospective father-in-law, the unwontedly severe aspect of the old gentleman, and the grave manner with which he received him, took him so completely by surprise that he quite forgot his oration and could not open his lips.

"Be seated, sir," said the doctor.

Lovell dumped himself down on the nearest chair.

" My friends, you may retire," said the doctor to Professor Malpost and Mrs. Strongitharm, who were with him, and who looked significantly at Lovell as they left the room.

" I was about to send for you, sir, when you opportunely came in," said the doctor. " I have been grieved — deeply grieved — at the reports that have reached me concerning your conduct towards one of the sisters. There is some doubt (in my mind at least) as to the extent to which your criminality has gone, and, in fact I am loth, extremely loth, to believe that the tempter can actually have found his way amongst us, and was desirous of personally inquiring into this lamentable affair before taking any action in the matter."

" I know not what you have heard, sir," answered Lov-

5*

ell; "but I can assure you that my intentions are strictly honorable; and I have come to you to-day for the purpose of asking your consent to our marriage."

A benevolent smile passed over the doctor's face.

"Ah! my dear young friend," he said, "I knew that my informants must be mistaken. Their rigid sense of propriety has doubtless led them to take an unfavorable view of actions, not only innocent, but meritorious, when prompted by proper motives. But have you duly weighed all the momentous responsibilities of the step you think of taking? Have you taken into consideration your own youth and the lady's age?"

"Since she is old enough to love, she is old enough to marry," replied Leander, somewhat joyously, for he felt encouraged by the favorable turn the doctor's remarks seemed to be taking.

"Undoubtedly," said the doctor, "sister Minerva is old enough to marry."

"Miss Griffin, sir?" cried Lovell, jumping up; "I have never thought of Miss Griffin. I have hardly ever spoken a word to her. I don't care a tinker's d— for her."

Miss Minerva, who was scribbling in the room overhead, was attracted by the mention of her name, and, with the curiosity which is said to have been inherent in her sex since the days of Eve, promptly placed herself beside the stove-pipe hole. It is from her journal that we extract the rest of the conversation.

"It is Charity, sir," continued Leander, "my own dearest Charity, whose hand I ask."

"My daughter!" said the doctor, with surprise. "Really I do not comprehend the matter. Why, my dear boy, you are too young as yet, to think of becoming a father."

"I am quite indifferent to children, sir," answered Lovell, "and as Charity seems rather delicate, I would really prefer not to have any."

"Then, pray, for what reason do you wish to marry her?"

"Because I love her."

"You love! Why, that is against the rules of the establishment."

The doctor slowly turned round in his chair, raised his spectacles from his nose to his forehead, stuck his quill behind his ear, crossed his legs, and rubbed his hands together, which actions poor Leander knew too well were the promonitory symptoms that foreboded an eruption of the Greeks and Romans; so he folded his arms, and stood resigned to a patient and passive resistance.

"I perceive with regret," said Dr. Goodenough, "that you have not yet dwelt long enough amongst us to overcome the desires of the flesh. It is the evil spirit of man that has been aroused within you. My daughter unfortunately is comely, and I see with sorrow that you are far from being a true Harmonian. You are not yet imbued with the spirit of the New Utopia. Had you pondered over my studies on the Development of Healthy Offspring, you would be aware of the folly, if not wickedness, of seeking the premature gratification of a mere appetite at the expense of generations yet to be. The Lacedæmonians did not permit young men to marry until they were twenty-five years old. Plato informs us that the proper age is thirty; but Aristotle fixes it at thirty-seven. I waited until I was forty. As to this 'love,' as you call it, Avicenna tells us it is 'a mere disease, a melancholy vexation, or anguish of mind.' According to Villanovanus, it is 'a continual cogitation of that which is desired, with a confidence or hope of compassing it.' 'Est orcus ille,' says Plutarch, 'vis est immedicabilis, est rabies insana.' The part affected, according to Arnoldus, is the fore part of the head, but Longius is of opinion that it is seated in the liver. Others hold that the disease is in the spleen, while some think that the trouble arises from an inflammation in the heart.

"To overcome this malady, which is extremely dangerous in youth, eight rules have been prescribed, all of which are more or less efficacious.

"1. Abstinence and diet, and, in extreme cases, fasting.

"2. Hard work. 'Vacuo pectore regnat amor.' Love tyrannizeth over an idle person.

"3. Light clothing in cold weather. (St. Origen carried this precept to the extreme.)

· "4. Hair-cloth worn next to the skin. (Doubtless on the principle of a counter-inflammation.)

"5. Camphor internally administered, with syrup of hellebore, and an occasional clyster of ice-water.

"6. Absence from the cause of the mischief; as persons fly from districts in which they are subject to fever.

"7. Avoidance of amorous thoughts.

"8. Phlebotomy. The ancient Tartars were accustomed to draw the blood from behind the ears, others took it from the legs, while some preferred leeches on the perinæum.

"You now, my dear boy, clearly perceive the folly into which youth and its unbridled impulses were leading you, and how easy it is to cure your complaint. You have merely to follow one or more of the prescriptions I have given you. If you are much affected I would advise you to try them all. Look at me. You see me at nearly seventy years of age, calm and tranquil, because I am able to keep under the control of reason those passions that cause so much trouble to mankind."

"Nothing, sir," answered Leander, "can ever weaken my love for Charity ; I adore her."

"Do not make use of unseemly language, sir, in Harmony Hall," replied the doctor ; "I find nothing peculiar in the diagnosis of your case. You are affected as thousands have been before you, and the remedies that cured them will cure you.

"Retire now to your apartment, with this copy of the 'Regeneration of Man.' Its perusal will strengthen your mind ; and, if you take a strong dose of the sweet spirits of nitre with a little rhubarb and magnesia, the medicine will cool your hot blood, and excite in you quite different feelings from those that now agitate you."

"Then, sir, you refuse me the hand of Charity," said Lovell.

"Most decidedly, sir," answered the doctor. "Even if I thought it prudent to select you for her husband, I would not be at liberty to do so, since she is already promised to another, — to one, who, to unbounded benevolence, and the most perfect acquiescence in all my views, has learned to suppress the promptings of the flesh, and regards marriage merely as a means to an end. She is to be united to brother Nicholas Malpest."

Poor Lenny's heart was too full for words, and he silently stole out of the study, a sadder if not a wiser man. He was seen soon afterwards walking up and down the garden in a highly excited manner, gesticulating wildly, clenching his fists, and anon striking at vacancy.

"D——n the fellow," he exclaimed. "To think of my being refused for a beggarly upstart adventurer, — a scoundrel, who I believe has deliberately led Dr. Good-enough into this Foufouville business, solely for selfish purposes of his own. But I'll unmask the villain; I'll unmask him, or have his heart's blood. He shall find that Leander Lovell is not a man to be trifled with. Ugh!"

CHAPTER IV.

*Some curious and interesting Papers never before presented
to the Public.*

WE now propose to lay before the reader a few of the
original documents from which this narrative is compiled.
It is true that on glancing over the pages already written,
and seeing the somewhat dramatic form that the work has
unavoidably taken, we feel a strong inclination to continue in the same style. We have the lovesick maiden,
the despairing lover, the partially successful rival, who is
also the villain of the piece, the tyrannical father, and two
or three makeweights, whose characteristics being comic,
form an admirable contrast to the pathetic portions of the
story. In the first chapter we have described the locality,
and brought the *dramatis personæ* on the scene; in the
second, the introduction of the domestics would seem a
master-stroke of policy, like clearing the decks for action,
and leaving the company entire freedom of movement;
by the end of the third, we have got our ingredients pretty
well mixed up, that is to say, the plot has begun to develop itself, all sorts of passions have been brought into
play, and almost everybody has got at loggerheads with
somebody else. We repeat, that when we consider all
this, we feel strongly tempted to give way to our fertile
imagination and, taking the few actual facts for a basis,
to spin a plain, unvarnished tale into a three-volume
novel; but our respect for the memory of the late Dr.

Goodenough, our desire to defend his reputation against the criticisms and sarcasms of the witless journalists of an unscrupulous press, and our sense of duty to an intelligent public shall restrain us from thus seeking after literary fame under false pretences, and we shall rigidly adhere to our first intention, and simply give a matter-of-fact record of the most important events connected with the experiment at Foufouville. Moreover, since the years of man's life are but threescore and ten, and we do not possess the lucrative faculty of saying something when we have nothing to say, we shall study concision in every way possible; a study, we regret to say, that is too much neglected by modern writers, whose chief aim seems to be to make a whole volume out of incidents and thoughts enough for a single chapter only; a fault that has led readers into the reprehensible (though, under the circumstances, excusable) habit of skipping. In pursuance of this plan we shall give the original documents whenever they are of sufficient interest, or whenever they exhibit the causes of the decline of Harmonianism as clearly and concisely as a synopsis would do; and whenever we deem it preferable we shall digest our authorities.

These may be divided into eight classes, as follows: —

1st. Letters from members of the society, or parties connected with them.

2d. The books of the phalanstery, comprising one blotter, one day-book, and one ledger. These are all in the handwriting of Prof. Nicholas Malpest.

3d. Vouchers for the expenses of the phalanstery. Most of these show indubitable evidence of having been tampered with (as will be explained hereafter), and are consequently of little value.

4th. Plans, specifications, etc., in the possession of Palladio Styles, Esq., N. A. A., architect and builder.

5th. Records of the proceedings of kindred societies.

6th. The "Journal of an Ennuyée," by Miss Serena Minerva Griffin (not intended for publication).

7th. The press of the time, particularly the Comic Weekly and Monthly Squib.

8th. Oral testimony. We have collected this at no little personal trouble (and regardless of expense), having visited Foufouville for the sole purpose of interrogating those who lived there during the brief existence of the New Utopians, as such; for it should be borne in mind that the transactions, now for the first time narrated to the public in an authentic form, all took place within the memory of men still living. That well-known individual, the oldest inhabitant, remembered the Harmonian era perfectly, and had, on one occasion, even seen Dr. Goodenough himself. Two highly respectable retired oystermen, who lived at Communipaw at the time of the events of which we are writing, but who were accustomed to pay frequent visits to Foufouville (where they married a fishmonger's daughters), gave us much valuable information. We are also indebted to John Smith, Esq., now cashier of the National Bank of Foufouville, who recollected being frequently engaged, when a boy, in nocturnal expeditions with youths of his own age, for the purpose of robbing the hen-roosts, or of committing depredations on the apple-trees at the Hall. We have also conversed with all the surviving Harmonians, except Professor Malpost, whom we have been unable to find, and who, it is therefore highly probable, is now defunct.

Of our MS. authorities, some have been for a long time

C

in our possession; others have been kindly lent to us by Leander Lovell, Esq., president of the Oil Ocean Petroleum Co., and a few, belonging to the Jersey City Historical Society, have been politely placed at our disposal for perusal by the urbane and gentlemanly librarian.

The reader will observe that the following papers are not given in strict chronological order. We have preferred to follow the method adopted by other superior writers, as Gibbon, Prescott, Tacitus, etc., and have grouped them with reference to the events of which they treat.

"CIRCULAR.

"To all Mankind and future Generations, *Greeting:* The Society of Harmonians, for the regeneration of man, has a practical existence. Foufouville is the new Eden where the tree of knowledge has been planted. Its fruit is free to all. O ye who are still wandering in the wilderness of Ignorance, who are tossed on the stormy waves of Passion, who are lost in the desert of Doubt, in danger of being swept away by the simoon of Sin, come to this earthly Paradise, this haven of refuge, this oasis where all is verdant.

"Without, ye have endless strifes, contentions, heart-burnings, lusts, envy, hatred, and all uncharitableness; within, only brotherly love, harmony, peace, and good-will.

"Hasten, then, to the new fold; the door is open; come one, come all.

"J. Goodenough.

"Given at Foufouville, this 1st day of the 1st month of the 1st year of the Harmonian Era."

DR. J. GOODENOUGH TO PROF. GUMMP, LEIPSIC.

"FOUFOUVILLE, 4th 1st Mo., A. H. 1.

" RESPECTED FRIEND AND BROTHER, — The fame of your translation of the New Utopia has reached America. I thank you, in the name of humanity, for the boon you have conferred upon your fellow-man, and the special honor paid to my unworthy self. I am proud to think that henceforth my name will be indissolubly associated with that of Gummp. I knew that the German mind would not fail to appreciate the mighty truths I have humbly endeavored to inculcate.

" You are doubtless aware that the Society of Harmonians has at last a local habitation as well as a name. The dream of my life is being realized. We are now dwelling in the first phalanstery, and others are to be erected as soon as the number of proselytes who have joined us reaches one thousand.

" Here we are gathered together, a chosen few, and in this tranquil retreat, entirely dissevered from mundane thoughts and pursuits, we find that peace which the world cannot give, with its snares, its temptations, its bickerings, its unholy passions ; that perfect serenity of mind for which mortals have hitherto sighed in vain.

" I send with this, copies of my last two works, the " Regeneration of Man," and " Studies on the Development of Healthy Offspring."

" Farewell, respected friend and brother.

" J. GOODENOUGH.

" P. S. I enclose a pamphlet containing our circular, together with our rules and regulations, and would advise that it be translated into German, and from fifty thousand to one hundred thousand copies printed for general distribution."

"We, the undersigned, constituting the Woman's Union Association of Lebanon, have received, with unbounded satisfaction, tidings of the glorious enterprise inaugurated under the auspices of the far-seeing and progressive Dr. Goodenough.

"The Age of Reason is indeed at hand. Woman will no longer be exposed to the neglect of the other sex.

"Profoundly impressed by the delightful prospect of happiness held out in the circular of Dr. G., we propose at once uniting our fortunes with yours, and write to inquire the cheapest route to Harmony Hall.

"We deem it proper to state (however unimportant the fact may be) that we shall not be able to contribute pecuniarily to the resources of the society; but do not doubt that the noble example we shall set to the world, and the moral influence gained by our presence will more than counterbalance the want of mere lucre.

"Your sisters in love,

"Miss MARY ANN KETCHUM.
"Miss CLEOPATRA GROSBECK.
"Miss EVERGREEN WAITE.
"Miss SOPHONISBA HOPE.
"Miss MARTHA VALENTINE.
"Miss PATIENCE STAAHL."

(No date.)

PROF. NICH. MALPEST TO THE WOMAN'S UNION ASSOCIATION
OF LEBANON.

"HARMONY HALL, April 25th, 1850.

" *To Miss Mary Ann Ketchum and Others:*

" LADIES, — It is with inexpressible regret, — owing to
the great moral influence that would accrue to our community could we have the benefit of your presence amongst
us, to say nothing of personal gratification, — it is, I repeat, with the deepest regret that I am constrained to
inform you, that, in consequence of the heavy outlay to
which we have been put in preparing for the thousands
of New Utopians whose arrival is daily expected (by Dr.
Goodenough), we must for the present deprive ourselves
of the advantages and pleasures of your society.

" Accept, ladies, the assurance of my distinguished
consideration.

" NICH. MALPEST,

"*Cor. Sec. of the S. of H.*"

MRS. ELIZABETH STRONGITHARM TO THE HON. ANDREW
JACKSON JONES.

"FOUFOUVILLE, April 19th, 1850.

" SIR, — I shall endeavor to be present at the coming
convention of the Female Rights Association.

" Your bill for extending the franchise to woman meets
my approval.   It is encouraging, in these degenerate days,
to find one man of enlarged ideas.

" How differently legislation would be conducted if
women had the making of the laws !   Instead of the present contentions that disgrace our assemblies, all would be
love.

6*

" The abominable tariff now imposed on silks, satins, laces, feathers, and other articles of female necessity, would be at once repealed.

" The amassing of excessive wealth would be prohibited. Those who possessed more than a competency would be compelled to bestow the surplus on portionless young women.

" Every man who attained the age of thirty years without having taken a wife, would be obliged to support at least one foundling or orphan, and an additional one for every year thereafter that he persisted in celibacy.

" Whiskers being a symbol of· manhood, no bachelor would be permitted to wear them ; nor would any such be eligible to any public office whatever.

" A suitable and becoming costume (such as is worn by me) would be made obligatory on the female sex.

" Theatrical exhibitions would be put down, as having an injurious influence on public morals ; or at least they would be held under severe restrictions. Males alone would be allowed to perform in ballets.

" Those abominable institutions called clubs would be broken up (unless women were admitted to them), and they would be closed at nine o'clock, p. m. No card-playing or billiards would be tolerated in them.

" Those houses — likened by Miss Martineau to harems — would be torn down, and the sites sown with salt.

" An army would be despatched against the Mormons to exterminate those American Turks.

" No religion would be tolerated save one founded on common sense.

" The shameful license of the press would be curtailed.

Editors who took a wrong view of the woman question would be put in the pillory, and their papers suppressed.

"The distillation of spirituous liquor, under any pretense whatever, would be prohibited.

"No vile tobacco would be imported or grown.

"Such, sir, are a few of the reforms that will follow the bestowing of the ballot on my sex. Think how much more happy mankind will be.

"Woman, instead of spending her life in beau-catching, or the pursuit of frivolities, as at present, will stand on her rights by the polls, armed with that palladium of liberty, the ballot, and, hurling it in the face of masculine injustice, will appear with a new charm in the domestic circle.

"I am, sir, yours, in progress,

"Elizabeth Strongitharm.

"To the Hon. A. J. Jones, Albany."

LEANDER LOVELL, ESQ., TO RICHARD LONGSHANKS, ESQ.

"Foufouville, March 29th, 1850.

"Dear Dick, — I have not joined the Macedonian Phalanx, as you insinuate, nor is it Mars, but rather Venus, who has brought me here. The truth is, I am engaged to the most beautiful, lovely, and fascinating of her sex, daughter of the celebrated Dr. Goodenough, author of several well-known works on social philosophy. I have not yet been converted to the doctor's peculiar views, and must confess that I am guilty of some little dissimulation in foisting myself into his society; but 'all is fair in love,' you know. O Dick, she is adorable! When or where the ceremony will take place I cannot tell, for untoward circumstances have prevented me thus far from asking the old gentleman's consent; but I shall obtain it in a day or two. She is perfection. To know her is to love her; she — but I won't expatiate on this charming theme to such a matter-of-fact individual as you are. You might call it a bore, and I should never forgive you. How lucky I am to be in existence at the same time as Charity, — for her equal never lived before! Her eyes are of that deep azure only seen in the sky of Italy at noon-day; her hair is auburn, and falls in natural ringlets over her alabaster shoulders; her delicately chiselled nose —" [we will omit the rest of this descriptive passage, as not being of sufficient public importance to warrant an insertion.] " I am the most happy and most fortunate man on the face of the earth.

" I have a sort of rival (but he has no chance), one Malpest, who calls himself ' professor ' — of what, I know not. He is the chief-cook-and-bottle-washer of the concern, and his actions, in some respects, appear suspicious; still, for all I know to the contrary, he may be a good enough fellow at heart. (Charity, dear girl, hates the sight of him.)

" A strong-minded harridan of a bloomer, with the man she protects, and an affected spinster, complete the inmates. The Strongitharm is abusing everybody from morning to night, and perpetually pecking at poor Peewit, whom she calls her co-partner. He has lately shown symptoms of insubordination. The forlorn Griffin goes about expressing the loftiest disdain for mankind (how different she would be if she had a good stout husband, and half-a-dozen yellow-haired brats around her!), and contrasting her own contented condition with the bickering existence of Stongitharm & Co.

" The two women, of course, are at sword's points.
" Why do you bore me about business, and say you can't get along without me? What the mischief do I care about business when I am going to be married to the girl of my heart?

"Yours ever,   L. L."

MESSRS. WESTCOTT & CO., TO PROF. NICH. MALPEST.

"NEW YORK, April 1st, 1850.

" SIR, — On presenting your check on the National Bank for $325\frac{98}{100}$, given in payment of our bill for clothing, we were advised that your balance there amounted to but $1\frac{3}{100}$, and the check was consequently dishonored.

" Respectfully, your obedient servant,
" WESTCOTT & CO."

PROF. NICH. MALPEST, TO MESSRS. WESTCOTT & CO.

"HARMONY HALL, April 4th, 1850.

" GENTS, — I trust that my inadvertence in overlooking the state of my bank account when I gave you my check, may not have subjected you to any inconvenience. It is a matter of astonishment to me that the officials should have hesitated to allow my account to be temporarily overdrawn, as it is customary to do with heavy depositors, and I shall have no further dealings with a moneyed institution so blind to its own interests.

" My funds at the present moment are all locked up in one of the most promising speculations of the age ; but I am making arrangements by which I hope in a few weeks to render them available.

" Your obedient servant,
" NICHOLAS MALPEST."

RICHARD LONGSHANKS, ESQ., TO LEANDER LOVELL, ESQ.

"NEW YORK, April 5.

"Dear Len, — Our business really requires the undivided attention of both of us, so that one may always be present at the office. We have lost some good chances lately in consequence of my temporary but unavoidable absences ; so hurry up and get married if it is necessary for you to commit that act, in order to recover your wonted serenity and go to work.

"Meanwhile congratulations, — felicity, etc.

"Yours,   R. L.

'P. S. — I've hung up our shingle 'Longshanks & Lovell, Brokers.' "

LEANDER LOVELL, ESQ., TO RICHARD LONGSHANKS, ESQ.

"FOUFOUVILLE, April 21.

"Dear Dick, — I am the most miserable man in existence. A malignant fate seems to pursue me. Old Goodenough has actually resolved to throw away his Charity on that double-distilled villain, Malpest. But the deed shall never be consummated, *never*, Richard, NEVER. Charity has obtained a delay of one month, and in that month something shall be done, for I must have her ; cost what it may, I must have her. She won't consent to a clandestine marriage, because she clings to her father in the most childish manner, and says she could never forgive herself should any act of hers cause him pain. Under these unprecedentedly embarrassing circumstances, I feel the need of a friend to lean upon. Let me hear from you without delay.

" As to that despicable miscreant who pretends to her hand, should he give me the shadow of an excuse, may my right arm be withered if I don't thrash the black-hearted scoundrel within an inch of his life !

" Had I not better call him out at once? Will you be my friend on the occasion? If so, come down as soon as you can with the hair-triggers.

"Yours,   L. L."

RICHARD LONGSHANKS, ESQ., TO LEANDER LOVELL, ESQ.

"WALL STREET, April 23d.

" DEAR LEN, — On the 5th inst. I wrote you a congrat-ulatory letter under the impression that the affair was settled, but I perceive, by yours of the 21st, that this was an error.

" The truth is, you have fallen in love, which is the most silly thing a man can do, particularly when the girl on her part preserves her senses ; and it is clear to my mind that Miss What's-her-name don't care a pin for you since she won't run away with you. In fact, I think it most likely she is smitten with that other fellow. He has pater-familias on his side, which is a great advantage.

" The best thing you can do is to take the matter phil-osophically, as I should do under the circumstances, and forget the young woman entirely. To accomplish this nothing more is necessary than not to think of her at all. So come back to town like a sensible man and go to work again.

"Yours,   R. L."

LEANDER LOVELL, ESQ., TO RICHARD LONGSHANKS, ESQ.

"FOUFOUVILLE, April 25th, 1850.

" SIR, — I expected to find in you a sympathetic friend, instead of an indifferent man-of-the-world. Having never seen the young lady, of course you cannot enter into my feelings ; but that was no reason for casting a slur on her character, — for such I regard your insinuation that she has become attached to another.

" Sir, your philosophy I despise. I could not, and would not if I could, forget her until my latest breath. It is my intention to demand satisfaction from the scoundrel, and had hoped that you would second me ; but now I shall look elsewhere for that act of friendship.

" Sir, our acquaintance is at an end and our partnership dissolved. Be pleased to remove my name from the shingle.

" Your obedient servant,

" LEANDER LOVELL."

RICHARD LONGSHANKS, ESQ., TO LEANDER LOVELL, ESQ.

"WALL STREET, April 27th.

" MY DEAR LEANDER, — What is the matter with you? I didn't know how unreasonably savage love made a man. I must get into that condition myself in order to find out the sensation. But, seriously speaking, I had no intention of wounding your feelings, and if my note has done so (I certainly expected it would have a soothing effect), I must ask you to excuse it.

" As to challenging Mr. Malpest, I really do not think you have justifiable grounds for doing so. You wrote to me yourself that it was impossible to see Miss Goodenough without loving her; and such being the case can you blame the professor? If you fight him what will you gain? If you wound him, you excite pity for him, and pity is akin to love; while, if you kill him, you find yourself in serious trouble. If he wounds you, I don't distinctly see where the satisfaction comes in; while, if he kill you, you certainly will not be able to marry the lady, but on the contrary *he* may do so.

"I shall go down to Foufouville as soon as business will allow, in the hope of being of service to you in some way. If Malpest should appear to me half as bad a man as you imagine him to be, I'll gladly help you tar and feather him.

"Believe me, yours ever truly,
"RICHARD LONGSHANKS."

EXTRACTS FROM THE "JOURNAL OF AN ENNUYEE," BY MISS SERENA MINERVA GRIFFIN.

"*April* 20*th.* — The heart of woman is a soundless sea. Man, coarse man, cannot fathom its depths. She was born for duality. Like the clinging vine she yearns for a protector; she is ever searching for sympathy; yet, according to the false customs of society, she must ever conceal in her bosom those emotions that fain would find utterance in — [illegible]. · ' The heart, like a tendril accustomed to cling,' etc. Man must be the one to propose. How absurd! The sturdy oak must seek the frail vine, not the vine the oak. Is this right? Is it proper? The untrammelled promptings of gifted souls answer indignantly, NO.

"21*st.* — This has been a trying day. To think I could have been so mistaken in that man. But dearly have I paid for my error. It is far better for woman to exist alone. ' Few are the hearts whence one same touch,' etc. Her nature is profoundly analytical. She perceives those invisible shades of character, that are lost to man's less delicate vision, and thus discriminates with unerring judgment the hidden motives of human action. [The villain, to have deceived me so grossly! Why was I so blind? I was indifferent to him before; now I hate him. I despise him].

"22d. — Oh, this aching head! My temples throb. I must apply ice to the region of the cerebellum. The events of yesterday will never fade from my mind while memory retains her seat. It is the warm hearts that suffer most in this cold world, yet are they ever ready to forgive and kiss the hand that wounds. Such is woman. [May I live a hundred years to torment him!] I am much concerned for poor little innocent Charity. She seems inclined to yield so implicitly to the will of her father. She lacks strength of mind. Of course he cannot have any real feeling for such a mere chit. His views are mercenary. I must warn the simple-minded doctor, and put Mr. Lovell on his guard. The poor young man seems to be madly in love. What a pity he has so little knowledge of the world! [The wretch! I shall be avenged on him. He shall know that Minerva Griffin is not to be treated lightly].

"23d. — Confined to my bed. That hateful Strongitharm came in with her affected condolence. How foolish I was to become reconciled to her! But woman was ever forgiving.

" ' No strong-minded woman,' said she, ' would allow herself to be made sick by a man.'

" ' What do you mean, madam?' I asked.

" ' A true woman would conceal such weakness in her own bosom,' she continued ; ' *I* never would give in.'

" When I asked her if she called physical suffering a ' weakness,' she had the impertinence to insinuate that my headache was not owing to a disordered stomach, but to a disturbance of the heart. I requested her to leave me to myself; on which she called me an ' ungrateful thing' to make such a return for her sympathy. Sympathy indeed! She rejoices in my sufferings. They enable her to assume airs of superiority. Alas! it is not from her own sex that woman in misfortune must look for sympathy.

" 23*d.*—Still confined. Mr. Peewit looked really sorrowful when he came limping in with the gruel. He said he had made it himself with the assistance of the cook. He is a kind soul is Peewit.

" The good doctor also came to see me, and prescribed ipecac. He does not comprehend the delicacy of the female organization. It might work well with a man. His pains are merely physical. Only a woman understands the organic difference between the sexes. Yet is the doctor a well-meaning person. · [The monster! I see him in the kitchen window talking to the cook. *I* cannot think of eating at this time. Pity is the only feeling I have for him.]

" 24*th.* — Still reclining on my sofa. Oh, how wearily drag the long hours! Heigh-ho! This day I am [erased] years of age. *He* had the effrontery to send to inquire how I was, and the maliciousness to choose Strongitharm as his messenger. She happened to come in just as I was trying on my new green dress. Green is very becoming to my style of — that is to say, to delicate blondes.

The yellow dahlia Mr. Peewit sent me, and which was placed on my bosom, heightened the color considerably, and contrasted well with the light-blue trimmings and the red coiffure. I looked — no matter how. So I told her I was perfectly well as she saw. She went out with a disappointed air. Was it envy? Mr. Peewit said he wished his ogre (though that is not the exact word he used) dressed like me. He is a man of taste.

" *25th.* — I see from my window Mr. Lovell and Charity in the grove. He is very demonstrative. It is a pleasure to watch them, — love is so rare. What a passionate attachment his seems to be! How strange that a mere chit of sixteen should inspire such ardent devotion, when those in whom maturer years have developed all the full yearnings of woman's nature are comparatively neglected! Where are man's boasted powers of reason? Alas! he has none where woman is concerned. [The only sentiment he excites is repulsion. I will follow him to the end of the earth for the sake of vengeance. He is talking to the cook again.]

" *Afternoon.* — I have spoken to Mr. Lovell about him. He said he believed he was a mere adventurer ; ' after her money,' was the expression he used ; that Charity positively abhors him. The dear child! Lovell has more discernment than I gave him credit for.

" I also spoke to the doctor on the same subject. He told me I was nervous and excited, and had better go to bed. He also wanted me to take a teaspoonful of soothing syrup, and prepared a powerful dose of salts, which he insisted on my drinking. Mr. Peewit, who was present, and observed the repugnance expressed on my countenance, took advantage of the doctor's back being turned

for a moment, and swallowed the nauseating mixture
himself. Few men would be capable of such self-sacrificing devotion. My looks expressed my gratitude, and
Joseph looked happy. Tears of contentment stood in his
eyes. To reward him, I asked him to stroll with me in the
garden, for he is able to walk, although still somewhat
lame. I leaned upon his arm, being weak from my recent
illness. He seemed delighted at first, but in about half
an hour became embarrassed in his manner, and appeared
ill at ease. We sat down under the trees ; but he continued restless, as if .anxious to go away in spite of my
cheering conversation, and, after a while, suddenly jumped
up and left me abruptly. Did he fear to be overcome by
his feelings? Men are such singular beings! I really
begin to believe that Joseph appreciates me.

"26*th.* — Feel almost well to-day, but think it prudent
to remain in my room. Bridget brought me my breakfast,
with a bunch of wild flowers, from Mr. Peewit. She said
Mr. Malpest was such a 'nice gentleman.' Ignorant
creature! She judges only by externals. Behold Peewit!
He is not exactly handsome, yet is his a nature simple,
perhaps, but generous, and even possessed of a certain
amount of penetration. He has discovered my superiority to that odious she-dragon who has appropriated him.
He would not attempt to deceive a trusting heart.

"THOUGHTS FOR MY LECTURE ON THE CO-RELATION OF THE
SEXES.

" How beautiful are the home affections! They move
in perpetual harmony, like the heavenly orbs (and are
they not heavenly in their nature?) ; and when the fatal

7*

shaft takes one away, it leaves a void that, like the place of the lost Pleiad, can never be refilled.

"What the sword of Alexander was to the Gordian knot, so is a harsh word to that of true love. [A pretty conceit.]

"Chemistry tells us that sometimes, when we mingle two elements together, a portion of one will combine with the other, while a portion still remains free. If this latter come in contact with its affinities, it will all be absorbed in chemical unions.

"Thus, few or none of us find all our sympathies responded to by another; some affections remain unsatisfied, or go to waste. Hence we sometimes see a husband and wife, who are in many respects congenial, seeking in others the satisfaction of those sensibilities that meet with repulsion at home.

"In an all-absorbing love (if such there could be), the loss of the beloved would be a total shipwreck of the heart. Usually, only a portion of the cargo is lost, and even that is sometimes recovered, though in a damaged condition.

"The negative pole of the magnet repels the negative, while there is a mutual attraction between it and the positive. How like the apparently singular physiological fact, that the strongest attachments are between those of dissimilar or opposite temperaments! Didst ever see a child's block-map? 'Tis thus that the affections of the happily mated become interlocked. [There is deep thought in this.]

" Behold the hands of a timepiece! The one pursues the other, only to leave it when overtaken. Alas! how like is the conduct of man to woman!

" As the ignorant, seeing not the hidden springs, think that the pendulum makes the clock go, so do the superficial judge of our motives by — [erased]. [To be worked up.]

" Woman cannot enter into the feelings of woman to the same extent as man. [Profound.] The male and female were formed to be united. Separate, like blue and yellow, they may be complementary to each other, but joined together, they make one homogeneous whole, their natures blended in verdant harmony.

" Some men look upon women as mere nothings. Well, conceited being, granting this were true, nothing (0) united to one (1) increases its value tenfold (10). [Happily put.]

" Like the Arabic numerals, the language of love is understood by all nations. To use an algebraic expression, the eyes are the exponent of this first power of nature.

" Marriage is a sort of Binomial Theorem, in which, if the man is negative, the woman is certain to be positive. They increase by unity, until the leading power (feminine) reaches 45.

" A vulgar man, like a vulgar fraction, is not a perfect

entity. His faults may be called his denominators, — the greater they are, the less he is worth.

"As we go up in a balloon, we find that all is frigid and serene in the upper atmosphere. Thus, when man soars into the lofty regions of philosophy, he looks down with disdain, from his intellectual elevation, on the petty miseries of earth; but those cold, calm regions are not suited to the tender nature of woman. Her affections freeze [rather strong, say wither] when she seeks a higher sphere than the domestic hearth.

"The poet admires the uncultivated charms of Nature, while the practical man has an eye [I don't like this expression] for the well-tilled field. Thus the trifler looks only at youth and beauty, while the philosopher prefers those in whom the furrows of time indicate the fruitfulness of reason.

"As light ploughing suits a thin soil, so shallow people require but little love. A deep affection would be wasted upon them; it would meet with no adequate return. The feelings of such may be easily harrowed, but a few raindrops of tears efface the impressions of the past.

"The most saccharine vegetables ripen under ground, and, alas! how much sweetness do we often find in some humble home, buried, as it were, from the eyes of the world.

"Methinks that the heart, like the earth, hath its hills and its vales; but the poorest soil is on the hill-tops, yet they are most often caressed by the wandering zephyr, while the rich soil in the glen below rests undisturbed in its calm seclusion. [Zephyr is a pretty word ; bring it in again.]

" A deep lake, — sylvan, volatile zephyr, — only passes lightly over the surface, — profound depths, — unmoved, oysters hidden there, with pearls in 'em, — gold-fish too, no, not gold-fish, — might seem an allusion to filthy lucre, and perhaps even make the audience think of eels. [Work this up.]

" In winter you behold only a landscape of snow ; yet what rich meadows, what germs of fruitfulness lie dormant and concealed beneath it ! Thus does a cold and formal manner oft mark a loving nature, in which the warm affections, the marital and maternal yearnings of women rest undeveloped by the rays of love.

" If cold hearts sought cold climates, and warm ones the tropics, the women would all be congregated at the equator.

" In the starry heavens there are distant worlds which to the eye of ignorance seem as one, but which the learned know to be binary ; and how many couples are there who appear to be happily united, but whose hearts in reality move in widely separate orbits !

" Our present laws make the connubial tie, a hard knot, easy to do, difficult to undo. How much better were it merely a beau-knot, to be tied or untied at pleasure !

"The passions of man act upon his heart like acids on a metal, while the ennui of prolonged maidenhood is like the rust of time, slower in its operation, but none the less consuming.

"Yet it is better for a superior woman to exist alone, than to be united to an inferior man. In the one case she preserves her purity undimmed; in the other, like an alloy of silver with a baser metal, she becomes lost in the union and her beauty is tarnished. [Belle — bell-metal, — something can be made out of this.]

"Potassium brought in contact with ice, unites in combustion with the oxygen which it separates from the hydrogen; thus those who are coldly united in the bond of matrimony may become inflamed with love when a stronger affinity appears. [Very fine — scientific.]

"Man yearns for a congenial mind; woman for a congenial heart. Is not this a metaphysical subtlety? Is not the heart (in a poetical, not an anatomical sense) a figurative expression for certain qualities of the mind? Let us then say: man looks for kindred intellectual powers; woman for kindred sympathies. Yet how can we reconcile this with the old adage that people like their opposites? Does not this apply only to opposite sexes?

"Man (when successful) is happy in the love that he feels; woman in that which she inspires. [Only partially true.]

"A red-hot poker is painful to the touch; toss it in water, and the heat, being diffused among the particles of the liquid, will not burn. Thus, if our affections are divided among many, we may pass through life without sorrow; it is only when they are concentrated on one object that love becomes a consuming flame. [Good; but the poker is objectionable. Substitute something else for the poker.]

"As a little match will kindle a great fire, so doth some trifling act of kindness, on the part of the opposite sex, start the flame of love.

"Mr. Peewit says that a married couple should be called three, instead of one; because the woman is won, and the man too. But this is a vile pun. I thought Joseph was above such nonsense.

"What respiration is to the body, so is love to the soul; an involuntary function, yet woman cannot exist without it.

"Platonic love is an *ignis fatuus*. People may think to grasp it, but no one ever felt it.

"Jealousy and love may exist together, like an amalgam of mercury and gold; but the warmth of true affection drives away all trace of the ignoble portion of the compound, and leaves the other pure.

"A mirror may diminish our vanity; but love is only increased by reflection.

"The imagination is the pilot-fish of love.

" There may be women who care nothing for men ; but none are indifferent to Hymen. Marriage is said to be a lottery ; but to enter into it without love, — to marry for the sake of a husband, instead of the individual, — is like throwing your money into the sea. Yea, more, — it is like throwing yourself into a sea where all is bitterness.

" Woman would rather be adored than adorable.

" The yoke of love, like a yoke of oxen, is a good thing for the husbandman.

" To her who is indifferent, all men are men ; to her who loves, there is but one man in the world ; all the rest are merely human beings.

" If men knew all that women thought, and women all that men thought, how very differently — [Erased]. [This idea leads to such frightful conclusions, that I shrink from pursuing it.]

" A woman with only beauty to recommend her is like gilded copper.

" More women are lost by curiosity than by passion. [How few men are aware of this !]

" ' The altar of Hymen,' says Mlle. Sophie Arnauld, ' is the extinguisher of Love.'
" Is it not rather his dark lantern, where the flame may still burn brightly, although not displayed to the world?

" 27th. — Observed Charity sitting under the trees, watching the proceedings of Messrs. Lovell and Peewit in the melon-patch beyond. Saw *him* leave his office, cross the garden, and enter into conversation with her. Wishing to speak to Mr. P., I was necessarily obliged to pass through the grove. As I did so, Charity caught me by the hand, saying, —

" ' I want a witness. Listen !

" ' You can give me your answer at another time,' said he.

" ' No, sir,' she replied, ' I shall give it now ; and it is the only one you will ever get. I declare to you, in the presence of Miss Griffin, that I am utterly indifferent to you, and that, come what may, I will never consent to be your wife.'

" He bowed and left. But as he turned to go I caught his eye. Oh, the triumph of that moment ! What mortification and rage were shown in his face ! Truly I may say that for once I have experienced happiness. Charity is really a superior girl. No wonder Lovell is so infatuated.

" Partook of a hearty meal at noon in my room.

" Evening. Went down to dinner for the first time since my illness. The good doctor took me by the hand, and kindly expressed his joy at seeing me about again. My indisposition, he said, was owing to my not having become accustomed to the perfect harmony and entire absence of all mental agitation of our new life. Heigh-ho ! How little man knows of the secret workings of a woman's heart ! I could not eat ; and Joseph seemed much concerned on my account.

" 28th. *Sabbath.* — Mr. Malpest at the breakfast-table

8

looked ill at ease, yet, with characteristic dissimulation, he ate heartily. What an effort it must have been! I have quite recovered my health and spirits. Wore my green dress, and Joseph could not take his eyes off me. He was about to pay me some handsome compliment, when Mrs. S. asked him to pass her the beans. She said she once had a parrot whose colors matched mine exactly. The malicious bloomer! I told her I once saw an organ-grinder with a dressed-up monkey, from whose costume I presumed she had copied hers.

"Charity remained in her room, and Mr. Lovell had no appetite. The doctor was in high spirits. Everything, he said, was working so harmoniously.

"At ten o'clock he assembled us in the oratory, and gave us a learned discourse on the prophets. He told us that after forty years' hard study of Revelations, and of Daniel's prophecy in relation to the four prophetic secular monarchies of the Gentiles, the Babylonian, Medo-Persian, Grecian, and Roman, he had at last found the key by which the portals of these mysteries were to be unlocked; that the explanation of the whole system was now clear to him, both in its application to the past, the present, and the future. From the incipient disintegration of the Roman Empire, the 1260 days foretold (which mean years) point clearly to the year 1866 as the beginning of the end of the Pope. The Napoleonic dynasty, being the seventh symbolical and the eighth apocalyptic head of the Roman Empire, will achieve universal dominion preparatory to its final overthrow. Louis Napoleon, being the true 666, is the last Anti-Christ, and the final depository of Papal authority (for the Euphrates evidently means the Seine, — Paris, as we know, being the modern Babylon).

He and Monsieur Rothschild (who is typified, as the dullest understanding can see, by the golden candlestick with seven branches) are to lead the Jews back to Palestine, and annihilate the Turks, Mormons, Quakers, and all other heretics, on the field of Armageddon.

" The crucial point of the scheme is the year 1866, when there will be a general cataclysm of nations, after which the Millenium will begin. From Revelations, third chapter, he proves conclusively that the glorious period will be inaugurated at Foufouville ; for Laodicea, being rich with gold, evidently stands for New York ; Philadelphia is mentioned by name, and Foufouville, being midway between them, is clearly indicated under the symbolical name of Sardis.*

" Professor Malpest, who has doubtless passed a restless night, fell asleep during the discourse.

" Mr. Lovell, strange to say, did the same.

" Joseph, who dislikes sermons, because, as he says, they weary him, slipped away before the doctor began. While taking a walk, he found a kitten, to whose tail some mischievous youths had tied a tin cup, and who were amusing themselves by stoning it and otherwise maltreating it. (Such is human nature !) Joseph took the unfortunate waif away from them and presented it to me. What a kind heart he has ! Being a tom I named it Joe.

" *Afternoon.*— One Mr. Longshanks, a friend of Mr. Lovell's, arrived at noon. He is a fine-looking person and I should think a man of sensibility. I wonder if he is married. He and Lovell have been walking up and

---

* This discourse was published some years afterwards in a New York newspaper, but, with the characteristic unscrupulousness of a piratical press, was not credited to Dr. Goodenough. — *Note by the Author.*

down the garden for more than an hour, the latter apparently somewhat excited. What can be the matter? It is so close in my room that I will go and rest awhile in the grove.

" *Evening.* — As I was passing through the garden, I caught the following words.

Lovell. — ' — Right arm be withered — have her — fair means or foul.'

" Longshanks. — ' Keep cool, my boy; keep cool. Look at me and see how cool I am. I'll have an interview with the old man, and perhaps may affect a change in his views. What works did you say he had published? Studies on the generation of Utopians, and what else?

" Lovell. — ' No, no. You've got them mixed up. The New Uto —'

" At this moment they entered the house so that I unfortunately heard no more."

CHAPTER V.

A Discussion between Dr. Goodenough and Mr. Longshanks.

FOR the report of most of the following conversation we are indebted to Miss Griffin, and, as we know from other sources that it took place immediately after the incidents related at the conclusion of the last chapter, the inference is unavoidable, that, led by her inquiring mind and ardent desire to seek for the truth under all circumstances, that young lady must have hastened from the garden up to her room, where, as we know, there were peculiar facilities for finding out what was going on in the doctor's study below.

In order not to take up valuable space, we omit the preliminary words of mere politeness with which the dialogue began, and which ended in Dr. Goodenough and Mr. Longshanks being seated opposite to each other.

LONGSHANKS. — " I have made this pilgrimage to Harmony Hall, sir, in the hope of being permitted before I die to enjoy for once the society of the author of those philanthropical, those sublime, those immortal works, the delight and solace of my life, the ' Generation of Offspring' — I mean the — the — "

DR. GOODENOUGH. — " The Regeneration of Man? "

LONG. — Yes, sir. That's it, ' The Regeneration of Man,' and ' Studies on the Development of Healthy Utopians.' "

8*

Doctor. — "Offspring."

Long. — "I mean 'Offspring,' sir. You see I am some-what confused at finding myself in your presence for the first time. Man cannot gaze on the sun, and preserve an unruffled countenance. The great luminary is too much for him."

Doctor. — "Stop, my good friend. Such language should not be used to a mortal. I am but an humble individual striving to benefit my fellow-man. If any thanks are due for the success of my efforts, give them not to me, but to the source of the inspiration that penned those works. I am gratified to hear that they have had so great an influence upon you. Thousands, nay, millions are destined to be affected in the same way. I presume you contemplate joining our society at once?"

Long. — " I regret to acknowledge, sir, that just at present it is impossible for me to break the ties that bind me to the world, however great may be my desire to do so. It is to my friend Mr. Lovell (whose admiration of your works is equal to my own) that I am indebted for this happiness, the privilege of being here to-day. He is a superior young man."

Doctor. — " Brother Leander is a worthy youth. His instincts are good, though I fear he is yet somewhat under the sway of his passions; but I have given him some sage advice, and do not doubt that he will yet over-come them with the aid of reason."

Long. — " He is honorably connected, has excellent principles, and is well educated."

Doctor. — " I cannot agree with you on the latter point. Why, sir, he actually does not understand Greek!"

Long. — " Of what use is Greek, sir, to a man in business, — that is, — I mean, who expected to go into business?"

Doctor. — " Sir, Latin and Greek are the foundation of all knowledge."

Long. — " But are they worth the time and trouble it takes to acquire them? What do you gain that is an adequate compensation for years spent in the study of dead languages?"

Doctor. — " The discipline of the mind."

Long. — "' To discipline,' according to Dr. Johnson, means 'to educate, to regulate, to keep in order, to reform, to chastise.' Now, whichever of these words may be substituted for ' discipline' in the above expression, it is evident that the effect — whatever it may be — is to be produced either by the application and labor necessary in learning these difficult languages, or else by reading the books that are written in them. As to the application and labor, as much, if not more, are required to master mathematics, and the natural sciences ; but if it is the study of a language, — of mere words without ideas, — that is wanted to produce this peculiar effect of ' disciplining the mind,' we have modern languages, two of which, French and German, are considered nearly if not quite as difficult as Greek and Latin.

" If this ' disciplining the mind,'— whatever it may mean, — is to be effected by reading the writings of antiquity, it may be done by means of the very excellent translations that have appeared. It is true that a foreign phrase cannot always be given in English, word for word, and that certain idiomatic expressions may occasionally lose something of their force ; but in a good translation the spirit and ideas must remain essentially the same as in the original, and as the benefit to be gained is derived, not from the mere words, but from the ideas, it must remain the same, no matter in what tongue they are expressed."

DOCTOR. — "You forget how much our pleasure is enhanced by reading the thoughts of the great minds of former times in their own language."

LONG. — "It would be a pleasure dearly purchased by years of preparatory study; besides, if every one could read these works in the original, how few would have either the time or the inclination to do so! or, if they had is it certain that their perusal would repay them ?"

DOCTOR. — "Not repay them? Herodotus, Plato, Pliny !"

LONG. "All the historical works of the Greeks and Romans are filled with misrepresentation and superstition. They frequently give long and tiresome harangues of ambassadors to ambassadors, or generals to their troops, which were never really spoken. Suppose Mr. Bancroft should write interminable disquisitions, and represent them in his 'History of the United States' as orations delivered by General Washington; would his work be considered trustworthy? On the contrary, the very men who defend this fault in the ancient, would condemn it in the modern writer.

"These old histories have other and more important defects ; and he who reads them for the sake of information becomes confused by the conflicting accounts of the same events, the exaggerations and the prodigies related as facts. He knows not what to believe, nor what to disbelieve, and finishes them with a feeling of dissatisfaction, if not of disgust. To become acquainted with ancient history, we must turn to the pages of Gibbon, Nie-

buhr, Milnor, and others, men of research and discrimination, who have studied and sifted the writings of antiquity, and, rejecting what is evidently false, reconciling the
contradictions where it is possible to do so, and where it
is not, adopting the most probable version, have given us
works on which we can rely."

The doctor's face assumed as strong an expression of
contempt as was possible to appear on his benevolent
countenance.

Doctor. — " Perhaps, sir, you do not regard the philosophers of ancient times as sages?"

Long. — " The philosophers of antiquity have a high
reputation among the admirers of the classics ; and those
who have not read their writings doubtless imagine they
were the prototypes of the philosophers of modern times.
Excepting in regard to their mathematicians, there can
be no greater error.   They were sometimes men of virtuous
lives, — according to the ideas of the age in which they
lived, — and their discourses undoubtedly contain some
words of true wisdom, — some beautiful and sublime
thoughts ; but, for each grain of these, the reader must wade
through an immense amount of chaff in the shape of long
and wearisome disquisitions, usually in the form of dia-
logues, full of hair-splitting differences of opinion on matters sometimes utterly unfathomable by human wisdom, and
sometimes easily solved, in this nineteenth century, with
but a school-boy's knowledge.   Macaulay says that ' all
the metaphysical discoveries of all the philosophers, from
the time of Socrates to the Northern invasion, are not to
be compared in importance with those which have been
made in England every fifty years since the time of Elizabeth.'   John Adams says that after reading all these

metaphysical subtleties of the ancients we have ' learned nothing; and economy of time requires that we should waste no more in so idle an amusement.' Says Jefferson, ' When Plato puts into the mouth of Socrates such quibbles on words and sophisms as a school-boy would be ashamed of, we may conclude they were the whimsies of his own foggy brain.' How puerile and nonsensical their rigmaroles appear, compared with the works of a Bacon, a Locke, or a Humboldt!"

Mr. Longshanks had evidently become excited with his subject. He rose to his feet, inadvertently kicking over his chair as he did so; and, with one foot planted in his hat, which he had crushed on the floor, one arm akimbo, and gesticulating rapidly with the other, he continued his diatribe. As to the doctor, he was perfectly aghast, and sat with open mouth, and spectacles on top of his head, without proffering a word; like the Aztecs, who, when the Spaniards were pulling down their favorite idols, were so taken by surprise at the audacious profanation, that they seemed as if transfixed with horror and astonishment, and could not move to their assistance.

Mr. Longshanks continued, as follows, —

" The best of the ethics of these long-winded old heathens can be found in fewer words and clearer language in the ten commandments. But if it is a waste of time to read their moral philosophy, even though it be correct, the same can hardly be said of their natural philosophy, for if one-half the information they give us in physical science is founded on fact, then the philosophers of modern times hold some very erroneous opinions, and the sooner they go through a course of Plato, Socrates, etc., the better. The wonders revealed by the telescope and microscope, and by chemical analysis, are insignificant when compared to some of the discoveries claimed by the sages of Greece.

" The ' Timeus' of Plato is looked upon by pedants as one of the most profound works ever written. Such is its profundity, that persons whose mental vision is limited by common sense are unable to see anything whatever in its muddy depths. In this learned effusion we are informed that there are just four elementary bodies, of which all other substances are formed, namely : air, earth, fire, and water ; and, moreover, that three of these elements are composed of scalene triangles, and the fourth of isosceles triangles.

" One Anaximenes taught that the heavens were a vault of solid crystal, in which the stars were inserted like nails. The sun, he said, was about the same size as the earth. But Anaxagoras looked upon Anaximenes with contempt, because he could prove that its diameter was no greater than that of the Peloponnesus ; while Heraclitus considered them both ignoramuses ; for, in his eyes, it was only as large as a house. Anaximander believed the moon to be on fire ; Empedocles, that it was as far from the earth as from the sun. One of these old wiseacres tells us that the earth is square and flat ; another, that it is shaped like a soup-plate ; and another that it has the exact form of a kettle-drum. Zeno says that it is the centre of the universe, and that the firmament revolves around it ; and this was the general opinion of the ancients.

" Now, there once lived an English gentleman, named Newton,— Sir Isaac Newton, — who is considered pretty good authority on matters of natural science. And it was the belief of this Sir Isaac Newton that these ancient hypotheses were utterly false and absurd. The fact is that in those days people had but little correct information on physical matters. While they excelled in sculpture and architecture, and had made considerable progress in mathematics, and even in astronomy, notwithstanding some erroneous notions, their geographical knowledge was limited almost to the shores of the Mediterranean ; medicine was in its infancy (and perhaps is still) ; surgery was but a branch of butchery ; while chemistry, geology, and other kindred sciences were utterly unknown. Lord Bacon had not yet inculcated the principles of inductive science ; and the so-called philosophers of the time, instead of seeking to discover facts on which to found theories, began by fancying some whimsical hypothesis, which they pretended to prove by reasoning, more or less logical or illogical, or by a statement of facts which they found, not in Nature, but in their imaginations ; and it would seem that just in proportion as their imaginations were vivid, did their equally ignorant, but less imaginative followers look up to them as sages, and regard them with veneration.

"In the idle and ignorant population of Athens, these old rhapsodists easily found a few followers, as Jane Southcote, Mother Lee, Joe Smith, and other worthies have done in more recent times ; but they and their doctrines were contemned by the more sensible of the people, at least we may infer that such was the case, from the writings of contemporary dramatists.

"Aristophanes, in his farce of the 'Clouds,' treats some of the principal among them, and their teachings, with the most unmeasured ridicule and contempt, not only lavishing upon them such epithets as 'imbeciles,' and 'charlatan vagabonds,' but directly accusing them of

crimes against the morals of the people, and the religion
and laws of the State. The admirable dialogue between
impersonifications of justice and injustice is a biting criticism on the ethics of the philosophers. Now, if these
gentlemen had been held in any estimation by the Athe-
nian public, it is hardly credible that Aristophanes would
have deliberately ventured to revile and ridicule them in
so merciless a manner. We may, therefore, conclude that
by all their contemporaries, excepting their immediate
followers, they were looked upon in very much the same
light as the crack-brained individual who, some years ago,
was accustomed to hold forth from the steps of the city
hall in New York, calling himself the Angel Gabriel.

" It was not discovered that they were sages until they
had become ancients.

"One somewhat unorthodox modern writer, named
Anthon, calls their notions ' a train of fanciful conceptions, numbers, ideas, proportions, qualities, and elementary forms, in which philosophers took refuge as the
asylum of ignorance.'

" In reading their absurdities, one is tempted to fancy
that if the individual who asserted that the moon was
made of green cheese, or old Mother Goose, who declared
that the cow jumped over it, had been so fortunate as to
have lived a few thousand years ago, they also might
have set up for philosophers.

" These old fellows appear to have written their lucubrations rather for the sake of displaying their rhetorical
or argumentative powers, than for any useful purpose ; in
fact, they constantly assert, in their works, that it is *beneath the dignity* of philosophy to endeavor to alleviate
the physical sufferings, or to add to the material comforts

of life. The learned men — that is to say, the men of science — of modern times, write, and not only write, but study and labor in order to discover facts that may benefit their fellow-men ; and the classical scholar, who studies by gas-light, who travels by steam, who sends an important message by the electric telegraph, who undergoes a surgical operation, which, owing to the influence of chloroform, seems like a pleasing dream, or who has been saved from the small-pox by vaccination, is certainly unappreciative and ungrateful, if he does not acknowledge that the men to whom he owes these blessings have done more for his happiness, and are more deserving of admiration than all the stoic, epicurean, platonic, peripatetic, laughing and crying philosophers that ever lived."

Longshanks now paused to take breath. The doctor, who was still in a bewildered state of mind, could only say, in an indignant tone, " Go on, sir, go on."

So Mr. Longshanks went on.

" Those who have not read the celebrated ' Natural History' of Pliny sometimes labor under the delusion that it is a standard work on this subject.   Such is not the opinion of Monsieur Cuvier.

" Some of the statements of Pliny are undoubtedly correct, such as that a cow has horns, an ass ears, etc. ; but his work is chiefly filled with monstrous accounts of dragons, winged horses, the phœnix, basilisks, salamanders, mermaids, and fish that are connoisseurs of music. Cuvier, one of the most profound and exact naturalists that ever lived, and who gave the animal kingdom its present classification, treats the work of Pliny with the utmost contempt, calling its author ' a compiler devoid of genius, research, or discrimination, or any personal knowledge of the subject on which he wrote, who collected in a confused mass, mingling what was false with what was true, all the vulgar errors and superstitions of his time.'

" Should some future biographer draw a Plutarchian parallel between Pliny and Professor Agassiz, it would, doubtless, be like this: 'If these great men resembled each other in their lives, inasmuch as they both interested themselves in natural history, they differed in their manner of acquiring information. While the American sought for facts by direct observation and experiment, the Roman contented himself with noting down the silly superstitions of an ignorant people. If the modern is correct as to his facts, and his theories are logical deductions from them, those of the ancient are unworthy of belief, and his speculations on them ridiculous. Lastly, if the writings of Agassiz are invaluable to the student, those of Pliny are as worthless and as incredible as the stories of Baron Munchausen.'"

The doctor's indignation now became stronger than his astonishment. However, he choked down his rising wrath and with an effort at calmness, said, —

"I am astonished; such paradoxical sentiments I never heard expressed before. What is the world coming to? Now, granting for the sake of argument that the ancient chroniclers are untrustworthy, the natural historians given to the supernatural, the philosophers unphilosophical, what say you to the poets, dramatists, orators, etc., — are not their works worth reading?

LONG. — "Many of them are, for some of them are among the finest ever written; but most of them contain passages, or sentiments, so licentious and gross, that if

found in a modern book, they would cause it to be ban-
ished from a respectable library.

"The indiscriminating admirers of the classics are
generally pedants who have been educated in the idea
that these works are the perfection of human genius, and
judging everything by its comparison with the ancient,
every modern performance appears to them defective just
inasmuch as it differs from their false standard; as the
Hottentot, comparing the missionary's white wife with
his own sable mistress, objects to her fair complexion,
and clear blue eyes, and deems no article of her dress so
becoming as the ring in his lady's nose.

"These pedants sometimes have sufficient discernment
to detect the real faults in a contemporary work, but
their perverted judgment can see none in one written two
thousand years ago. In every silly platitude or ridiculous error they fancy some occult meaning. As Thack-
eray sarcastically observes, 'They would mention Pythag-
oras' precept to abstain from beans, and say that he
probably meant to insinuate thereby that wise men should
abstain from public affairs;' or Dean Swift, —

> "'As learned commentators view
> In Homer more than Homer knew.'

"This propensity to admire the old, apparently only
because old, at the expense of the new, has always prevailed. Even some of those whom we now regard as
ancients complained of this as an injustice to themselves.
Thus Horace, in his first epistle to Augustus, speaking
of some poem written several centuries before his time,
asks, 'Are verses like wine which time renders better?'
And again, in the same letter, 'Is it reasonable that peo-

ple should go into ecstasies over a long poem for a brilliant word here and there, or a few verses that run smoothly?'

"If what I have urged against ancient literature be false, and all the classics, unreliable historians, ignorant philosophers, immoral poets, and all deserved to be read, and. it were worth while to learn Latin and Greek in order to read them, there would still remain an argument against the enforced study of these languages, which is wholly disconnected with the value, or worthlessness, of works written in them; this is, that of all those who are obliged to spend so much time in poring over Latin Grammars and Greek lexicons not one in a thousand acquires sufficient proficiency to read Latin and Greek with any fluency, or consequently any pleasure; and of those, but a very small portion ever go through a course of classical reading, or, in fact, ever read one quarter of the standard works in their own language; while, as to the great majority of students, they who cannot or will not become proficients in the dead languages, school and college days over, the classics are thrown aside forever, and the mass of words forced into unwilling minds, at the expense of so much time and trouble, are soon forgotten in the turmoil of business and society. Hence, whatever advantages there may be in knowing Latin and Greek, they are lost to them, and the years they were obliged to waste in endeavoring to learn them, and which might have been profitably employed, have been spent in vain."

Longshanks' flood of words was apparently too much for the doctor. He appeared to be almost overcome, and made but feeble efforts to stem the torrent.

Doctor. — "We sometimes meet learned foreigners

9*

who do not speak English, but understand the dead languages."

LONG. — " Sir, you might as well learn Hebrew in the hope of some day having a chat with the Wandering Jew."

DOCTOR. — " Think how much a classical education adds to our appreciation of the beautiful, architectural, and sculptural remains of antiquity."

LONG. — " Think how much a knowledge of French adds to our appreciation of Paris fashions, and how much speaking Chinese would improve the flavor of tea ! "

DOCTOR. — " The study of Latin and Greek facilitates the acquisition of modern languages."

LONG. — " This is true ; but it is absurd to offer it as an argument for learning them. You might as well say that a man should learn to ride on an elephant that he might the more easily learn to ride on horseback."

DOCTOR. — (With an air of triumph,) " THE DERIVA-TION OF WORDS."

LONG. — " Many of our words are derived from Latin and Greek, and many more from French, German, etc. ; but none of these are original languages, and suppose they were, what of it? Of what advantage would it be to know the derivation of words? "

DOCTOR — " It would give us a clearer comprehension of our own tongue."

LONG. — " I think not, sir. While many words have the same meaning as their foreign or ancient derivatives, others have changed or modified their signification, and are still doing so, as any person who has read works written in English a few centuries, or even a century ago, must be aware. Now if a word conveys precisely the same idea in English as its derivative, it is impossible that a knowledge of the language of the latter can make its meaning any clearer to us ; while, if the derivative has a different sense, it is plain that an acquaintance with that fact must cause the English word to carry less precision of signification to the mind, by confusing us with two ideas at once. We do not experience a double enjoyment by listening at the same time to two different pieces of music.

" But supposing this was not so, and that understanding the dead languages was an advantage to us in English, would not this be a very trifling return to urge as a reason for giving up years to their study?

" To a lexicographer a knowledge of the derivation of words is essential, and the more he knows of Greek, Latin, Hebrew, Sanscrit, French, German, High Dutch, Low Dutch, Saxon, Norse, Danish, Persian, Chaldee, etc., etc., etc., the better. But we do not all intend to compile dictionaries ; and it may well be doubted, if, to those who do not, it would be of any more practical utility to have at their tongues' end the derivation of every word in the language, than when eating an apple-pie to know where the apples came from."

The doctor sank back in his chair and actually gasped for breath. It was some minutes before he recovered from the shock his feelings had received.

DOCTOR. — "The dead languages are a good basis to the various pursuits of life."

LONG. — "There are few pursuits to which such a basis is worth its expense. A four-story house may require a foundation fifteen or twenty feet in depth ; but a man would be a fool who built one equally deep for his hen-house.

" Among the professions in the study of which Latin and Greek are supposed to be of the greatest service, are medicine and law; yet many physicians and lawyers have risen to eminence without them. It may, indeed, be asserted that classical learning would have been of some assistance to them ; but it can be said, on the other hand, that the time which, under other circumstances, they would have spent in acquiring it, was doubtless passed in gaining knowledge more directly useful. It is true there are some Latin and Greek words and phrases, that a physician or lawyer is obliged to understand; but these are so few that they can easily be learned in studying the rudiments of his profession. To learn a whole language for the sake of a dozen words is no more reasonable than it would be to gather a whole orchard of apples to make the apple-pie just spoken of.

" There will doubtless always be found some persons to maintain that a knowledge of Latin and Greek is neces-sary in their particular avocations. Whether they be right or wrong, let them study these languages if they will; let them become perfect Porsons if they can; but because they think this learning useful to them, — a few, —•is it right that its attempted acquisition should be made obligatory on everybody else? It is no more just than it would be for the whole world of M. D.s, D.D.s, LL.D.s, and all to be forced to waste a portion of their lives in learning to turn back somersets or to walk on their heads, because they are accomplishments required in the calling of a clown. In fact, considering the little attention given to physical development in the United

States, I think that these gymnastic performances might be substituted for the dead languages with great advantage, not only to the bodily but to the intellectual progress of the rising generation.

"Yet this supposition that Latin and Greek are of use in a few professions is one of the principal pretexts for making everybody study them. Would it not be wiser to confine the efforts of young scholars to the gaining of information useful to all, leaving it to those who think they will need these languages, the time, trouble, and expense of learning them?"

A smile of complacent scorn passed over the doctor's face.

"Happily, sir," said he, "your absurd notions are not shared in by others."

Long. — "You are mistaken, sir. I have in my pocket a paper on education, by the Rev. Sidney Smith, and as his profession, his reputation, and his known moderation, learning, and ability add weight to his words, I will take the liberty of reading a few passages. He says, 'There never was a more complete instance in any country of such extravagant and overacted attachment to any branch of knowledge than that which obtains in England with regard to classical knowledge. ... Now, this long career of classical study you may, if you please, denominate a foundation; but it is a foundation so far above ground, that there is absolutely no room to put anything upon it. If you occupy a man with one thing till he is twenty-four years of age, you have exhausted all his leisure time. He is called into the world and compelled to act, or is surrounded with pleasures, and thinks and reads no more. If you have neglected to put other things into him, they

will never get in afterwards. If you have fed him only
with words, he will remain a narrow and limited being
to the end of his existence. . . . When a young man
has finished his education, the great system of facts
with which he is most perfectly acquainted are the in-
trigues of the heathen gods, . . . talents for speculation
[*speculation*, so useful to an American], and original in-
quiry he has none, nor has he formed the invaluable habit
of tracing things up to their first principles, or of collect-
ing dry and unamusing facts as the materials of reasoning. . . . A classical scholar is a man principally acquainted with the works of the imagination ; . . . all the
solid and masculine parts of his understanding are left
wholly without cultivation.' Speaking of classical pedants, he says, ' Their minds have been so completely possessed by exaggerated notions of classical learning, that
they have not been able, in the great school of the world,
to form any other notion of real greatness ; . . . their object in life is not to reason, imagine, or invent, but to
conjugate, decline, and derive. . . . The English clergy,
in whose hands education chiefly rests, bring up the first
young men in the country as if they were all to keep
grammar schools. . . . An infinite quantity of talent is
thus annually destroyed in the universities. . . . In those
who were destined for the church, we would undoubtedly
encourage classical learning more than in any other body
of men ; but if we had to do with a young man going out
into public life, we would exhort him to contemn, or at
least not to affect, the reputation of a great scholar. He
should learn what the constitution of his country was,
how it had grown into its present state, the perils that
had threatened it, the malignity that had attacked it, the

courage that had fought for it, the wisdom that had made it great.' Sidney Smith wrote only for England; but if this excessive devotion to classical studies is uncalled for there, where so large a portion of those who go through it are born to hereditary fortunes, and are consequently at leisure to pass their lives in the cultivation of literary tastes, or in doing nothing, how much more useless must it be in America, where so few can afford to be idle?

"The majority of men in the United States are engaged in mercantile or agricultural pursuits. Now, granting that a knowledge of the dead languages may be of some assistance in two or three professions, will any one assert that they can be of as much use to a merchant or farmer as the modern languages to the former or the natural sciences to the latter?

"Thomas Jefferson,—a man of wealth, of classical learning, and an admirer of the best writings of antiquity, who lived while the paramount utility of classical studies was still unquestioned, before science had perfected the steam-engine, the electric telegraph been thought of, or Liebig published his researches in agricultural chemistry, —when asked his opinion as to the study of Latin and Greek, spoke doubtingly in its favor, adding, 'For the merchant, I should not say those languages are a necessity; ethics, mathematics, geography, political economy, history, seem to constitute the immediate foundations of his calling; the agriculturist needs ethics, mathematics, chemistry, and natural philosophy.' But there is no hesitation in his mind when speaking of French. 'The French language,' he says, 'become that of the general intercourse of nations, and, from their extraordinary advances, now the depository of all science, is an indispensable part of the education of both sexes.'

" He gave a practical illustration of the comparative value he placed on different branches of study by the course he proposed should be pursued at the University of Virginia. The students being supposed to have received an elementary education, only a part of the first year was to be given to languages ; the rest of that year, and the whole of the two following ones were to be devoted to mathematics and scientific studies, particularly chemistry, geology, botany, and mineralogy ; ' but the students were not to be all held to one prescribed course of study. Elementary qualification only was required in general knowledge, while they were at liberty to apply themselves more exclusively to those branches which were to qualify them for the particular vocations to which they were destined.'

" Now, if these studies were worthy of the high comparative position thus assigned them fifty or sixty years ago, of how much greater importance must they be at the present time, when such advances have been made in all of them?

" It is not to the men of classical learning, but to the men of science that we are indebted for nearly all the comforts of civilized life.   The mere classical scholar may possibly be an ornamental, but he certainly is not a useful, member of society. A Davy, a Watts, a Fulton, a Franklin, the inventor of a reaping or sewing machine, a steam plough, or a method of lessening the cost of cotton, iron, or any other commodity, contributes more to the happiness of mankind than all the Porsons, Bentleys, Heynes, or Mezzofantis that ever lived.

" Few discoverers or inventors have been men of classical attainments. If they had been, it is possible that many of them would have frittered away their lives in weighing the value of Greek particles, in hunting for ' anapæsts in the wrong place,' or in muddling their brains with the ' Sylburgian method of arranging defectives ; ' civilization would be fifty years behindhand ; it would take a week to go from New York to Albany ; our Brussels carpets (if we had any) would be soiled by grease spots from our tallow candles ; vanity or love would pay a hundred dollars for a portrait, or go without it, instead of getting a photograph (which is better) for fifty cents ; our matchless city press would be confined to a single newspaper about the size of the ' Foufouville Gazette,' but costing four times as much ; and land would not be worth as many hundreds as it is now worth thousands of dollars."

Longshanks again paused. He evidently thought (to use a metaphorical expression) that he had laid the doctor out flat, but he found that the old gentleman was not to be put down so easily.

DOCTOR. — " Let natural philosophy, botany, astronomy, chemistry (organic, inorganic, analytic, and synthetic) ; agriculture, horticulture, arboriculture, and all the other cultures ; mineralogy, geology, physiology, conchology, paleontology, ichthyology, ornithology, zoology, and all the other ologies ; geography, photography, topography, and all the other ographics ; optics, acoustics, mathematics, — the whole course ; — arithmetic, algebra, geometry, ditto, descriptive and analytic ; mensuration of surfaces and solids ; equations of the point and straight lines ; conic sections ; line and plane in space ; general equation of the second degree ; surfaces of the second order ; spherical

10

projections (particularly useful to military men) ; trigo-
nometry, plane and spherical ; the calculus, differential
and integral ; surveying ; plane, geodesic, trigonometric,
and maritime ; mechanics ; hydraulics ; lights and shadows ;
perspective, linear and angular ; engineering ; theodolites ;
transits ; protractors ; prismatic compasses ; circumferen-
ters ; logarithms ; sines and tangents ; traverse tables,
plane tables, and puzzling tables, — let them all be studied,
with French, German, and Spanish, too ; but why give up
Latin and Greek? Why not learn them also?"

This fearful volley of words staggered Longshanks.
He dropped into his chair, and his battery was silenced
for the space of a full minute. He muttered to himself
" the life of man is but threescore and ten years." Then
he spoke aloud.

Long. — "There can be no Admirable Crichtons, no
men of universal knowledge in this nineteenth century ;
life is too short, and memory too limited ; a selection
must be made, and since some attainments have to be
rejected, would it not be wisest to let them be such as
are of no practical utility, confining our attention to
those that will be most likely to aid us on our way
through the world?"

Doctor. — "Sir, I would not permit a daughter of
mine to learn French ; there are too many vile books
published in that language."

Long. — "Then, sir, for the same reason, you should
not teach her to read English, and still less, Greek and
Latin. Sir, every advantage that can truthfully be urged
in favor of the study of dead languages applies also to
modern ones ; while a knowledge of the latter is attended

by many benefits, to which no one can pretend that the former have any claim.

"If understanding the former enables us more easily to learn the latter, the converse of the proposition is also true; that understanding the latter enables us more easily to learn the former; and if both are worth acquiring it is surely best to begin with the most useful ones.

"If we sometimes meet with a Greek or Latin phrase that it would be well to understand, for every such phrase we see whole books in French, German, Spanish, or Italian, that it would be well to read.

"The pitiful argument of satisfying vanity, applies to the one as well as to the other.

"But the great and most important advantage that a modern language has over an ancient one is the fact that it is spoken by existing nations, and may be of service, not merely as an amusement for idle hours, but also in the professional or business relations of life. We constantly meet Europeans who do not understand English, and we are deprived of a pleasure, and perhaps of a profit, when we cannot converse with them; but there is no danger that we will ever meet with an ancient Greek or Roman (unless through the agency of a spiritual medium, and as ghosts, the whole of them, Cæsar, Pompey, Homer, and all speak English, more or less grammatically). When I hear a man boast of being a good Greek and Latin scholar, I cannot help thinking as of a good billiard-player, 'Alas! how much time he must have wasted.'

"For more than a thousand years they have been dead languages, doctors of law have thoroughly dissected them, is it not time that they were buried in oblivion?"

During the latter part of Longshanks' diatribe the doctor's wrath and indignation were gradually getting the upper hand of him. He endeavored to maintain his equanimity, and grew red in the face from his efforts to do so; but when Longshanks had the audacity to propose to bury in oblivion the languages of Homer and Horace he could no longer restrain his anger. Jumping up, in a high state of excitement, he exclaimed, —

"Stop, sir. I will listen to no more. Patience has ceased to be a virtue. I did not suppose that such ignorance, conceit, and folly, existed in the world. Sir, you are a — a — but pardon me, pardon me. I am forgetting myself."

Long. — "Pardon me, sir. It is I who have forgotten myself, or rather who forgot you. In the heat of argument I became oblivious of the fact that I was in the presence of the author of that sublime work, 'Studies on the Regen—'"

Doctor — "No more compliments if you please, sir, for as the eloquent Tusculan says, 'Quanquam ista assentatio, quamvis perniciosa sit, nocere tamen nemini potest, nisi ei, qui eam recipit atque in ea delectatur.'"

Long. — "I do not quite comprehend all that, sir, for I do not speak Greek."

Doctor. — "You see now what you have lost by not devoting three or four years to the study of dead languages. Allow me to present you with this copy of the New Utopia. I hope you will read it with more attention than you seem to have given to my other works. You will find that its perusal will strengthen your powers of reason, and enlarge your views considerably."

Long. — "Accept my thanks, sir, for this invaluable work. I am impatient to begin the study of its sublime truths, for, as the sage of Geneva says, 'Il y a tant de contradictions entre les droits de la Nature et nos lois sociales, que pour les concilier il faut gauchir et tergiverser sans cesse.' "

DOCTOR. — "What language is that?"

LONG. — "French."

DOCTOR. — "French! Don't talk French to me, sir. The French are all infidels. What do they know about social philosophy, or anything else? Listen to the words of Socrates — "

LONG. — "Socrates be hanged, sir. Socrates was a fool compared to Voltaire or Rousseau."

DOCTOR. — (Stamping his foot with rage.) "Leave these premises, sir. You will contaminate this peaceful, God-fearing community. Away, sir — away."

LONG. — "I go, sir. And here (flinging the New Utopia on the floor) take your confounded Utopian nonsense."

So Mr. Longshanks went out, slamming the door, and leaving the doctor striding up and down the floor in a state of violent agitation. Longshanks found Leander waiting for him in the hall, and also much agitated, for having heard loud words between the two gentlemen, and naturally supposing himself to be the object of them, he was in much perturbation of mind as to the result of the interview. So the moment he saw Longshanks emerge from the study, he rushed up to him and grasping his hand, anxiously inquired if "it was happily settled?"

"What, Len, what?" asked Longshanks, who was still rather bewildered after his violent altercation with the doctor.

"'What!' you ask me 'what'!" said poor Leander.

"Oh! Ah! Your scrape with Miss Goodenough — well

10*

—well — yes — no — now I remember. No, I cannot exactly say that we did arrange the matter — that is to say — not definitely."

"Tell me what was done," said Leander. "Why do you keep me in suspense? What did the doctor propose?"

"Nothing."

"Nothing!"

"My poor Lenny," said Longshanks, the truth is, he got me on the subject of dead languages, my *bête noir;* and being pretty well primed, for I delivered an oration thereon last week before the 'Young·Men's Debating Club' of Mackerelville, I floored him easily, but as ill-luck would have it, I became excited in the heat of discussion by the old gentleman's absurd arguments, and entirely forgot what I went in for, — never thought of you or your affair, — 'pon honor, but wasted an hour in trying to convince the doctor that he was a regular old fool, and got kicked out of his office for my pains."

Leander ran his hands through his hair, though he did not pluck any out by the roots, as some despairing lovers are said to have done.

"What can I do? What can I do?" said he.

"Cut the whole crew," answered Longshanks, "and come back with me to Wall Street."

"Leave her," cried Lovell; "never while life endures. And do you, my friend, intend to desert me at this moment?"

"Now just be reasonable," answered Longshanks, "I can be of no use to you here, with her father exasperated against me; and, even were it otherwise, our business makes it imperative on me to be in town to-morrow morning, so I must take myself off as soon as possible."

Longshanks left; and Leander, hoping to find relief from the thoughts that oppressed him, in bodily exertion, went to work in the melon-patch; but he soon became wearied, and sitting down on a stone, like Marius on the ruins of Carthage, or Achilles mourning for Briseis, sat ruminating on his blasted hopes until the shades of night had fallen.

CHAPTER VI.

A Convention of the Female Rights Association.

"By Venus! the republic will henceforth be happy."
ARISTOPHANES, *in " The Assembly of Women."*

THE seventeenth annual convention of the Female Rights Association was held about this time; and, as some of the Harmonians figured therein, an account of what took place may expose some of the causes that brought about the unfortunate termination of the philanthropical experiment at Harmony Hall, which, as we have seen, began so auspiciously. We will, therefore, compile from the newspapers of the day a report of the proceedings, conforming as much as possible to the language of our authorities, but omitting whatever may be irrelevant to the object we have in view.

MORNING SESSION.

Dr. Mary Mott called the meeting to order, and proposed as chairman that noble champion of right, that sincere friend to woman, Professor Nicholas Malpest.

This gentleman, whose lectures on reform have been listened to by hundreds of admiring auditors throughout the rural districts, would doubtless have been chosen without opposition, had it not been for a Miss Griffin, who rose in an excited manner and objected to a man being called upon to preside over an assembly composed principally of the opposite sex.

"When," said she, "has a woman (though men sneer at her fondness for talking) ever been chosen Speaker of the House of Representatives? When was any woman ever admitted into any of our legislative halls, excepting as a mere spectator, to listen to interminable arguments on dry political or financial questions, any of which she could answer without thought? [Cries of 'Hear, hear!'] Is it because woman is inferior to man? Is it because she has nothing to say for herself? [Indignant shouts of 'No, NO!'] There is no reason; and until men vote for women, I shall vote for no man." [Cries of "Good, good!" and great applause.]

Professor Malpest now rose, and stated that his name had been proposed without his sanction, and much to his surprise [Ironical cries of "Oh, Oh!" from the gallery], and that he would gladly waive any claims he might have to the honor sought to be conferred upon him in consequence of his humble though arduous efforts in the glorious cause of woman, and he begged to propose, as a fitting candidate for the high position of chairman, that ornament to her sex, Mrs. Elizabeth Strongitharm.

Mrs. Strongitharm was elected by acclamation, although there was one dissentient voice, supposed to have been Miss Griffin's, as she was heard to say she "would rather have a man."

The meeting being organized, Miss. Lucy Blackball, perpetual secretary to the association, proceeded to read some of the letters of excuse.

The first one read was from that well-known hu-

manitarian, Dr. Jonathan Goodenough. It was as follows, —

" FOUFOUVILLE, 14th 2d Mo., A. II. 1.

"RESPECTED MADAM AND SISTER IN PROGRESS, — The
engrossing duties attendant on the happy realization of
my grand scheme of human regeneration, in preparing for
the influx of the coming multitudes of rejoicing Utopians,
will prevent me from taking part in the convention.

"I regret this the more, as I had contemplated delivering a discourse which would have conclusively demonstrated to all nations the advisability of at once estab-
lishing phalansteries in every part of the globe.

"Accept for the Association, with my best wishes for
its success, the accompanying copies of my works, and
believe me,

"Respectfully,
"Your brother in progress,
"J. GOODENOUGH."

The following were then read in order, —

"WALL STREET, May 1st.

"Mr. Richard Longshanks regrets that previous engage-
ments will prevent him from accepting the polite invitation
to be present at the convention of the F. R. A., trans-
mitted to him by the kindness of Miss Griffin.

"Whatever airs of superiority may be arrogated to
themselves by other men, Mr. Longshanks begs to
assure the ladies that he will ever acknowledge himself
their slave. Woman shall ever be his mistress."

"LEBANON, May 2d, 1850.

"MADAM, — I respectfully decline further attendance at the meetings of the F. R. A., and beg to withdraw my name from the list of members; my views in regard to the objects sought to be obtained having undergone a material change.

"Yours, sincerely,

"MARY ANN KETCHUM.

"P. S. It will doubtless afford you great gratification to be informed that I have decided to change my condition, considering it a duty that every woman owes, not only to the present generation but to those yet unborn, and have therefore accepted — after mature deliberation — the honorable offer of Mr. John Shaker.

"M. A. K."

This letter called forth much animadversion, and several ladies, among whom Miss Griffin and Miss Crane were conspicuous, became quite excited and insisted that it be publicly burnt and the writer expelled from the Association. After considerable discussion the subject was dropped, as most of the gentleman seemed quite indifferent to it.

The secretary then favored the audience with this eloquent and characteristic epistle from Ralpho Bunsby, Esq.

BOSTON, April 29th, 1850.

"'*Non facio.*' — The finite and the infinite are incommensurable. It is predicable that man's-battle cry is 'Tally-ho!—Such is the physiological sequence of woman's alliciency. Who shall solve the social problem? Society cannot be crystallized. It is too carbonic. What is the man of society? A sham. All barber and tailor. What is the woman of society? A sham. All is artificial. I prefer woman in a state of nature. Know thyself. So be it; So let it be. What is the soul? Read Homer; read Plato; read Aristotle; read Dante. Such is the *prima philosophia.* The Platonic is the poetic tendency. 'Tis quite certain that Brigham Young is a Platonist. Is not his system corporeally spiritual? Bacon and Locke were true poets. So were Arkwright and Watts. Poets of the cotton-loom, and steam engines. But the word cannot be applied to Byron and Moore. Shakespeare was received with apathy, which demonstates the elevation of the British intellect in the sixteenth century, as I have observed in my 'Bovine Traits.'

"Whoever requires facts on which to base an argument is wanting in the poetic faculty, — in ideality. Woman is an idealist. Hence she is superior to man. Yet she cannot exist without him, nor he without her. Without him, she would be a human Sahara, — a barren waste. Without her, his entity would become intangible. United they make one, and then proceed to make many. The vacuist vainly strives to vaticinate futurity. The *epoptæ* of the mystic Eleusinia of Nature are not cis-Styxian. Psycho-Pompos can alone initiate us. The age is full of nonsense. I want common sense.

                                    "R. B."

Mr. Peewit rose and begged to inquire what Mr. Bunsby meant.

The chairman requested the gentlemen to take his seat.

Several persons desired to know whether or not Mr. Bunsby was coming. ·

The chairman asked if the letter itself was not sufficiently explicit, and said that she "had never heard a more lucid and philosophical discourse from the pen of that profound thinker."

The secretary, with a look of contempt at the inquirers, offered to read the letter again; but somebody having stated that it was clear Mr. Bunsby was coming, the proposition was unanimously voted down.

The subjoined communication from the President of the United States was now listened to with marked attention.

"TO THE SECRETARY OF THE FEMALE RIGHTS ASSOCIATION.

"WHITE HOUSE, May 1, 1850.

"MADAM, — I have had the honor to receive your polite invitation to attend the seventeenth annual convention of the F. R. A., for the purpose of considering the . best method of obtaining those social, political, and religious reforms, that are demanded by the enlightenment and progress of the nineteenth century.

"Although deeply sympathizing — as every patriot must — with all movements that tend to increase the honor and welfare of our beloved country, I am nevertheless constrained to express my regret that the heavy pressure of public duties will deprive me of the pleasure of assisting at the convention of the F. R. A.

"I have the honor to be, madam,

"Very respectfully

"Your ob't serv't."

11

[The original of the above lies before us. The signature has been cut out by some enthusiastic autograph hunter.]

On motion of Miss Griffin, seconded by Miss Crane, it was

" *Resolved*, That a vote of thanks be presented to the President for the sympathy, and elevation of character displayed in his letter."

Next came an epistle from the Hon. Wm. H. Steward; but as it covered twenty-four pages of letter-paper we cannot afford space for it.

This was followed by a letter from that rising statesman, the Hon. A. J. Jones.

TO THE SECRETARY OF THE FEMALE RIGHTS ASSOCIATION.

"ALBANY, April 29, 1850.

" MADAM, — " It is with heartfelt regret, that I find myself obliged to forego the honor and pleasure of attending the next caucus of the F. R. A., in consequence of important political business that requires my personal attention in this district. The election comes off next week. My friends are sanguine of my success, though it will, doubtless, be a close contest. Nothing but a profound sense of duty to the country would induce me to deprive myself of the inestimable privilege of listening to the discussion of those wrongs under which woman labors. But, if she cannot vote, she can at least direct the votes of others, and I trust that every member of the association will exert her influence in favor of that candidate who may appear to her most deserving.

"I am, etc.

" ANDREW JACKSON JONES."

On motion of Mrs. Allbone, it was

" *Resolved*, That in consideration of his self-sacrificing patriotism, the Hon. A. J. Jones deserves well of the country."

The secretary then read the following, —

"ATHENS, N.Y., May 1, 1850.

"DEAR MADAM, — "Since I was last with you, a year ago, Divine Providence has at last blessed my long union with Mr. Doolittle, and I have become the happy mother of twins. I cannot conscientiously take upon myself the serious responsibility of neglecting maternal duties by attending the future meetings of the Association. My doing so was always contrary to the wish of my respected husband.

"Yours in progress,   .
"VICTORIA DOOLITTLE."

Mr. Peewit jumped up and offered a resolution declaring that Mrs. Doolittle "deserves well of the country," but the chairman sternly called the gentleman to order, and he subsided.

Miss Griffin proposed to amend the resolution by adding to it the name of Mr. Doolittle.

This was loudly seconded by all the gentlemen present; and in spite of the opposition of Miss Crane and Mrs. Allbone, as well as of the chairman, who seemed to think the proceeding in some respects irregular, the resolution, as amended, was carried.

The reading of the letters having been finished the convention proceeded to business.

Upon motion of Miss Blackball, it was

" *Resolved*, That the statement in the preamble to the Declaration of Independence, ' that all *men* are created free and equal,' in omitting to mention woman, is a disgrace to the American Eagle, and an insult to the Genius of the Nineteenth Century."

Mrs. Allbone offered the following, which was adopted.

" *Whereas*, According to that atrocious instrument, the Constitution of the United States, woman is denied her just coequal right with man in framing those laws that are applicable to both sexes alike ; therefore,

" *Resolved*, That a petition be presented to the President to so amend the Constitution that the franchise be secured, upon equal terms, to both sexes."

Mr. Peewit expressed some doubts as to the power of the president in the premises, but the chairman promptly put him down.

In supporting the resolution Miss Griffin said that " the ballot to woman means self-protection. To the daughter, it means diversified employment and speedy marriage ; to the wife, the control of her own person ; to the mother, an equal right with man to children.

" The present state of society is radically false. There is not enough sympathy between man and woman. This is partly owing to our defective educational system. The sexes should be brought up together. They would thus enter sooner into each other's feelings.

" It is time for us to cease being nothing more than house-keepers and nurses. Woman should insist on an equal partition in all the duties of man, while he participates in hers.

" Why are our textile fabrics so tasteless ? Because there are no designing women.

" Why are our shops attended only by the male sex? Because the men don't want their wives to sell themselves.

" Why is our country so backward? Because woman does not put herself sufficiently forward.

" Why does our decennial census show such a meagre advance? Because woman is not free to act as she would.

" Why should the forum, the pulpit, the bar, the bench, be monopolized by man, to the exclusion of woman? It is said she cannot bear the close labor; but what woman ever objected to being confined?

" Shall we continue to endure such injustice? I hear on all sides the indignant ' No.' Man has too long had his own way. It is time for woman to arise and strike for her proper position. Where would man be without her? (Cries of, ' Hear! Hear!') He would be nowhere. She is his greatest want. Without her he is an incomplete being, — a mere chrysalis. Why, then, in this so-called free country, is she denied the right of suffrage? What is her fault? She is found guilty, not of a crime, but of a sex. She does not want reason, intelligence, or virtue, but she wants — whiskers."

The eloquent speaker sat down, amidst cheers and some laughter from the galleries.

The chairman directed the sergeant-at-arms, Mrs. Allbone, to turn the laughers out of the room, if their conduct was repeated.

The chairman now introduced the Rev. Scipio Africanus of South Carolina, who had just arrived by the underground railway. He spoke as follows, —

Mrs. CHAIRMAN, BELOVED BROTHERS AND SISTERS, —

" *Firstly.* Why is the black man no' 'lowed to vote?
11*

That's the question, as Hamblet says. If this is a white man's country, why did they tote us culled persons into it? Ha! I pause for a reply. It was no fair. They say we got no soul; no go to Heaven whar the angels all clothe in white. How then they raise all the cotton thar for dress all the angels in white, if no culled man thar? Ha!

"*Secondly.* They call America a free country. Then, I ask, whar is America? whar is that land of freedom? The Honorable Andrew Jackson Jones, I heerd him say it was bounded on the norf by the Norf Pole, and on the souf by the Souf Pole, and thar was a liberty pole stuck up in the middle, on which was perched the American Eagle with the cap of liberty on his head, the thunder and lightning in his claws, and the rejoicin' nations was a playing on the banjo and dancin' the Virginny reel around it. But whar is that land of freedom, whar nobody work no more? I can't find it. It isn't whar we 'uns live. It don't seem to be where you 'uns live.

"*Thirdly.* What does the blessed Saint Paul say? 'Pay unto Cæsar all that is Cæsar's.' But they don't do it. They make Cæsar, and Pompey, and Cuffee, and all on 'em work free, gratis, for nuffin. But the day of Jubilee is comin', when the culled gentleman work no more. When he hang up the shovel and the bow forever. Glory, Hallelujah!

"*Fourthly.* The good Book says, 'By the sweat of your brow shall you get your livin';' but the black man down souf, he get no sort of livin at all by the sweat of his brow. It say, 'Do unto others as you would have others do unto you.' If the white folks down thar do that, they must have very peculiar tastes; for they give the

poor laborer nuffin' but a little pone and bacon, and old
clo' for the sweat of his brow. But the day of Jubilee
will come. Then the Lord, sittin' on the Judgment Seat,
will say to the massa, 'You jes pay Scipio six bits a day
for his time, or St. Peter no let you in.' Then massa
mighty skeered, will whisper, 'O Lord, my money all
spent in New Orleens. Then the Lord will open his mouf
and say, ' You go to de Debbil.' Ya! Ya! Glory, Hallelujah ! "

Brother Scipio Africanus continued on to sixteenthly,
by which time he had worked himself into a furious state
of excitement, when the chairman informed him that his
hour was up.

His proposition to pass around his hat was disallowed.

AFTERNOON SESSION.

The proceedings were opened with a mystical, transcendental *farrago* of long words, called a poem on the Millenium, by Miss Lillie Emerson. The idea involved in it
(if there was any) might perhaps have been found out
with the aid of a dictionary. The following four lines
were the only ones comprehensible to ordinary understanding, —

> " There is a joyful time at hand
> When love alone shall rule the land,
> When all men shall embrace as brothers,
> Women true sisters be, and mothers."

The secretary then stated to the audience that she had
received a document which exhibited a state of affairs

truly pitiable, and calculated to awaken the sympathies of every true woman. She then read the following, —

"PETITION OF THE INDIGNANT YOUNG LADIES SOCIETY OF MANSFIELD, MASS., TO THE F. R. A.

"This township contains a population of two thousand males and three thousand females, yet notwithstanding this alarming deficiency of the stronger sex, our young men are constantly emigrating to the distant West, there to lead lives of toil and celibacy, doing nothing for their country.

"Although personally quite indifferent to the matter, we hereby protest, in the name of humanity, against this wholesale deportation of mankind, and declare that if it continue we will emigrate in a body to Utah, where we will stand some chance of being appreciated.

"It is a matter of vital interest to the future prospects of our town, the injury being not merely temporary, but one that will entail loss on generations yet to come.

"Man is becoming too materialistic. He thinks if he cultivates his fields he is relieved from the obligation of cultivating the affections of a wife and family.

"Your petitioners therefore pray that some means may be devised whereby this continued exodus of able-bodied young men may be checked, being convinced that such action will add greatly to the happiness and contentment of your petitioners, as well as of thousands of their suffering sisters, for they feel themselves fully capable, and are in fact anxious, to fulfil all the duties required of them by society, but are unable to do so by themselves alone.

"And your petitioners will ever pray, etc.

"Miss Ariadne Lorne,
"   Betsey Jane Willing,
"   Kate Krauss,
"   Aurora Roe,
"   Mary Lillywhite,
"   Desire Mann,
"   Seraphina Bell,
"   Polly Darling,
"   Margaret McCoy,
"   Olivia Blossom,
"   Priscilla Prim,
"   Susan A. Roseinblüm.

The petition was ordered to be put on file.

Dr. Mary Mott then addressed the convention. She said it was a melancholy fact that there was an alarming decrease in the number of marriages. Yet this was not the fault of woman. She was ever ready to do her part; she had never shrunk from the performance of the duties imposed upon her by her being. She had been accused of extravagance, but she (Dr. Mott) indignantly denied the aspersion on behalf of her outraged sex. Does woman spend millions annually for vile cigars, for champagne, for whiskey? Does she waste her time loitering in clubs and bar-rooms? Does she spend her pin money in those abominable —

Here a gentleman in the audience called the speaker to order and desired to know what was before the house.

The chairman stated that the question was what action should be taken on the petition just read.

This brought a Dr. Bernhard to his feet. He was a stout, burly-looking individual, and spoke with much vehemence of manner. He said that the petition of the hapless young women of Mansfield moved him greatly. He felt his indignation rising within him. It was man's duty to double himself four times.

Mr. Peewit. — "Like the india-rubber man?"

Chairman. — "The gentleman will not interrupt."

The doctor, without heeding the interrogation, said, that the deplorable case to which the attention of this convention had just been called showed that the means were at hand, but owing to our unnatural social laws could not be brought into action. What would we think of a general who needed all his forces in front, and yet held a large portion of them in reserve, doing nothing? When an army longing to be engaged in active operations is set to work digging ditches and entrenchments, the men lose strength and die, and the loss is greater than in a battle. Woman and her affections are like that host. If she cannot bring on an engagement the best of them wither away. She buries them under the dust of years, and, entrenched in her pride, repels the advances of man. We condole for the loss of property caused by a fire, or a shipwreck; but this " waste of feeling unemployed " is made light of; yet it is the cause of more heartfelt sorrow than any sacrifice of material wealth. As a remedy for the deprivations under which woman suffers he would propose " an amendment to the constitution to the effect that every man be allowed to have six wives."

This atrocious proposition created a tremendous commotion in the assembly, particularly among the women, thirty or forty of whom instantly jumped up, some of them standing on the benches, and all began talking at once. Cries of " infamous," " abominable,"

" wretch," " Mormon," and " monster " were heard on all sides. It was in vain that the chairman hammered on the desk with her mallet; it only seemed to increase the uproar. In the midst of the din the shrill voice of Miss Crane was heard screaming. " The hypocrite! he would make slaves of us all; but my spirit is not yet broken; I never shall be sacrificed."

" Such infidel Turks," cried Mrs. Allbone, "deserve to be — I won't say what. Sisters we must band together to resist their further advances." ·

" Man was ever thus," said Miss Griffin ; " always striving to keep woman in subjection ; but if we all stand by each other, such beings as Dr. Bernhard will find it difficult to put us down. Our numbers will be too much for him. He doubtless considers himself a Lord of the Creation, and believes that woman was designed ·to be his serf, and would like to keep her ever in an inferior position. He may have met with some chicken-hearted creatures who would consent to be trodden upon ; but he shall find that all women are not alike. Some can assert their prerogatives, and will not be imposed upon without a struggle."

Mr. Peewit now moved that the proposition before the house be laid upon the table.

" On the table ! " yelled Miss Crane ; " let it be hurled upon the floor and trodden under foot."

Dr. Bernhard now rose and begged leave to explain his motion. He stated that much of the dissatisfaction with which it had been received was doubtless caused by a misapprehension of its meaning. He had not intended to propose that any man should be allowed to have more than one wife at a time.

This explanation seemed to be perfectly satisfactory to the gentlemen, and even many of the ladies appeared to deem the proposition, as explained, not unreasonable, for the noise and clamor perceptibly began to subside; but the lull in the storm was only temporary, for Peewit being heard to say that he thought " one wife sometimes too many," the hubbub instantly recommenced, and with greater violence than before, — his remark exciting even a more lively indignation than the motion of Mr. Benhard. Some of the exasperated females, who were nearest to him, appeared from their actions anxious to lay violent hands on him; but he slunk away in the confusion, in the midst of general execrations accompanied by hisses and hootings and cries of "Turn him out!" "Turn him out!"

Peewit having thus acted as a lamb of sacrifice, and drawn upon himself the concentrated wrath of the audience, Dr. Bernhard escaped without further remark.

EVENING SESSION.

It had been announced that Miss Griffin would, on this occasion, deliver her long and anxiously expected lecture on The Co-relation of the Sexes, but the lady stated that her feelings had received so great a shock from the atrocious proposition that had been enunciated during the afternoon by one of the opposite sex (here she looked significantly at Peewit), that she felt quite unable to do herself or the subject justice that evening.

The disappointment appeared to be general.

Mr. Peewit now rose for the purpose of explanation, but was received with such a storm of hisses and reproaches that he could not make himself heard.

The chairman finally ordered him to sit down.

Dr. Mary Mott then proposed the following resolution, —

Whereas, A Convention is about to be called for the purpose of framing a new State constitution ; therefore,

" *Resolved*, That we recommend to the people that they elect their delegates to the said Convention irrespective of sex or complexion."

DR. BERNHARD. — " If female candidates are voted for, it will be useless to advise the people to pay no regard to complexion. Those who have the fairest skins will certainly be elected."

MRS. ALLBONE. — " Are men such ninnies ? "

MISS GRIFFIN. — " Alas ! I fear they are."

The resolution was passed.

The subject of education came next in order, and *apropos* of this, Prof. Nicholas Malpest read his learned and appreciative review of the " Timeus " of Plato. As it contains some novel ideas and may serve as a a rebuke to the materialistic tendencies of the present age, we herewith give the document entire, printing from the original MS.

" PLATO.

" BY PROF. NICHOLAS MALPEST.

" The works of Plato, with notes by Dr. Solomon Bigwig. Minerva Press, Oxford, 1850.

" Œuvres de Platon, chez Tête-de-chou. Rue de l'Hibou, Paris, 1750.

" Platos Briefe übersetzt. Leipsig, 1600.
Opera Platonis. Roma A. U., 748.

" Τίμαιος ἤ περὶ φύσεως. Athens, 99th Olymp.

Etc. etc. etc. etc. etc. etc. etc. etc. etc. etc. etc.

12

" A whim seems to be taking possession of men's minds in favor of the study of physical sciences as taught by the moderns, instead of the lucubrations of the philosophers of ancient times ; and we regret to say, that of late years, this delusion appears to have been steadily gaining ground, and even to have received the commendation of some of the most distinguished names in literature, art, and science.

" The writings of Plato have engaged the study and excited the admiration of the scholars of Oxford and Cambridge since the days of Alfred, and we now propose to recall to the reader's attention, some of the most striking passages of his immortal works, — works that will be universally read and esteemed when those of the Newtons, Herschels, and Faradays, are forgotten, — though we fear, if the new-fangled ideas prevail, — not till then.

" The 'Timeus' of Plato is acknowledged to be one of the most profound emanations of ancient wisdom ; in fact, such is the depth of its profundity that much of it is utterly incomprehensible to modern understandings.

" It is known that a couple of Frenchmen by the names of Buffon and Cuvier have elaborated a complicated system of Natural History, in which the mind of the student is bewildered with kingdoms, genera, species and varieties *ad infinitum*, with vertebrate, invertebrates, mollusks, etc. *ad nauseum.* How much simpler and more satisfactory to the classical scholar is the system of the learned Greek ! It is expounded in the 'Timeus' in the following language, —

" There are four species of animals, namely, the celestial race of gods, birds, fish, and beasts, that walk upon the land.' [Timeus. Edition of Schwalbé. Page 505.]

" One Tyndall, a professor in the Royal Institution of London, has (we have been informed) published a work on heat in which the modern theory is developed, — a theory based on an almost infinite number and variety of experiments, and a close observation of the workings of nature, but in which many questions are left unsolved.

" Now behold how, unaided by a single experiment, but guided only by the light of transcendental wisdom, the great Plato lucidly accounts for the phenomena that so perplex our modern philosophers.

" ' In the first place, it is evident to everybody that air, earth, fire, and water are bodies. What is more, every kind of body has depth, and depth necessarily implies a plane nature. Now every perfectly plane surface is composed of triangles, and all the triangles are derived from two other triangles, each of which has one right angle and two acute angles ; one of these triangles has on each side a part of the right angle divided by equal sides, the other has the unequal parts of the right angle divided by unequal sides. Such is the origin that we give to fire and other bodies, basing our opinion on reasons both probable and certain.' [p. 523.]

" After this brilliant scintillation of genius, the sage of Ægina vouchsafes us some information that we respectfully recommend to the attention of the learned.

" 'Let us now take the two triangles, of which the body of fire, and the bodies of the other elements have been formed, the isosceles and the scalene, of which the square of the greatest side is three times that of the smallest. The four species of bodies appeared to us to spring from each other ; but this was an error. These four species are formed of the triangles that we have mentioned, namely, three of them from the scalene triangle, and the fourth from the isosceles triangle.' [p. 524.]

" Mark how different is his explanation of the reflection of light from that given in text-books at present.

" ' As to the images that are formed on mirrors or polished surfaces, it is very easy to give the reason. In effect, when the interior fire and the exterior fire unite together, and, the latter renewing itself without cessation, applies itself several times to the polished surface, the images of which we spoke are formed necessarily, because the fire which starts from the visage mixes itself up on the polished surface with the visual fire. Then the right of the object appears the left, because the contact does not take place according to ordinary laws.' [p. 513.]

" There is nothing here about those angles of incidence and angles of reflection that so puzzle the classical scholar. Who, we may triumphantly ask, after reading this fiery passage would hesitate to choose between the Optics of Plato and those of Brewster.

" Many volumes have been written on the origin of the various ills that afflict mankind. Had the authors consulted Plato, they might have saved themselves much trouble, and we earnestly call upon the Academy of Medicine to give heed to the following words, —

" ' As to the origin of maladies, anybody can easily find it. In effect, as there are four elements of which bodies are composed, — namely, air, earth, fire, and water, — the excess or the deficiency against nature of these substances, their transposition, the properties contrary to their nature acquired by fire and the other elements, for there are several, all similar accidents engender disorders and sicknesses, since each one of the elements changing its nature and position, that which was at first cold becomes warm, that which was dry becomes moist, that which was light becomes heavy, and all undergo all sorts of changes.' [p. 261.]

" What depth of reasoning is displayed in this exposition ! How admirably the effect is deduced from the cause ! We know of nothing that can be compared to it out of the Chinese. How unlike it is the style of the Harveys, the Coopers, and the Motts, who in these days are looked upon as authorities !

" Having accounted for the ills of the body, the sage rises to a loftier theme, and informs us of the origin of those of the soul. He says, —

" ' When bitter and salt phlegm, sour and bilious humors spread themselves throughout the body without finding an issue, and, pressed from the interior, mix themselves up and disturb the revolutions of the soul by their vapors, they engender all sorts of maladies in the soul.' [p. 567.]

" What a knowledge of hidden causes is displayed in the following passage !

" ' The gods foresaw that we would be inclined to great intemperance in eating and drinking ; so, to prevent us from making ourselves sick, and killing ourselves by over-eating, they arranged that receptacle called the belly as a sort of store-house of superfluous food, and gave the intestines an immense number of circumvolutions, from the fear that if the victuals passed through them quickly we would immediately begin eating again, and thus would have no time for the muses and philosophy.' [p. 549.]

" How the divine Plato rises above the vulgar anatomical reasons that would be given by a modern M.D. ! Instead

12*

of descending to chyle and bile, he soars into the regions of the muses and philosophy (ancient) ; and how suggestive, too, is the whole passage ; for it is clear that if the rectum and intestines formed a straight continuation of the stomach and œsophagus, so that food passed out of the body about as fast as it was taken in, we would have no time for anything but eating. We would be lower in the animal scale than rabbits. Every man would have to be his own Delmonico, and keep an unlimited supply of food on hand, and even then would be in danger of starving to death, unless Nature provided some way of seizing it flying (as it were) on its rapid course through the jejunum. The human race would sweep over the earth like devouring locusts. The flocks and herds would be swallowed up ; horse flesh would be at a premium ; the Chinese would not be alone in their taste for cats and rats ; and even the partiality of the Digger Indians for grasshoppers might come generally into fashion ; oysters would go down by the bushel ; the poor would all starve to death ; and, to cap the climax, we would have been deprived of the inestimable privilege of studying Plato, for his brilliant lucubrations, having been written on parchment, would undoubtedly have been devoured by somebody long before our day, — a misfortune that would have prevented modern men of learning from digesting them.

" What an abyss of mysticism is contained in his view of creation !

" ' It was in order to give birth to Time that God made the Sun, the Moon, and the five other stars that we call planets ; in order to determine and preserve the numbers which measure it, and, after having made these bodies, God placed the whole seven of them in the seven orbits,

that the nature of the other describes in its revolution;
the Moon in the first orbit that surrounds the earth, the
Sun in the second, Venus and the star sacred to Mercury
in the orbits in which they revolve with a velocity equal
to that of the Sun, but in a contrary direction to the order
of signs.' [p. 503.]

" No mind less profound than that of Plato could have
conceived the idea of the creation of the Sun, Moon, and
five other planets before Time was ; and what classical
scholar will not consider his astronomical theory more in
accordance with the perceptions of our senses, than that
of Copernicus and his followers, who go so far as actually
to deny that the Sun revolves around the earth, notwithstanding the daily evidence of our eyes to the contrary?

" But it is in his description of the manner in which the
Creator formed the soul, that the incomprehensible genius
of Plato attained its highest flight. We trust our readers
will pardon us for giving an English translation of it, as
it is possible there may be some among them not sufficiently versed in Greek to appreciate the full vastidity of
the ideas in the original.

" ' Here is the way God formed the soul. With the essence indivisible, always identical to itself, and with the
essence divisible, variable of bodies, he composed a third
kind of intermediary essence, which partakes of the nature
of the same and of the other, and thus he established it
in the midst of that which is indivisible and that which is
divisible ; after having taken these three kinds of principles, he mixed them up in order to reduce them to a single kind, by forcibly uniting the rebellious nature of the
same to that of the other; and when he had mixed the
same and the other with the intermediary essence, and

out of these three things had made one whole one, he
divided it into as many parts as were necessary; so that
each one of these parts was composed of the same, of the
other, and of the intermediary essence.' [p. 499.]

" Now it will hardly be credited, but it is nevertheless
true that a celebrated French author has had the temerity
to pronounce this quintessence of sublime, metaphysical
transcendentalism to be ' sheer nonsense!' (galimatias!)
and this opinion we regret to say, seems to be that of
most of the learned men of his country, who indeed do
not hesitate to speak in the most disrespectful manner, not
only of Plato himself, but of the ancient philosophers in
general, — nay, they even go so far as to LAUGH at them!
Such hardihood might be expected from a people so
deeply infected with the teachings of modern science as
the French.

" The few extracts we have given from the ' Timeus,'
are, we trust, sufficient to show the nature of that sublime
work; and when it is borne in mind that all the productions of Plato, and indeed of most of the philosophers
of old, are conceived in a similar lofty and mystical spirit,
we feel assured that enough will have been done to enable
the intelligent reader to draw a correct conclusion as to
the comparative advantages between the study of their
lucubrations, and the works of modern men of science.
The former disdained to stoop to experiment, but, relying
on their intuitive perception of truth, did not shrink from
the boldest speculations, with what success the extracts
we have given demonstrate. How different was their way
of theorizing, from the method by which philosophers in
those degenerate days seek to penetrate the arcana of
Nature! The latter would reduce everything to weight

and measure, and refuse to accept the smallest fact until
it has been proved by actual experiment; moreover, they
value a discovery just in proportion as it tends to ameliorate the condition of mankind, — a low consideration
quite beneath the dignity of ancient philosophy.

"The Turks believe that those who are afflicted with
mental hallucination are favored by the Almighty, and
gifted with a peculiar wisdom. This idea of those infidels seems to receive some confirmation from the fact that
the only productions we ever met with that could be compared to those of Plato, for the extreme profundity of
their sublunated mysticism, were the original articles in
the journal published by the inmates of the Asylum for
Aliénés at New Bedlam.

"In conclusion we will observe that as the human body
after death is resolved into its original elements, and by
then entering into the composition of plants and being
eaten, may actually assist in building up and form a part
of some other and living body or bodies, may we not —
reasoning from analogy, and taking into consideration the
doctrine of the conservation of force — suppose that the
soul or mind may pass through a similar change? A scientific man in the nineteenth century would doubtless
decline to trouble himself about this question unless he
could catch a soul to experiment upon, but an ancient
philosopher would not have hesitated to pronounce his
decision, and we can easily picture to ourself the solemn,
long-bearded, barefooted sage, muttering his oracular
sentences with upturned eyes, while his open-mouthed
auditors are dumfounded by such a display of ineffable
wisdom; we can even fancy that we hear the lucid and
convincing argument.

" ' The soul being composed of isosceles triangles, it is clear that the indivisible essence is permeated by the same, and consequently the divisible essence is to the intermediary essence as $\frac{14}{7}$ are to the square root of the first principle, — consequently twice two are four. Now, since the world is an animal, and a soul without a corporation is minus individuality, and fire is a neutral conglomeration of scalene triangles, each containing eighteen obtuse angles, it is obvious that by the intermixification of the primary principles the resultibus is one ex nihility ; so that by the natural ratiocination of secondary ideas, anybody can see that the sequence to the manducation of mundungus must be a jactitatious lumbago of the diaphragm.

" Having proved so much by reasons clear and incontrovertible, know now that an infinitesimal hypothenuse from the zenith to the umbilical region of the nadir would cause a hiatus of heterogeneous gnomonics throughout the universe ; hence it is evident that the homologousconcatenation of sesquilateral xylobalsamums being equal to one hundred and seventy-seven perpendicular parallelopipedons, therefore my confabulation must excite oscitancy, wherefore I will incontinently proceed to exsiccate."

Prof. Malpest's address was received with much applause although one hiss was heard (supposed to have come from Miss Griffin).

The secretary then stated that she had received a letter of declination, which came too late to be given with the others, but which she proposed to read now, as the writer — a gentleman named Lovell, and evidently a mere man of the world — most unwittingly exposed the shallow sophistries by which the man of the present day endeav-

ored to stifle the promptings of conscience, and to up-
hold that iniquitous system by which woman is kept in
degradation.

This puerile epistle would serve as a warning to the
Convention, and by showing the exact strength — or
rather, weakness — of the enemy's position, would give
encouragement to the female mind in future struggles
against the advances of the foe.

Miss Blackball then read the following letter, —

"HARMONY HALL, May 2d, 1850.

" *To the Secretary of the F. R. A.:* —

" MADAME, — I regret that a previous engagement,
which makes my presence here absolutely necessary, will
debar me from the pleasure of assisting at the Convention.

" I beg to decline the honor of being proposed as a member of the Association, from the fear that my views are
not in sufficient accordance with those of the ladies composing it. Although I will not deny woman's abstract
right to the franchise, I have doubts of the advisability of
her obtaining and exercising that right. [Some signs of
indignation among the ladies.]

"Although in politics a firm Republican [Cries of 'That's
enough!' 'Stop!' 'Stop!' 'The vile Radical!' ' 'So am
I!' 'Go on!' 'Go on!'], and therefore holding that government derives its theoretically just powers only from the
consent of the governed, I nevertheless believe that
government to be the *best* which adds most to the happiness of the people, no matter what its form may be.
History shows that these two principles, like oil and water,
are generally antagonistic. Education is the alkali that
makes them run smoothly together. In some countries
Republicanism has been tried and found wanting. The

mass of the people were, perhaps, not sufficiently intelligent or advanced. They were, politically speaking, boys, and still required masters, or a master with a sceptre for a rod. In our own glorious and enlightened land [Male voice 'Good!' feminine ditto, 'Enlightened indeed!'] the two principles do not clash, and a system founded on the will of the people is the most just theoretically, and at the same time the best practically, and makes us the freest and happiest people in the whole world. [Boy in gallery 'Hurrah!' Several ladies, 'Founded on the will of the *people*, indeed!' Old lady, 'Aren't women-folks people then?' Professor Malpest was heard to mutter something about 'Sunday,' and brother Scipio Africanus was seen to shake his head negatively, but whether in response to the query of the old lady, or to the last paragraph in the letter, your reporter could not determine.]

"Applying these two principles to the subject of the political disabilities of woman, and granting that no just reason can be urged against her *right* to vote, the question arises, Would the happiness of man ['Man!' 'Man!' 'Only man!' 'What does he care for woman!' 'The selfish thing!'] that is to say, mankind in general — both sexes — be increased by the exercise of that right? I think not. [Strong marks of dissatisfaction. Miss Griffin observed that the writer was a young and very inexperienced person.]

"The most delightful charm in life is found in the relationship between the sexes as it exists in civilized countries, and this charm is actually heightened by the differences between them. Sensible women do not admire effeminate men; men do not admire masculine women. Each sex has its peculiar duties. This assertion does not necessarily imply an intellectual superiority in either ; for one person may have a talent for the law, another for mercantile pursuits, another for the arts of design, each be wanting in the special gifts of the others, and yet all be of equal mental calibre.

"The strong arms of man can accomplish work for which the delicately moulded limbs of woman are quite unfitted. [Mrs. Allbone, ' He can't!'] She has work to do that cannot be done by him. [Several gentlemen, 'What is it?' 'What is it?' Mr. Peewit ventured to suggest, "Wet-nurse;" the chairman frowned, and he shrank into a corner, looking as frightened as a boy in a church-yard, at night, at the sound of his own voice.] In barbarous states of society there is some equality between the amount of labor done by the men and the women. But is the condition there of the latter desirable? Does the most strong-minded sister envy it? The convention-alities of civilization have given us different fields of toil. If you were to break down the barriers that separate us, so that men and women should be in all respects as much on an equality as human efforts could make them, you would break the charm that attracts them towards each other [Mrs. Allbone, 'Charm, indeed! No man ever charmed me!']; marriage would cease to be valued as a sacred and enduring bond, and would be regarded as a mere temporary convenience ['Or inconvenience!' said Mr. Peewit, for which interruption he was sharply rebuked by the chairman], to be assumed or cast off at will."

" Moreover, it is very doubtful if the exercise of the franchise by the ladies would have a beneficial effect on our political affairs [' Of course not in the opinion of such persons,' said Miss Crane, tossing her head], for women

13

of culture and refinement, whose perceptions of right and wrong are far superior to those of the average male voter, would generally shrink from the squabbles of the polls, while the brazen, ignorant denizens of the purlieus of our cities would swarm out to make use of their privilege, thus doubling the strength of that portion of our population which is the least qualified to understandingly exert its power.

"Men, in their actions, are guided chiefly by their interests; women, by their feelings or prejudices; and surely in politics the former are a better guide than the latter (except where the prejudice is in favor of honor); for, in a republic, if every man knows his interest and votes in accordance with it, the majority are benefited by it. [Several voices, 'The majority of the *men.*'] I assume that the interest of the wife is, or ought to be, the same as that of the husband. ['The outrageous assumption!' 'It is!' 'It isn't!' 'It never can be till women make the laws!']

"In the southern section of our country the politicians are said to be plotting secession, impelled by motives of fancied personal interest. The women, from a prejudice in favor of their peculiar institution, or from devotion to their fathers, or husbands, or brothers, are in full accordance with them. If war were to result, the women would have more to lose than the men; for while the latter would risk their lives, the former would risk the loss of those on whom they depend for support, and in whom are centred those affections whose satisfaction alone makes life desirable. Yet is it probable that they would endeavor to have a restraining influence over the men? Would not their passions be more powerful than their interests? *

"Your voting, mesdames, would not augment, but would rather diminish, your influence over us ; and, believing that influence to be for the best, I wish to see it increased. The more truly womanly you are, the greater it will be. We are now with some truth called your slaves, and willing slaves we are ; but make yourselves to all intents and purposes one of us, and the chains are broken. We might jog along together amicably, perhaps, united, like partners in business, by reasons of interest and mutual convenience, or even of friendship, but not by the stronger ties of the heart.

"If you have wrongs, they can and will be rectified ; and impartial justice is more likely to be done by intelligent men, who have mothers, and wives, and sisters, and daughters, than by the majority of those of the gentler sex who would be most prone to do battle at the polls. Believe me, you can obtain more as women than as voters.

"Men know that it is sometimes best not to make use of an admitted power or privilege. Your right to vote I will not dispute. I have a right to cut off my own nose, if I will (having no wife) ; but I would be very foolish to do so.

"Nothing human is perfect. If the franchise could be confined to the educated men and women of our country, it would probably be better for us all. There would be less corruption in office, and a higher tone in all our affairs. But this cannot be.; and since such is the case, and we claim to be more prosperous and contented than any other people, would it not be wise to leave well

* The event justified Mr. Lovell's fear. — NOTE BY THE AUTHOR.

enough alone at least, until we have a stronger surety than exists at present, that the change you desire would increase the general welfare and happiness?

     " Yours respectfully and sincerely,

               " L. LOVELL."

A silence of several minutes' duration followed the reading of this letter. Several of the ladies were heard to say that their indignation was so great that they could not find words in which to express it. Miss Griffin was the first to recover her equanimity, or, at least, the entire power of speech.

"Such," said she, " are the pitiable subterfuges with which our tyrant has too long beguiled us. But the hour of deliverance is at hand. Woman has only to be true to herself to see man at her feet. Why should she be constrained to mope by her lonely hearth, while he goes about where he will? Why should she be frowned upon for that which is passed over lightly in him? If a single life was for him the reality that it is to to her, I fancy there would not be quite so many useless bachelors." ·

At this point an excited individual in the gallery (evidently an outsider) jumped up and exclaimed, —

" You say there is a different standard of morality for men and for women ; that what is venial in him, is unpardonable in her. You have only yourselves to blame. Men do not make our social codes. The days of sniveling Puritans are over. The laws of society are not decided by ballot. It is you, not us, who prevent the ' unfortunate ' from retrieving the errors of the past, while he, who shared her fault or misfortune, goes comparatively unscathed. Would you pardon neither, but condemn both equally, hoping thereby to reform the world? If such is your aim, you should call a convention in heaven, and induce the Almighty to change human nature."

Here the chairman ordered the sergeant-at-arms to put the interloper out. Mrs. Allbone obeyed the mandate, amid cries from the boys in the gallery of "Out with him!" "Hustle him off!" "Bully for you!" etc.

"Alas!" said Miss Griffin, "there is truth in the words of the stranger. Woman is her own greatest enemy. Custom is the Kali — the evil-genius of the sex. In China, from time immemorial, her every step in life has been one of torture, in obedience to its absurd and cruel behests; in India, it sacrificed her upon an altar of fire; in Europe, it keeps her in lifelong bondage to man; her mind, not permitted to expand, cannot emerge from the chrysalis state, but remains confined in the cocoon of decorum. Let us hope that in America she will become fully developed, and attain the age of reason." [Several voices, "She has!" "She has!"]

MR. PEEWIT. — "Then, when she gets out of the cocoon, she will be a beautiful butterfly?"

DR. BERNHARD. — "And be guilty of indecorum?"

MISS GRIFFIN. — (With a look of contempt.) "Man cannot understand woman."

The chairman now read an "Appeal to the Women of the World," in which she set forth in clear terms the objects sought to be attained by the Association, and demonstrated the necessity of co-operation on the part of the sex in all countries, in order to enable woman to head off the futher encroachments of designing man on her natural rights.

The appeal was adopted with great enthusiasm and
13*

ten thousand copies directed to be printed in each of twenty different languages.

In order to obtain funds for this purpose, it was now stated that a collection would be taken up.

As it was growing late, the audience began moving towards the door, and in fifteen minutes the room was almost vacated.

So ended the Convention.

As the comments of the press of the time may be of some interest to the reader, we will give a few extracts from the editorial columns of two of the leading city papers, —

[From the Protean Herald of May 18th.]

" That heterogenous conglomeration of foufouites, phalansterites, ideologists, transcendentalists, spiritualists, free-thinkers, free-lovers, strong-minded women, and weak-minded men, known as the F. R. A., have held their annual confabulation. Society in general, and the male portion thereof in particular, seemed to be the peculiar object of feminine vituperation. One would suppose that the sight of that abominable animal — man — had a similar effect upon these ladies as a red banner upon a mad bull. Notwithstanding this, various projects were devised for providing all forlorn damsels with husbands. That unfortunate document, the constitution of the United States, was, figuratively speaking, torn to pieces. What imbeciles our forefathers must have been! Why did they not attend to their shops and their farms, and leave it to their wives to settle the affairs of the state?

" Letters were read from various individuals, known and unknown to fame (mostly the latter), including a patriotic effusion from the Old Public Functionary at the

White House. The Chevalier Malpest opened our eyes as
to the merits of an ancient Foufouite named Plato ; the
Baron Von Bernhard proposed to start a harem, which
brought the whole house down on him in the most harum-
scarum manner ; and poor Peewit having rashly given utterance to a sentiment derogatory to the amiable sex, was
obliged to fly for his life. If any one of these gentlemen
will pay us a visit at our hospitable mansion on Harlem
Heights, he shall be received with all the honors due to
his exalted merit, and we will show him how it is possible
in this sublunary sphere to jog through life quite com-
fortably with nothing but cash and common sense.

"A proposition to pass around the hat caused a general stampede for the door. Our reporter at first thought
the house was on fire ; but the apparition of half a dozen
grizzly, hirsute individuals, with their hats in their hands,
pursuing the flying crowd, showed him what was the
matter. We know not what was the contemplated object
of the contemplated contribution ; but the most worthy
charity we know of, and one of which we will gladly
head the subscription list with the munificent donation
of ten cents, would be for the purchase of a bran-new white
hat, overcoat, and box of blacking for our philanthropical contemporary, the Foufouite Mormon philosopher of
Spruce Street, so that his appearance might be in some
sort of keeping with the name of the street in which he
holds forth.

"Seriously speaking ; if this noble army of martyrs,
male and female, really wish to be of use to their country,
let the men immediately set themselves to work cleaning
the streets of our city, and, when they have raised the

wherewithal, let them present each one of the women with
a patent sewing-machine."

[From the Tribune of the People of May 19th.]

"The Convention of the F. R. A. has finished its labors.
The objects sought to be attained by the lofty-minded
men and women who conduct this movement for reform,
deserve the serious consideration of every progressive
and patriotic American. If we would behold this glorious union advance for the enlightenment of mankind in
the future as it has done in the past, we must give heed to
the warning voice of reason. If we would see our rum-
shops closed, the fetters stricken from the limbs of the
oppressed, our manufactures fostered, our rising generation of young men and women free, virtuous, and happy,
we must listen to reason.

"We notice that the 'Satanic Press,' as might have been
expected from that shallow sheet, treats this profound
subject of reform with its customary superciliousness ; its
personal strictures we shall pass by without notice, that
being a matter between man and man, with which the general public has nothing to do.

"If we wear a shocking bad hat, it covers a head
filled with good thoughts.

"If our coat is white, so is our conscience.

"As to understandings, we consider polished manners
of more consequence than polished boots.

"With regard to the infamous insinuation that we have
become a convert to Mormonism, we indignantly hurl
back the false aspersion in the teeth of our calumniator."

CHAPTER VII.

Some Adventures of Mr. Peewit.

On the day after the Convention broke up, Mrs. Strong-itharm, considering it incumbent on her to return without delay to her house-keeping duties at Harmony Hall, placed fifty dollars in the hands of Mr. Peewit with instructions to purchase for her a few needed articles of female apparel, and rejoin her at the phalanstery in the evening. This was the first day the gentleman had been left to himself since he became a Harmonian, and he determined to take advantage of the opportunity to put in execution a design that had for some time past engaged his thoughts. Purchasing a copy of the "Protean Herald," he ran his eye rapidly over the columns until he came to the following advertisement, —

"WONDERFUL. — Madam Demain, seventh daughter of a seventh daughter, born with a caul, the greatest living clairvoyant. Reads the past, present and future, reveals your thoughts, tells lucky numbers, gives advice on business and theft, describes whom you will marry, etc."
"Ladies, 50 cents, — Gentlemen $1.
"1001 *Mulberry St.*, 4th Floor."

Mr. Peewit cut out the advertisement, put it carefully in his waistcoat-pocket and directed his steps to the locality indicated. He found it to be a dirty, tumble-down, four-story tenement house; sheets, shirts, and stockings were hanging from the windows to dry, and dozens of tow-headed children were playing around the gutter in front. After looking up and down the street once or twice, as if he feared to be seen, he at last ventured to go up the steps and to give a gentle tap with the knocker. No response being made, he tapped again, and, after waiting five minutes longer, gave a positive knock. A woman now poked her head out of a basement window, and, speaking with a decided Irish brogue, asked, —

"An who are ye afther seeking?"

"Does Madam Demain live here?"

"Sure its up the alley ye'll find her, in the rare buildin'."

So Peewit passed through the narrow open passage-way alongside of the house, and saw at the back of the yard a four-story dwelling, of a more dingy and weather-beaten aspect than the one in front. This was the "rare building," and the door being open, and unfurnished with either bell or knocker, he walked in and ascended the rickety stairway. Having reached the fourth floor he knocked at the first door he came to. Some one was grinding a hand-organ within, but the noise now ceased and a heavily bearded man, with a wretched-looking monkey on his shoulder and a small switch in his hand, opened the door an inch or two, and asked, in a petulant tone, —

"Vat ish it?"

"Madam Demain," answered Peewit.

"Up shtairs," replied the man, slamming the door.

So Peewit mounted to the attic. He there saw a tall, gaunt woman, about forty-eight years of age, with keen gray eyes, heavy, overhanging brows, uncombed, frizzled black hair that stood out in every direction like the snakes from the head of Medusa, and dressed in a dirty, black frock, soiled stockings, and slippers down at the heel. When he arrived she was bending over a small stove frying sausages.

" Madam Demain, the meedjum?" said Peewit.

The female immediately assumed a look of dignity, and, striding across the garret with a theatrical air, opened a low, narrow door and said, in a lofty tone, —

" Enter."

Peewit obeyed, though it was necessary for him to stoop in order to do so. He would now gladly have found himself once more in the open street, — for the place reminded him of descriptions of the mouth of Hell, and he felt exceedingly ill at ease, — but the door had been closed after him. It was too late to retreat. He found himself in a contracted attic room, lighted only by a small dormer window from which several panes had been broken, and the apertures stopped with a hat and some old clothes. At first he could hardly distinguish more than the dirty panes of the window ; but, as his eyes became accustomed to the obscurity, he perceived by a dim light a small, square table in the centre of the room, with a couple of chairs on opposite sides of it. Into one of these he let himself drop, for a tremor came over him, and he felt as if he had put himself, body and soul, in the power of the evil one.

A hissing sound without added to his unpleasant sensations, for he could not distinguish whether it was made by venomous serpents or sausages. He sat for some time perfectly motionless, hardly daring to raise his eyes from the table, for he fancied he was surrounded by grinning skeletons, stuffed toads, lizards, dragons, antediluvian reptiles, and other frightful objects, like the alchemist in

Hogarth's picture. When at last he ventured timidly to look around, he was quite surprised to find that the walls were perfectly bare, being covered with nothing but dirt and cobwebs. In about ten minutes, the gaunt female glided in by a side door, and, seating herself in a chair opposite to him, held out her hand across the table. Peewit, supposing this was a demonstration of amity, grasped it with his and shook it.

"Dollar," said the woman.

The fee was paid, and the conjuror taking a dirty pack of cards from her pocket, arranged them on the table in a circle.

"Your hand," said she.

Peewit extended his hand, and the lady passed her fingers rapidly over it, at the same time scrutinizing his face.

She then raised her eyes to the ceiling, and for the space of a full minute her attention appeared to be absorbed in gazing fixedly at a fly-speck.

"You have known some happy days," she said at last, fixing her keen gray eyes on Peewit, as if she would look through him. "You have known some happy days, and many that were not so. You have had trouble and been in doubt. You are in doubt at this moment. There are many perplexities in business. People lose much by theft."

She looked hard at Peewit, who appeared earnestly attentive.

"But the great source of trouble," she continued, "is the human heart."

The gentleman changed color.

"Ha!" cried the sibyl, "I see a lady,—a dark lady,—whose destiny is mixed up with yours."

Peewit looked uneasy, and the muscles of his face twitched nervously.

"Venus and Mars are in conjunction," continued the woman; "but Mars is not favorable to you. Venus, however, can overcome the malignant influence of the other when the Ecliptic cuts the Zenith at the Vernal Equinox. Ha! Here is a number. Beware, beware of 4–11–44."

"Forty-four!" exclaimed Peewit; "why, that is just about her age."

"Beware of forty-four, I tell you; it is your unlucky number. The dark lady is before me still. She is not young. She wears spectacles."

"Now?" said Peewit, with surprise.

"I am looking into futurity," answered the clairvoyant; "at present her eyesight is good. Her hair is dark. She is destined to have an effect upon your existence."

Peewit looked sad.

"Is there not," he asked, hesitatingly, "is there not *any one* who cares for me?"

The sorceress shuffled the cards about, and, taking a piece of chalk from her pocket, drew a circle on the table within that formed by the cards, and within the circle she described a number of cabalistic characters. She gazed upon these intently for a few moments, and then started back, exclaiming,—

"Ha! behold, I see another,—a younger lady,—very different from the other."

Peewit's countenance at once brightened up.

"She is not a dark lady—no—not dark—she has light hair—yes, light hair and blue eyes."

14

" Blue?" inquired Peewit.

" No, not exactly blue," answered the seventh daughter, gazing alternately at the mystic figures on the table and into the face of Peewit, " in fact, on looking more closely, I should pronounce them hazel, — no — no — they are not hazel, — yet are they not quite black, — no — not black — ah! now I have it — they must be — yes, I see more clearly, — they are a sort of gray — yes — that's it, gray."

" Wonderful!" said Peewit.

" She is younger than the other," continued the medium, " yes, much younger; in fact, a mere girl."

Peewit looked disappointed, and he muttered audibly, " It can't be her."

" Interrupt not the flow of the magnetic fluid. I am looking into the past. She was younger once than she is now. Yes — she was a child, — a happy child; then she became a girl, — now she is a woman, — yes, she is a full-grown woman."

" True!" exclaimed Peewit, striking the table with his fist. " It is as true as the gospel — and is she," he continued with some embarrassment, " is she — thinking of any one in particular?"

The seeress again fumbled with the cards; drew some more necromantic figures, and said, —

" The planets are propitious; Venus is in the ascendant. Yes, — she is thinking of some one at this moment. She thinks of him whenever she sees the dark lady. He is an undersized gent, — just as large as you, — he looks like you; he has on a blue coat with brass buttons, and he wears a white hat. His hair is light-colored and straight — an undemonstrative nose — large ears — ha! it is — it is yourself; she is thinking of you at this moment."

"Miraculous!" exclaimed Peewit, "miraculous! And will I — that is to say — will she be happy?"

"She will have some happy days, and some unhappy days. Your fate will be mixed up with hers. More definite information I cannot give you until the Zodiac points to the Pole star; come again. Adieu."

The Pythoness, or whatever she was, now rose, and with a majestic motion of the hand waved the awe-struck Peewit out of the room.

He had been so spellbound while in the presence of the sorceress that he had not been conscious of the emotions caused by her influence, — or his imagination, — and, on descending the rickety staircase, was surprised to perceive that he was in a profuse perspiration and trembling from head to foot. It was with a feeling of relief that he found himself once more in the light of day on the open street.

Whether it was owing to joy on account of danger past, or the gratifying nature of the information he had received, certain it is that he walked away with a light heart, and proceeded with an elastic step towards the lower part of the city, where he intended making his purchases.

As he was passing through Chatham Stree, he noticed a crowd in a shop, and heard the words, "Going — going — gone!" Curiosity induced him to enter. As he did so, the auctioneer, who had a decidedly Jewish cast of countenance, cried, "How much, gentlemen, for this magnificent ten-jeweled, patent lever, Lepine gold watch, with this heavy gold chain, how much am I offered — how much?" and as he spoke he exhibited the articles.

"That looks like a fine timepiece," said a respectable-looking middle-aged gentleman, who was standing by the side of Peewit. "Will you allow me to examine it?"

" Certainly, sir," said the auctioneer, handing down the watch.

"I do not like to make costly purchases," said the old gentleman, opening the watch and carefully examining the works, " without having made an inspection of the goods. Three years ago I bought just such a looking watch as that at this establishment for one hundred and twenty dollars, and it proved to be a most excellent time-keeper. I should like to find a similar one to present to my wife. By Jove! I believe this is its duplicate. It would be cheap at a hundred dollars."

" How much," cried the auctioneer " for this magnificent watch and chain? Who bids? Don't all speak at once."

Now we do not care to describe an operation, the details of which — or at least of similar ones — are published weekly in the newspapers, so we will merely state that Peewit was inveighed into exchanging his silver " turnip " (as Lovell called it), but which was a really serviceable timepiece, for what he supposed to be a superior gold watch and chain, worth at least one hundred and fifty dollars. Moreover, he paid forty-eight dollars to boot, so that he left the shop with only one dollar in money in his pocket with which to pay his way to Foufouville. Of course he would not be able to make the purchases for Mrs. Strongitharm, but he thought the great bargain he had made was a much better investment. Still, as he neared the ferry, he began to have some misgivings, for, judging the future by the past, it was more than probable that, right or wrong, that terrible female would not fail to find fault with him.

Just as he reached the wharf, a well-dressed young man suddenly stooped down beside him, and, tapping him on the shoulder, told him he had dropped his port-monnaie. As he spoke he held up a half-opened pocket-book, which he had evidently just picked up, as it was covered with fresh mud, and in which Peewit could see large rolls of bills, among which he caught a glimpse of two or three of the denomination of fifty or one hundred dollars.

" It is not mine," said Mr. Peewit.

" It must be yours," answered the stranger. " I saw it fall out of your pocket; just feel again."

Peewit felt in his pockets, and his eyes glistened as he looked at the well-stuffed port-monnaie, but he repeated the assertion that it was not his property, although he spoke hesitatingly and as if with an effort.

" I am going to Havana in the Moro Castle at five o'clock, and it's half-past four now," said the stranger; " the bills won't be of any use to me in Cuba — metallic currency there you know. I am sorry I have not time to go to a broker's and exchange them for gold. If I could get a couple of hundred dollars for them I would let them go."

Now Peewit in all his life had never done a positively dishonest act, — it is true he had never been tempted, — but the serpent had tendered him the apple at last, and there was consequently what fine writers would call " a terrible struggle " in his breast; but we think this is too strong language to apply to the species of ratiocination that was going on in his noddle whereby he succeeded in convincing himself that black is white, or at least nothing more than a shade of gray. The pocket-book did not belong to him; but neither did it belong to its present possessor. If the latter took it to Cuba with him, the rightful owner would certainly never see it again, while

14*

if he took it himself, he could return it to the unfortunate
individual who had lost it, whenever the said unfortunate
should advertise his loss, — which there was little doubt
of his doing, — and offer a reward proportionate to the
magnitude of the amount indicated by those thick rolls
of bills. Then there was a possibility — the thought of
which fairly made Peewit smile — that the luckless loser
might *not* make his mishap publicly known, or, if he did, it
might never be brought to the notice of the fortunate
Peewit (but this latter idea, was a sort of mental reser-
vation as it were, — a thought he tried hard not to think,
though he could not entirely suppress it. But who can
chide him? Is man more responsible for his thoughts —
wrong though they be — than for physical defects? Let
him who is without guile cast the first stone). Then the
vision of Mrs. Strongitharm loomed up before him. He
had not felt entirely at ease at the idea of appearing before
her without the articles he had been ordered to purchase,
even though he did show a gold watch instead of a silver
one ; but he knew that money, like charity, covers a multitude of sins, and if he could bring a hundred-pounder to
bear it would effectually silence her batteries. To be sure
to take the pocket-book might seem somewhat like taking
advantage of the young man's difficulty ; but such an
action — as he had often heard — was nothing more than
the way of the world (and, to tell the whole truth, Peewit,
the simple Harmonian, felt a peculiar sort of self-com-
placent gratification at the idea of outwitting a cosmopolitan). The money did not belong to the young man ; he
was evidently not aware of the large amount contained in
the pocket-book, and when he should discover it, its
retention would doubtless be a burden on his conscience ;

he seemed willing, nay, anxious to part with it, and would it not be doing him a positive kindness to relieve him of it? So Peewit thought and argued with himself, and finally told the young man, in the most disinterested manner in the world, that unfortunately he did not have two hundred dollars about him just at that moment, but that he had one dollar and a superb gold watch and chain worth not less than one hundred and fifty dollars.

The young man appeared to hesitate ; but just then the bell of a steamer was heard, and, saying it was too bad he had not time to go to a broker, he concluded to let the packet go for the dollar, the watch and the chain.

The articles changed hands simultaneously ; but the moment the young man examined the watch, he seized Peewit — who was making off — by the cuff, saying, — " Stop, — this won't do."

At that moment a policeman appeared, crossing the street, and the stranger let go of Peewit's sleeve, and, exclaiming, " D—n the luck ! " hastily left, doubtless from the fear of being too late for the Moro Castle.

Peewit now hastened towards the ferry-house with a countenance radiant with joy ; in fact, his mouth was wide-open with a broad grin. It seemed to him as if six inches had been added to his height. He walked with a proud step, cocking his hat over his right eye, for his happiness was complete, and, in the elation of the moment, he felt like hiring a special ferry-boat to carry him over to Jersey City.

Approaching the toll-house, he opened wide the pocketbook, and from a roll, consisting principally of ten, fifty, and one hundred dollar bills, took out a five, which was the lowest denomination he could find. On handing it to the ferry-master, the latter asked him if he had no change, and, on his replying in the negative, carefully examined the bill, then, giving Peewit a sharp, significant glance, he winked to somebody in the rear. Instantly a policeman seized the unfortunate Harmonian by the coat-collar, while another grabbed the pocket-book which he still held in his hand.

"Come along, you bloody counterfeiter," said M. P. No. 1; "we've been a watching for yer this long time."

It was in vain that poor Peewit expostulated and explained and referred, for his respectability, to Dr. Good-enough.

"Who's he?" said one of the M. P.'s; "the head of the band, I suppose?"

"Yes," answered Peewit; "we look up to him as our chief."

"He wants to turn State's evidence," said the other policeman, in a low tone; "we'll make a good thing of it. Where is the fellow's establishment?"

"At Foufouville," replied the prisoner.

No. 1 made a note of this information on a slip of paper, and then, followed by a hooting, jeering, mocking crowd the two guardians of justice dragged the hapless Peewit to the nearest station-house.

"We've nabbed one of 'em at last," they said to the magistrate as they entered. "Here's one of the most desperate 'and owdacious of the hull posse of them are counterfeiters. Why, he tried to shove the queer right under our very eyes."

"Counterfeiter!" said the justice; "why, he looks more like a sneak thief. Where is the evidence?"

"Here, sir," said policeman No. 2, handing up the

pocket-book, " and here is the very identical bill he give the ferry-master."

The justice, a stern, dignified-looking man, with an air of imperturbable gravity, glanced severely at the trembling culprit, and, putting on his spectacles, proceeded to examine the bill. Soon the muscles of his face relaxed, and a sort of grim smile passed over his countenance.

" I do not think this is a *very* dangerous counterfeit," said he ; " in fact, I doubt if it is a counterfeit at all in the eye of the law."

The two policeman looked exceedingly disappointed. He then held up the bill of which this is a *fac simile*, —

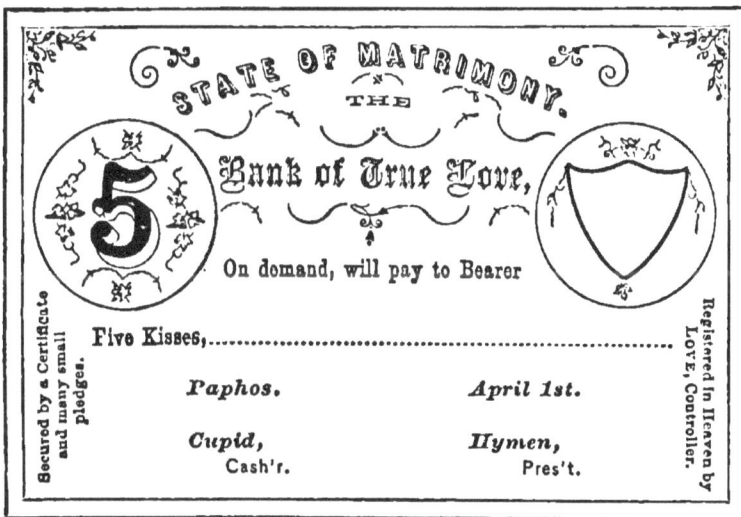

STATE OF MATRIMONY.

THE

Bank of True Love,

5

On demand, will pay to Bearer

Five Kisses,..

Secured by a Certificate and many small pledges.

Paphos. *April 1st.*

Cupid, *Hymen,*
Cash'r. Pres't.

Registered in Heaven by LOVE, Controller.

" I guess it's only a joke," said the judge.

"No, indeed ; " answered the unfortunate Peewit, " it's anything but a joke."

" In truth it's no joke at all," said policeman No. 2, " for the villain offered to turn State's evidence, and I took down from his own lips the name of the chief conspirator, one Goodenough, which I strongly suspicion is nothing but an *alias* of that slippery scoundrel, One-eyed Jake. Their operations are carried on secretly by night at Foufouville."

"Here is truly some genuine bogus," said the judge, opening a roll of bills from the pocket-book; "the case begins to assume a more promising aspect. Lock him up for the present in cell No. 6, while we concert measures for the arrest of the whole gang."

So the wretched Peewit, in spite of his entreaties and protestations, was incarcerated in cell No. 6. This miserable den was five feet by four in size, and was furnished with what had once been a three-legged stool, but of which two legs had been broken off.

The prisoner propped the stool up in a corner, and, seating himself on it very carefully, lest it should slip from under him, mused upon the mutability of human affairs.

In about half an hour a seedy-looking individual appeared at the grating and offered, for a consideration, to convey any message he might wish to send to his friends. Peewit, having no other paper about him excepting his collar, took it off and wrote on it a few harrowing lines to Prof. Malpest descriptive of his forlorn situation. The professor, he told the seedy one, would remunerate him for his trouble.

In about an hour — which seemed an age to the captive — the jailer unlocked the grating, and beckoned to him to come out. For a moment hope rose before him, but, like the ghost at the museum, the illusion was quickly dispelled, for, the moment he emerged from the cell, he was unceremoniously handcuffed, led into the yard, and, in si-

lence and darkness, — for night had fallen and no word
was spoken, — shoved into a sombre, rectangular vehicle
that stood before the door. As the prison van had no
opening whatever for the admission of light, it appeared
to the excited imagination of Peewit like a hearse, and
as it was driven rapidly over the stones, a sort of vague
apprehension seized upon him that he was being hurried
to execution. He quaked with fear; but his alarm was
groundless, for he was merely deposited in the prisoners'
reception room, — commonly called the receiving vault,
— at the Tombs. This was an indescribably filthy hole,
and was doubtless kept in that condition with the humane
motive of causing the inmate a feeling of positive relief
when he was removed to a cell. The one in which our
unlucky Harmonian was finally shut up was furnished
with a stool, a bench, and a pitcher of water. Here
he passed a sleepless night; but this was not altogether
on account of the hardness of his bed, that is to
say, the bench. It was his mental rather than his physical troubles that kept him awake, and surely these
were enough to cause him disquietude. He had lost his
watch and his money, and rendered himself amenable to
justice. It is true he was not aware of exactly what
high crime and misdemeanor he had been guilty; but this
incertitude aggravated his uneasiness, especially since it
was clear he had committed, or at least was suspected of
having committed, some heinous offence, and should he be
proven innocent, — which he hardly dared to hope, — it
would be like jumping from the frying-pan into the fire,
for he would escape the clutches of the law only to fall
into those of Mrs. Strongitharm.

In the morning a slice of brown bread, with a bowl containing a liquid that looked like swill, was given to him for breakfast; but he could not eat. His heart was full, and his stomach seemed to sympathize with it. Broiled partridges would not have tempted his appetite. Hour after hour passed wearily away, the captive sitting moodily on his bench, brooding over his unhappy situation.

About mid-day an old gentleman, with a benevolent face and a white cravat, looked in at him through the gratings with a pitying expression of countenance, and, handing him a pamphlet, walked away. The heartsick prisoner opened the pamphlet, hoping to find something that would distract his thoughts from the sorrows of his position. What was his disgust when he found that the document was a sermon on the sin of theft! It began with the poetical assertion that

"It is a sin to steal a pin, —
Much more to steal a greater thing,"

and demonstrated that thieving leads on to crimes of greater magnitude, which finally bring the wretch to the scaffold. A fearful picture was drawn of the last night. of the sinner on earth, and there was a coarse wood-cut representing the condemned dangling from the gallows.

Peewit, who had become morbid from his solitary confinement, was worked up to desperation by this last humiliation, and, hardly knowing what he was about, he sprang to the grating and yelled with rage after his reverend would-be benefactor.

"Where's the insinuatin' caluminator?" he cried as loud as he could bellow. "I don't want his libellous trash. I'm an honest man. Come back, — come back, you vile, unmitigated slanderer, you lying serpent, you personal reflector!"

The good minister, supposing the prisoner had lost his wits, almost broke his neck in hurrying down the steep iron stairway in order to make his escape before the maniac should break loose and pounce upon him.

Peewit continued his outcries, but in the midst of them two wardens rushed up, and, throwing open the iron door, soused him from head to foot with a bucketful of cold water.

"We'll teach yer to be obstreperous," said one of them.

"You'd better be quiet," said the other, "for if yer don't we'll jes' turn the whole Croton reservoir on yer, we will."

Poor Peewit was completely cowed by the shower-bath, and, throwing himself down on the bench, he covered his face with his hands and groaned in spirit.

Professor Malpost made his appearance not long afterwards, accompanied by an advocate of the firm of Sharpe & Kean, Attorneys and Counsellors at Law.

"Why, Peewit, my boy," said he, "you seem to be in a sorry plight. What's the matter?"

The crestfallen and thoroughly humbled Peewit, who looked like a drowned rat, moaned in anguish, for the tone of persiflage in which the professor addressed him seemed like a mockery of his misery.

He told his sorrowful tale, and concluded by expressing the conviction that he would be unable to survive an imprisonment of more than a year, and begging to know if some one would not intercede with the governor to

15

procure his pardon ; at which both the unsympathizing professor and the lawyer burst out laughing.

"You are in a very tight place," said the professor, assuming a serious air. "I am glad I don't stand in your shoes, for you will be lucky if you escape the knot. Nothing can be more dangerous than to tamper with the bank of True Love. When the president of that institution once catches a man he does not easily let go his grip. He is an inexorable jailer, and the cashier has been so often imposed upon by counterfeiters (after gold you know), that he is always on the watch for victims. His favorite mode of execution is by shooting the unfortunates through the heart. They often suffer untold anguish."

This fearful picture of his possible fate so affected Pee-wit, that, partly from alarm for the future, and partly from present cold caused by his drenched clothing, he quivered and quaked from head to foot.

The lawyer had more compassion than the professor, for, taking him by the hand he led him out of the cell and told him in a kindly tone to be of good cheer, for his case was not yet quite desperate.

Eventually the unfortunate gentleman was taken before a magistrate, and, it being clearly proved that he was the victim of misplaced confidence, the charge against him was dismissed, and he returned to Foufouville the same day, a sadder and a wiser man.

We will spare the reader an account of his meeting with Mrs. Strongitharm.

The doctor, as may be supposed, could not forego so favorable an opportunity of giving his flock a discourse on the advantages of remaining secluded in the true fold at Harmony Hall, instead of exposing their innocence to the manifold perils and dangers of the outside world.

The disasters that had happened to brother Joseph he hoped would be a lesson to the whole community.

It may be proper to mention, that Peewit said nothing about his interview with the female astrologer.

CHAPTER VIII.

The Doctor invests in the Fine Arts.

WE remember once in our boyhood, seeing a juggling clown at a circus toss three or four balls up in the air one after the other, and repeating the operation quickly with each one in succession as it came down, keep them all going at the same time for several minutes. All at once he stopped his performance, and stood holding out one hand and looking up into the air, as if one of the balls, which had gone up, had failed to come down. We can never forget our amazement when we first saw the trick, nor the impression, which remained on our mind for an indefinite period of time, that that ball was still pursuing its upward flight towards the zenith, perhaps never again to be seen by mortal eyes.

Now we cannot entirely free ourself from a sort of ill-defined apprehension that in the management of this narrative the reader may suspect us of imposing upon him a kind of literary sleight-of-hand. In the beginning we exhibited our balls — that is to say, our characters — to the public; in the third chapter we set them in motion and got them all in a beautiful whirl; we kept them pretty well in sight for ten or twenty pages or more; but in the fifth chapter we showed decided symptoms of breaking down; and, by the end of the sixth, one of them at least, Charity, had been entirely lost sight of.

Leander we left sitting on a stone in the middle of the

melon-patch, and we believe that Charity vanished from view going into her room several chapters back; but it was so long since that we really are not certain about it. Now this apparent neglect of a young lady and gentleman whom many will doubtless regard as the hero and heroine of our book, may perhaps be considered by some as a defect, in a literary point of view, and were we writing a mere work of fiction, we should endeavor to keep the most interesting characters — that is to say, those who love each other the most — prominently before the reader; but inasmuch as we have not undertaken our task in order to afford amusement to a few lackadaisical young women, but for the purpose of laying before the world an impartial statement of facts, we shall continue as we have begun, and shall jot down those incidents that we judge worthy of being recorded for the benefit of posterity, in chronological order, and just as they actually occurred, without making the slightest effort to diminish the truth, or to enhance its interest and effect by postponing the marrying and killing until the last page.

The records of what took place at the phalanstery during the convention week, when more than one-half the Harmonians were absent, are, we regret to say, quite meagre; but inasmuch as Mr. Lovell and Charity were left almost alone in the house, we presume that time must have hung heavily on their hands. We also infer (and there are corroborating circumstances to support our inference) that it was about this time that the doctor, visiting the city on business connected with his enterprise, happened to pass by the auction rooms of Messrs. Tuanhaff & Bangs, during a sale of some valuable original old paintings imported by Moses Levy & Co., the well-known German house. The doctor now recollected that Charity had complained of the gloomy appearance of the dark, bare walls in the large rooms at Harmony Hall, and the thought occurred to him that some of the fine pictures he saw put up for sale — such as "The Grilling of St. Lawrence," "The Stoning of St. Stephen," "The Martyrdom of the Eleven Thousand Virgins," and others — would give a different aspect to the blank spaces. So he entered the room and ranged himself among the bidders.

. . . . The doctor's purchases arrived at Harmony Hall on the very day when the members of the society who had attended the Convention had all returned from the city. The old gentleman's glowing account of his prizes excited the curiosity of all, and consequently the whole community was present when the huge cases were opened by John Long. The doctor stood by, catalogue in hand. "Ha!" he exclaimed, as the front of a case was removed. "Look at that. There you behold something that it is a pleasure to gaze upon. Listen to the description.

"'116. Cain Slaying Abel, — 64 by 87. Anacronismo Florentini. 15th Century. A glorious masterpiece. Abel has just been felled like an ox, and his blood and brains are gushing out. Cain stands a-straddle of the body, horror-struck. His eye is glaring wildly, the consciousness of his awful crime having just burst upon him. In his trembling hand he still grasps the club covered with the clotted blood and hair of his victim. On his brow is a great black mark.

"'This touching picture is full of that delicacy of conception and treatment so characteristic of this master.'"

" Papa," said Charity, turning away her head, " this is a horrible thing. I can't bear to look at it."

"You lack appreciation, my dear," answered the doctor. " For the enjoyment of such works you must be educated up to it. What can be finer than that execution?"

" The better the execution, the worse the picture would appear to me," said Charity. " How can a picture be attractive when the subject is repulsive?"

" Your very disgust," said the doctor, " is a proof of the artist's skill. It was his object to excite powerful emotions in the breast of the spectator, and he has done it. But you women have no judgement or appreciation. Your sainted mother was just like you. Notice the foreshortening of that club, and notice how the face of Cain is shown only in profile as if he were ashamed to look at his fellow-man. And then the accessories. Consider the depth of imagination displayed by them. In the distance you see an arch of triumph, typical of the triumph of virtue over vice, and it is copied from the arch of Constantine, which proves the artist's historical knowledge, for Constantine was the first Christian emperor. On the right hand you have the ruins of a Doric temple and a Turkish mosque, which are symbolical of the ruin of false religions, and on the left hand is a flourishing tree, — I cannot exactly make out of what kind, — which is intended to signify that the true faith shall never wither."

" It is a wonderful work, a wonderful work," said Professor Malpest standing off about twenty feet, and looking through his glass with one eye, while he closed the other with what appeared very much like a wink of derision.

"What is that they are cooking?" inquired Mr. Pee-wit.

"Sir," answered Mrs. Strongitharm, "if you cannot speak without displaying your ignorance, you had better remain silent."

"I once saw an engraving of the same subject, from a design by a French artist," said Lovell, "in which the body of Abel was partly concealed by the altar, the painter having evidently concentrated his efforts on the expression given to the face of Cain. In my humble opinion it was a better composition than this, for it did not create any unpleasant feelings."

"That proves the inferiority of the Frenchman," answered the doctor. "Here the strongest emotions of the human breast are provoked,—horror, aversion, dread."

"I thought love was the strongest," murmured Miss Griffin; but she spoke in so low a tone that her remark was not overheard.

Long now opened another case.

"Here we have a gem," said the doctor.

"'214. Landscape with Cattle,—48 by 56. Sebastian del Negrotinto — Spanish school.

"'A lovely picture of Arcadian life.'

"What say you to that my friends? those trees, and rocks, and mountains, and water are thrown together in the most miscellaneous manner. Did you ever see anything like it in this country?"

"Never," answered Professor Malpest. "Never."

"Were the skies green, and the leaves of the trees black in Sebastian's time?" inquired Mr. Peewit.

"Ignorant man!" replied the doctor, "don't you know

that this is the peculiar style of the Spanish school? Artists in those days did not content themselves with a servile copy of nature, — they drew upon their imagination."

Professor Malpest hinted that doubtless the colors had become darkened from the effects of time, the chemistry of pigments not having been well understood in former years.

"There is, perhaps, a slight change due to that cause," answered the doctor; "but the colors of the foreground were made dark originally in order to give distance to the background."

"But the background is dark, too," said Peewit.

"That," replied the doctor, "is for the purpose of preserving the same tone throughout the picture. Would you have your breeches black in front and blue behind? It is astonishing how little knowledge of art there is in this country. Our Churches, Bierstadts, Kensetts, Giffords, Durands, and Gineux don't paint like that."

"I acknowledge they do not, sir," said Mr. Lovell.

"A picture that truly resembled nature would please me more than this one," said Charity. "Not that I would have an artist copy every stick and stone and blade of grass, but I would have the general effect as it is in reality."

"That is because you are wanting in the ideal," replied her father; "but you can't help it. She was so before you. I have occasionally glanced at the landscapes in our modern exhibitions, but, pooh! what are they? Look at those cows. Did you ever see such cows? I never did. And then, the trees!"

"What kind are they, sir?" asked Peewit.

"Of no particular kind, sir," answered the doctor.

"A painter is not a botanist. With these great men, trees were simply conventional vegetation."

"Here is a pooty pictur'," said John Long. "It reminds me like of me owl moother in Llannwyddrygg, over agin Ben Caernelwyd."

"It's a gem!" cried the doctor, "a gem!

"' 71. — Interior 14 by 19, Paul Daub. Dutch School.

"' An exquisitely finished scene of domestic life. An old woman knitting; every thread of the ball of yarn is distinct; a cat is at her feet, — admire the hairs in the tail; overhead, a parrot eating a peanut, — the latter should be examined through a magnifying glass. Shelves, cups, saucers, and pewter spoons fill up the rest of this charming work of art.'

"There, my fine critics, there is reality for you! What can equal that for truth?"

"A photograph," answered Lovell.

"Pshaw! Mere mechanical work," replied the doctor. "What sentiment, what feeling is there in a photograph? Here you can figure to yourself the patient and laborious artist, working early and late for months over the creation of his genius. Why, there is a day's work on that peanut. Think of the time, think of the time necessary for such minute finish."

"I think it could have been better employed, sir," answered Lovell.

"Perhaps, then, you prefer the 'grand' style," replied the doctor. "Well, here you have it. The very perfection of high art.

"' 68. — Prometheus. 114 by 156. Taddeo Maccaroni. School of Naples.

" ' A grand conception. All is dark, gloomy, and sublime. The only specimen of this master in the country.'

" There is inspiration, there is force, there is power. Consider the chiaro-oscuro."

Mr. Peewit said he could see the oscuro, but could not make out the chiaro. He supposed it was a night scene.

" No, sir. It is broad day," said the doctor.

" Then it must be a very cloudy day," answered Mr. Peewit, "for I can't see anything but a colored man on his back, and a bird pecking at him. Everything is black."

" Mark the skilful management of the lights," said the doctor. " How the muscles are brought out ! "

" And the innerds, too," answered Peewit ; " the bird is a-devourin' of 'em. Ugh ! It makes me sick."

" That picture is a poem, an epic poem," said the doctor.

" What kind of a poem is that ? " inquired Mr. Peewit.

" If you want to know," replied Mr. Lovell, " you must read Swift's directions for making one."

" Now," said the doctor, " we come to the greatest bargain of all, a ' Virgin and Child,' by Raphael. That painting cost me seventy-five dollars, sir, seventy-five dollars (including frame), and warranted original by Tuanhaff himself. There is a copy in the Pitti palace at Florence. What do you think of that ? "

" No one can say anything against Raphael," answered Lovell.

" The design is certainly charming," said Miss Griffin.

" I can see nothing to admire in it," said Mrs. Strong-itharm.

"The child," said Charity, "is beautiful."

"It's the lady who takes my eye," observed Peewit. "She is perfectly angelic. You can see it was painted from the life. No man could imagine such a face. It is clearly an original portrait."

"Of an Italian contarini," remarked Professor Malpost. "The composition (being similar to that of the picture in the Pitti palace) is really most beautiful, and the flow of the lines is perfect."

"I know I had got a cheap thing when I bought it," said the doctor; "and here we have a companion piece, 'The Immaculate Conception,' by Domenichino. There is a perfect *fac-simile* of it (as to the design) in the Louvre. It is uncertain which of the two is the original, but I think there can be no doubt on the subject, for you see the master's name there in one corner in large letters."

"Domenichino," said Professor Malpost, "is universally acknowledged to have been one of the greatest painters that ever lived."

"I don't clearly comprehend the subject of this picture," said Peewit.

"Of course not," replied the doctor. "It is entirely beyond your depth; but, behold what is coming!

"'82. — Head, supposed to be a portrait of Cardinal Bembo. Michael Angelo.

"'This remarkable *chef d'œuvre*, unquestionably the finest specimen of this great master in America, was discovered while clearing out the rubbish from the garret of a pawnbroker's shop, over the Cloaca Maxima, Rome. It is so very much injured by the ravages of time, that it is difficult to make out whether it is intended for a male or a female head ; but this only adds to its value in the eyes of the *connoisseur.* Its authenticity is beyond dispute, the well-known monogram, $\mathcal{AB}$ being plainly visible in the left-hand corner."

"Mark the fire of that eye," continued the doctor, " (what a pity the other is so indistinct!) — and observe the force of the lines about the mouth, what power is displayed in them! The touch of the master is displayed in every line. Our Elliots, and Inmans, and Bakers don't exhibit such heads as that."

"They are quite incapable of it," said Professor Malpest.

"I can see little or nothing that is attractive in a faded, cracked, and dust-covered picture," said Charity ; "for no matter how good it may have been when first painted, its beauties have become marred, if not quite obliterated. A real face is not considered as being improved by cracks or wrinkles and loss of color ; and I cannot understand why a painted one should be."

"That," answered her father, " is because you are too realistic. The *connoisseur,* in his mind's eye, sees the cracks filled up ; the color restored ; the work, in short, as it came fresh from the easel of the master."

"It's a pity," said Mr. Peewit, " that we can't do that with the real thing ; for then a man could always see his wife as she looked when he was courting her ; and if he had a particularly vivid imagination, he might even fancy she was somebody else."

"Beauty, in the living subject, is only skin-deep," said Professor Malpest, " and time effaces it ; but in art, the ruins sometimes excite more admiration (or, at all events,

16

more commendation) than would have been given to the uninjured work."

" Art, then, in this respect is superior to Nature," said Charity.

" Yes," said Lovell; "if we are to give credence to men's imagination or vanity."

" I understand how the former can deceive," said Charity; " but I fail to perceive what vanity has to do with it."

" A cracked and defaced picture, or a battered and broken torso is found," answered Lovell, " and artists go into raptures over it. They think, by professing unbounded admiration for a mere remnant, to astonish the million by their profound knowledge of Art. I suppose that head, sir, was valued at a high price?"

" Thirty-three dollars, I paid for it," answered the doctor, " thirty-three dollars; and it was considered cheap at that."

" I think it was very dear," said Peewit, " a daguerreotype of Bembo would have been more satisfactory, for it would have shown us how the fellow looked."

" There is a charming head of Cupid in the windows of Kullers & Printz, that I would much rather have than this hideous old Cyclops," said Miss Griffin.

" I could understand your preference," said Mrs. Strongitharm, " if the parties were in the flesh; but remember they are works of Art, not of Nature."

" That which is the most beautiful in Nature must appear the most beautiful in the representation of it," answered Miss Griffin; " thus a portrait of yourself, madam, would hardly be as attractive as that of a good-looking woman ; in fact, the more it was like, the less it would be admired."

A withering glance was the response of Mrs. Strong-itharm.

" Here is a magnificent work," said the doctor, who was too much absorbed in the contemplation of his prizes to notice the passage-at-arms between the ladies.

" ' 26. Marriage at Cana, — 160 by 210. — Unknown. Flemish School.

" ' This superb painting formerly adorned the collection of Brian Boru, King of Ulster, and was brought to this country by his last-known descendant, Patrick O'Brien, Esq., who, having compromised himself in the Fenian movement of '98 (when he heroically endeavored to recover his lost rights), was obliged to fly to this country, and died some years since in Arkansas, where he was sheriff of Pikeville.

" ' Many of our best artists have expressed their opinions of this grand work. The figures are all the size of life. Some attribute it to Leonardo da Vinci, others to Teniers, and others again to Titian, for it possesses the merits of all three.' "

" What an interesting scene ! " said Miss Griffin.

" Why, all hands are drunk ! " said Peewit.

" You mean inebriated, I presume," said Mrs. Strong-itharm.

" Some of the positions may seem equivocal," said the doctor ; " but the artist merely meant to indicate the hilarity attendant on the joyous occasion."

" How superbly the bride is dressed ! " said Miss Griffin ; " what a pity those leg-of-mutton sleeves have gone out of fashion ! and those laces, how rich they are !

and how much those red high-heeled shoes add dignity to woman ; they give her elevation."

"I pity a woman," said Mrs. Strongitharm, "whose reputation depended on her heels, like a ballet-dancer's."

"Some people wouldn't have any," answered Miss Griffin, "even if they were mounted on stilts."

"Loftiness of soul, my dear sisters," said the doctor, "is of more consequence than elevation of body, and you acquire it by the contemplation of such a work as this. Look at the bride. I should pronounce her most excellent in conception, though the groom is perhaps the happiest figure in the group ; and in that female, standing on the left, their is food for an hour's study."

"Yes," said Miss Griffin, "I was contemplating that heavy yellow satin gown, and those rich point laces."

"They must have cost a heap," said Peewit. "But what queer head-gear they have ! One of them has on something that looks like a pair of horns, and another an immense extinguisher."

"That," said Professor Malpest, "was the female costume in the fourteenth century."

"And the men wore women's collars, I see," said Peewit ; "but where are their breeches ? "

"Probably," answered Lovell, "the ladies are wearing them, as some do to this day."

"No, no," said Peewit, "they have got them tucked up above the thighs like clam-diggers."

"Let me call your attention to the architectural details," said the doctor. "See that spire pointing upwards, signifying that even on the wedding-day we should direct our thoughts above. In the distance are arches on arches, and colonnade after colonnade."

"What a magnificent city Cana was!" said Mr. Peewit. "It must have been larger than Rome."

"And mark the transparency of shadow," continued the doctor, "and the luminous arrangement of the lights."

"Particularly in the window of the transept," said Peewit.

"That tracery," said the doctor, "is a study for an architect; it is a remarkably pure specimen of the flamboyant Gothic style."

"What talented fellows the Goths of Cana must have been!" said Peewit. "Why, there's the Pope!"

"Imbecile!" muttered Mrs. Strongitharm.

"That is doubtless intended for a Jewish Rabbi," said the doctor, "although the costume does resemble that of the Romish hierarchy; but how rich is the color, how deep the tone! It seems painted as it were with fused gems."

"The ear-rings of the bride are exquisite," said Charity.

"And the old clock in the corner," said the doctor; "how familiar it looks! and take note of the brilliant idea, — it marks one o'clock, symbolical of the fact that the married pair are one."

"But one hand points to twelve," observed Peewit.

"That," said the doctor with some hesitation, "that is typical of the future happy results of the union."

"What's this? What's this?" exclaimed several at once.

"This," said the doctor, turning over a leaf, "is the

"'379. Fall into Limbo, — 72 by 84 — Pietro Pintoretto. Time of Dante.

"'The damned are seen tumbling down, head first, sideways and in every possible position, arms and legs

16*

protruding on all sides. This is the picture so finely
characterized by Sir Joshua Reynolds as an " avalanche
of flesh." The devil is seen below stirring up his fires,
throwing on the brimstone, and getting ready his grid-
irons and ovens. The dove hovers overhead in a trian-
gular cage. Numbers of the lost are imploring for
mercy, but the Lamb glares at them ferociously, and St.
Peter averts his head, as if he was shaking it negatively
and saying, " You can't come in.' "

" What a dreadful imagination that painter must have
had ! " said Miss Griffin.

" It is truly a fearful thing to contemplate," said the
doctor; " and what a lesson it teaches us ! "

" Several lessons," said Lovell.

" I cannot bear to look at it," said Miss Griffin.

" See what a knowledge of anatomy is displayed," said
the doctor; " it is Nature itself."

Miss Griffin did not answer.

" We cannot be sure of that," said Lovell, " without
seeing the living models in the exact positions here repre-
sented, and that would not be easy to accomplish, for
some of the figures have got their limbs twisted together
(as if they were trying to tie themselves into hard knots)
in a way not possible to any but Japanese jugglers, and
others are flying through the air in postures seen only in
Hindoo devotees who swing themselves fifty feet above
ground, hooked through the back."

" How thankful we should be," said the doctor, " that
we are on the true road to glory ! Behold, in this picture,
how few are saved, and how many lost, notwithstanding
the efforts that have been made to rescue fallen man."

" The devil must be the most powerful of all," said Peewit.

" Here," said the doctor, " we have a very early work, and consequently very valuable.

" ' 24. Circumcision. (Tempera, w. g. b. g. 34 by 60.) Fra Domenic. About 1200,

" ' A most pleasing performance. The heads (all in profile) are excellent in design, the expression of the child undergoing the operation being particularly happy. Among the fine points we would call the *amateur's* attention to the knife, on which is seen a drop of blood. A young woman watches the proceedings with breathless interest.'

" And this will do for a companion piece to it.

" ' 18. Flagellation. (Fresco, 46 by 52).. Perugino Paletto. 1287—1329.

" ' The peculiar style of the period (before Raphael had debased the art) is here shown in all its perfection. The flesh has that fine light-bluish tint seen only in American marble. The figures are slightly idealized (being about thirteen heads in height), and the limbs are straight and rigid as becomes the subject. The little finger of the left hand of the principal figure is particularly well done. The expression of Pontius Pilate is masterly, the emotions of rage, hatred, and delight being shown in every lineament. The culverin in the back ground, astride of which is a ·Roman standard bearer, is extremely interesting, as proving that fire-arms were known in the time of Paletto.' "

" This is a painful picture," said Charity.

" It would be more so," answered Peewit, " if they did not all seem to be taking it so coolly."

"These subjects," said the doctor, "were chosen in order to do honor to the Almighty, which shows the elevation of sentiment possessed by the artists of that time. To appreciate them fully you must look at them with the eye of Faith."

"My taste," said Mr. Peewit, "is for mythological subjects. I love to look at Venuses."

"That simply shows that your taste is depraved and needs cultivation," said Mrs. Strongitharm.

"Here," said the doctor, "is a mere modern work that I inadvertently allowed myself to be inveigled into bidding for. It represents a pack of hounds, — in distemper, — after Sir Edwin Landseer."

"They don't look like mad dogs," observed Mr. Peewit ; "and where's Sir Ed——"

"Peewit ! Peewit !" said Mrs. Strongitharm.

"I could swear," said John Long, "they was portraits like of the dogs of Sir Owen ap Jones, whose kennel I kept at Glennwygrig ; it a'most seems as if I could hear 'em bark."

"How perfectly natural are the attitudes !" remarked Charity.

"That shows the superiority of the old masters," replied the doctor. "This thing is nothing but a copy from Nature ; there is no art whatever visible in it."

"Sir," said Mr. Lovell, "I would rather possess a pup of Landseer's, than a pre-Raphaelite virgin."

"What kind of a virgin is that ?" inquired Mr. Peewit.

"A very old one," answered Professor Malpest.

"A sort of old ma—" Mr. Peewit's words were cut short by a frown from Mrs. Strongitharm.

"Here is a glorious work," cried the doctor.

" ' 13. Susannah and the Elders. 108 by 120. After Rubens.

" ' This is a faithful copy by Von Beest, of the celebrated picture in the well-known gallery of Count Lackinwitz, near Antwerp. Although a mere copy, the exquisite delicacy and refinement of the original, is preserved throughout.

" ' The proportions of Susannah are colossal. There is nothing here of the pettiness of the modern French school, but everything is on a grand scale, majestic, sublime, like the mind of the master. The flesh is warm in tone, and hangs down in thick folds. (Winkleman calls it " flabby.") The drapery which lies at her feet is beautifully done, and so is the piece of soap on the edge of the bath-tub,—a remarkable instance of the care bestowed by this great man on his accessories.

" ' The two sly elders show by the direction in which they are pointing, and by the expression of their countenances, that their curiosity is being amply gratified. The one who is sticking out his tongue deserves the highest admiration, but both figures are in the best style of art, the action being especially worthy of commendation.' "

" That's my style," exclaimed Peewit. " That's what I call a picture."

" Von Beest's genius," said Professor Malpest, " seems to have spread itself there, to have borne him along as it were, under full canvas, with all colors flying."

" And laid on with a free brush," said the doctor.

" Regardless of expense," put in Peewit.

" And yet," continued the doctor, " nothwithstanding

the force, the energy displayed, what touching sentiment, what a feeling of refinement pervades the whole! "

" It is the only picture that has excited my emotions," said Peewit; "but what a whopper Susan is! How I should like to have seen her! "

The enthusiastic Peewit, becoming suddenly conscious that he had said more than prudence dictated, cast a furtive glance behind him; but his fears were groundless, Mrs. Strongitharm having left the room with the other ladies.

"It is a gorgeous work," said Professor Malpest, standing off at a distance, and looking as much as possible lost in admiration.

" Whatever may be the merits of the execution," said Lovell, " the design, in my opinion, is simply beastly."

"That," said the doctor, " is because your judgment has not been educated up to the appreciation of High Art. The true admirer of the old masters can see no fault in them; he looks *through* the subject, as it were, and sees only the genius displayed in its portrayal."

" But an artist of refinement," answered Lovell, " would either not select a coarse subject, or, if he did, he would so treat it as to conceal any want of delicacy in it. The beautiful picture of Diana and her Nymphs, by Professor Sohn, is an exemplification of my remark."

" Pooh! " said the doctor. " The modern German school."

" I consider Steinbruck's Adoration of the Magi the finest composition on that subject I ever saw," said Lovell.

" And yet," answered the doctor, " you have beheld the glorious conceptions of Signorelli and Squarcione! "

" There is no reason," replied Lovell, " to suppose that the human mind has degenerated during the last five cen-

turies; on the contrary, considering the advances that
have been made in civilization, it appears to me to have
improved; but, even granting that it has remained in
statu quo — "

" Like the Apollo Belvidere," suggested Peewit.

" In *statu quo*," continued Lovell, without heeding the
interruption, " artists of the present day have many advantages over their predecessors of the olden time. They
have the same beautiful nature around them and the
works of good masters to study from, with the writings
of able critics to guide them, besides some minor advantages in regard to materials. Among the ' old masters,'
which, in the popular estimation, means every one who
handled a brush some hundreds of years ago, I presume
there was just about the same proportion of good to bad
painters as at present; but as a class I do not believe
that they were superior in ability to the men of our day,
while, in regard to artificial acquirements, the latter have
the advantage. Macaulay says that as far as human intelligence is concerned, we are the true ancients, those
who lived in the early ages being the youths."

" Then," said Peewit, " Methusaleh was a youth at nine
hundred and sixty-nine years of age."

" In knowledge, yes," replied Lovell. " Now the fine
works of the old masters — and the bad ones too —
have long been collected in the galleries of Europe, com-
mented on by critics, and the place of all of them noted.
It is a very rare occurrence for a new one to be discovered,
and, when this happens, the fact is at once heralded over
the continent, and, good or bad, it brings a very high
price; yet hundreds of pictures bearing the names of
well-known early masters are annually imported into New

York. These may be divided into five classes, with the per centage of each as follows, —

" 1st. Bad copies of bad originals, 80, . worthless.
" 2d. Bad copies of good originals, 15,   "
" 3d. Good copies of bad originals, 3,   "
" 4th. Good copies of good originals, 2, of some value.
" 5th. Original works of old masters, 0.

100."

" Why do you speak of the fifth class as ' imported '? " asked the professor.

" If I were to answer you like an old Greek philosopher," replied Lovell, " I should say that the fifth class was ' nothing ' and ' nothing ' was imported ; but I have a better reason. I believe that occasionally stray *bonâ fide* originals (usually very inferior ones) do find their way into our market ; but the percentage of these is such a mere fraction that I felt justified in marking it 0 in the above classification.

" Besides the above, there are also imported for sale great numbers of acknowledged modern paintings. These may be classed and divided as follows, —

" 1st. Bad pictures by students or artists,   70.
              unsalable in Europe.
" 2d. Good pictures by students or inferior artists, 0.
" 3d. Inferior pictures by good artists (' Homer
              sometimes nods '),   20.
" 4th. Good pictures by good artists,   8.
" 5th. Fine works by artists of reputation,   2.

100.

" Copies, which sometimes resemble caricatures, of superior modern works which have become popular through the medium of engravings are weekly, if not daily, sold in auction rooms almost by wholesale. These are not imported, but are copied, in New York, from engravings, the artisan being paid for his work at the rate of about one dollar a foot. I have seen parties purchase these daubs under the impression that they were buying the originals."

" Is not all this rather beneficial than otherwise?" said the professor. " Does it not cultivate a taste for art?"

"It is about as beneficial," answered Lovell, " as it would be to cultivate weeds in a garden."

" Admitting, for the sake of argument, that what you say is true," said the doctor, " then but few persons in this country have any opportunity of gratifying their artistic tastes."

" Fine engravings can be had," answered Lovell, " and I am sure that a good engraving of a good picture is better than a bad copy or a bad original, and besides, many excellent paintings by Americans are annually exhibited. Our landscape painters, in my opinion, have no superiors. If old Andrea del Sarto, or Giotto, or any of those who came not long after them, had painted the ' Heart of the Andes,' or the ' Storm in the Rocky Mountains,' those truthful and most beautiful works would be worth their weight in gold (frames and all) ; whole volums would be written about them, and dictionaries ransacked to find terms strong enough to express their merits."

" But the works of the early painters," said Professor Malpest, " are interesting as showing the progress of art."

17

" Yes," answered Lovell ; " and matchlock muskets are interesting as showing the progress of fire-arms ; but a sportsman would not value one as highly as a breech-loader."

" That is not a parallel case," replied the professor ; " for an antiquarian might prize what a sportsman would not ; and, if there was as much gratification to the vanity in possessing a collection of old Spanish or Flemish musketoons, we would soon see them encumbering our walls, and imitations would be manufactured by wholesale."

" Now you have hit it," said Lovell ; " in order to gratify a petty vanity, founded on ignorance, we are unjust to our fellow-countrymen."

" I am glad of it," said Mrs. Strongitharm, who entered the room in time to hear the latter part of the sentence ; " for it may make some of them feel for the wrongs of their fellow-countrywomen."

" The city women have the hardest time," said Peewit.

This started the conversation on a new tack, — to speak nautically, — but our profound respect for the unities induces us to withhold it. Enough, however, has been given to enable the reader to draw several important inferences. In the first place, it is clear from Mr. Lovell's conversing in an amicable manner with Professor Malpest, that his blood-thirsty intentions in regard to that gentleman had become considerably modified. This we attribute to the influence of Charity, when they were left together during the convention week. In the second place, it is probable that the ignorance of art and want of appreciation shown by Mr. Lovell must have created an unfavorable impression against him in the mind of the doctor, especially when his presumptuous language was contrasted with the suavity and deep feeling for antiquity manifested by the professor. In the third place, we see that Mrs. Strongitharm and Miss Griffin still continued their bickerings, thereby demonstrating that the resentment of woman is more abiding than that of man.

CHAPTER IX.

Lively Times at Harmony Hall.

THE next morning it was resolved to mow the grass on the lawn in front of the house. This task fell to the lot of Mr. Peewit, for, as Mrs. Strongitharm observed, he and Mr. Lovell had undertaken to do the "light out-door work," and Mr. L. was at that time busily engaged in planting turnips, assisted by Miss Charity. So Peewit reluctantly took up the scythe. He began operations by slightly cutting his fingers in honing the implement, and being thereby convinced that it was sharp enough to set to work. After the first swoop of the scythe he stopped, and, visibly agitated, examined his legs, for he had a sort of nervous apprehension that he might cut them off. Finding them safe he made a second swoop, but the grass being rather short the blade passed above it, cutting harmlessly through the circumambient air. At the third stroke, he cut down the doctor's favorite peach sapling; at the fourth, the steel struck against a large stone, making the sparks fly, rebounding, and causing poor Peewit's arms to experience a sensation as though they had received a strong electric shock, his elbows feeling as if pricked by a thousand needles. He looked around piteously, in a bewildered state of mind, but, seeing the sharp eyes of Mrs. Strongitharm fixed upon him, he went to work again vigorously, or, to speak more correctly, desperately, slashing away right and left, sending the small stones flying in all directions, making deep grooves in the grass and in the ground, while tufts were left standing here and there, like the hair of a child's head which has been cut at home to save paying a shilling to a barber. The perspiration was streaming from him, but he kept on, heedless of consequences, though dreading every moment to find himself standing on his stumps. Jack, the poodle, excited by his awkward gyrations, leaped from the arms of his mistress and began to bark at him furiously, capering about, evidently much diverted by the performance ; but the mower, who neither saw nor heard anything, slashed away with his terrible weapon, hacking through grass, stones, sticks, and earth. All at once he was startled by a piercing yelp. *He had cut Jack's head off.* He dropped the scythe, and stood a moment transfixed with horror. He then slowly ventured to turn his head, and furtively looked over his shoulders at Mrs. Strongitharm. Pale and speechless she gazed at the severed carcass of Jack ; then scowled a moment at the dismayed executioner, and, shrieking " Wretch ! " sank fainting on the grass. Peewit's first impulse was to run away ; his second, to go to her assistance ; his third, to get out of sight before she recovered her consciousness. He acted on the latter idea, and instantly took to his heels, never thinking of his coat which was hanging on a tree, nor stopping in his terror-stricken flight until Harmony Hall was lost to view by an intervening hill. Like the wandering Jew, he might never have stopped at all had it not been for the want of breath. He was seen at noon sitting disconsolate on a stone by the roadside, near the entrance to the village of Foufouville, musing upon the vicissitudes of human life.

The day before he was a happy Harmonian ; now he

17*

was little better than an outcast. He had ruined John
Long's best scythe against the stones; he had cut down
the doctor's favorite peach-tree; he had killed Mrs.
Strongitharm's pet dog. What was he to do? Could he
ever venture to show himself again at Harmony Hall?
Could he stand up against the volleys of wrath and resentment with which he would be received? He shook his
head sadly in the negative, and muttered audibly, "Never,
never, never." He sat for hours wrapped in a seeming
lethargy.

He was aroused from his revery, by the approach of a
tall, stern-looking man, dressed entirely in black with the
exception of a white cravat and a pair of green goggles,
and flourishing a heavy walking stick.

"Sir, it is a fine day," said the unknown.

"It is, sir," answered Peewit, eying him suspiciously,
for he had strong misgivings that his sinister-looking in-
terlocutor was bent on highway robbery. However, as
he had not more than six or seven shillings in his pocket,
and was, moreover, in a sort of reckless frame of mind, he
sat doggedly on his stone, and though the next words
might be, "Your money or your life," resolved to resign
himself passively to fate.

But there was in reality no cause for his alarm, the
stranger who excited such serious apprehensions in his
mind being the Rev. Hieronymus Knox, incumbent of
All Saints Church in Foufouville, an earnest and conscientious worker in the good cause, whose stern and forbid-
ding exterior covered a breast filled with the milk of
human kindness. He had but recently returned from
fourteen years' service as a missionary to the Feejee
Islands, and was shocked to hear of the establishment in

the very midst of a Christian community of such a den of
abominations as Harmony Hall was popularly reported to
be. The erection of the phalanstery had at first merely
given rise to some curious and singularly erroneous sur-
mises among the people as to its object. Some said it
was to be an asylum for inebriates, or a factory of some
sort that would make everybody rich ; while others hinted
that the capital of the State was to be removed to Foufouville, and that the large building was the Senate
House. After the Harmonians took up their abode in
their new home, their habits of seclusion still further
piqued the curiosity of their neighbors, and when it was
found that they kept themselves rigidly aloof from out-
siders, abstaining from all intercourse with the world
around them, suspicion was added to curiosity, and
strange rumors of the doings within those secret walls were
whispered mysteriously among the people. The village
gossips had not failed to repeat to their pastor all the
miserable lies that obtained credence amongst them ; old
ladies over the tea-table had made Mrs. Knox's blood
run cold with harrowing accounts of the treatment of
women and children ; and a committee of vestrymen and
deacons had called upon the minister that very morning
to consult as to the best means to be taken to rid the
town of so great a scandal. When, as occasionally happened, Professor Malpest and the doctor drove through
the village on their way to the city, the small boys
glanced at them askant, young maidens timidly shrank
within doors, while grown men and women frowned as
they went by, and the old ones shook their heads and
looked knowing.

The Rev. Mr. Knox was on his way to visit some of

the poor and sick among his parishioners when he came upon the forlorn Peewit sitting by the road-side.

"You seem to be in trouble, my friend," said he. "It will gratify me if I can do anything to alleviate your distress. This life is one of suffering and trial to prepare us for a better world to come. Here none of us are free from sorrow; we must all bear our share of the burden. Are you in want of money?"

As he spoke, the kind-hearted parson held out a quarter of a dollar. Tears started to Peewit's eyes. He could not speak, but by way of answer slapped his pocket, making the silver jingle.

"Ah!" said the minister, "then your trouble is of the mind, not of the body. It is the peculiar province of my vocation, and my greatest happiness, to bring relief to those who are weary and heavy-laden."

Peewit thought of the ruined scythe, the destroyed peach-tree, the decapitated dog, the implacable Strongitharm, and groaned aloud.

"Unhappy man!" said the Rev. Mr. Knox, in a tone of deep commiseration, "whether it be crime or the cruel shaft of misfortune that has reduced you to your present condition, — whether you be suffering from the stings of remorse or from the pangs of sorrow, — I beg you to look upon me as a sympathizing brother. Do you reside in this vicinity?"

Peewit pointed to Harmony Hall.

"What! Do you come from that stronghold of Belial?" exclaimed the divine, shrinking back. "Are you one of those prodigal profligates, one of those licentious libertines? You have not the appearance of a radically bad man. Can it be possible that you are living in a state of sin with one to whom you have not been united according to the rites of the church?"

"Alas! sir, it is too true," answered Peewit, with a heavy sigh. "She just took me without any ceremony at all."

The good minister stood silent for a moment with an expression more of sorrow than of anger.

"You look dejected," said he. "Man cannot get rid of the qualms of conscience as easily as he throws off his coat. They cling to him more closely than his shadow, for they follow him day and night; yea, they pursue him even in his dreams. It would be strange if such guilt did not lie heavy on your heart. Do you sincerely repent of all your enormities?"

"Indeed I do, sir, indeed I do," answered the wretched Peewit.

"Then there is hope," replied Mr. Knox, as his severe if not harsh features relaxed with a smile of satisfaction; "for there is more joy in heaven over one sinner who repenteth, than over a thousand just men made perfect. Would you like to be released from the bonds with which Satan has bound you?"

"I should be rejoiced, sir," answered Peewit.

"I regret my friend that I cannot perform the good work to-day," replied the minister; "other and imperative duties call me hence; but, if you will meet me at the church to-morrow evening with your partner in guilt, I will unite you indissolubly in the holy bonds of matrimony, according to the forms ordained and prescribed by the convocation of bishops and deacons."

Peewit was struck dumb with astonishment, and, before he could recover his speech, the worthy missionary handed him his card, and bidding him farewell went on his way, happy in the belief that he had sown some good seed, which might perhaps take root and ripen, and end in the conversion of the whole heathen community at Harmony Hall.

Poor Peewit felt more miserable than ever. It seemed as if he had escaped from Scylla only to see Charybdis looming up before him. A feeling of utter listlessness was stealing over him when the gnawings of hunger roused him to exertion, for he had eaten nothing since morning, and he resolved to enter the village in search of food. He soon came to an oyster-stand alongside of a rum-shop and, being exceedingly hungry, ordered four dozen on the half-shell.

While Peewit was satisfying his prodigious appetite at the oyster-stand a group of idlers were lounging around the adjoining bar-room, discussing the merits, or rather the demerits, of their neighbors at Harmony Hall.

"Have you heard of the new sex we've got amongst us?" said one of them, who appeared to be a farm-hand. "They've built themselves a great barn of a house, and there they all live together like rabbits; and such carryings-on! I tell you it makes my blood bile to think on't."

"They are wus nor the Mormons, they are," said a red-faced young man, "for they keep all their women in common."

"They are a public nuisance, that's what they are," answered the farmer; "they don't buy nothin' from their neighbors like honest folk, but go to the city arter everything. What good do sich people do in the world? And then it's currently reported, it is, that they have six wives apiece. I tell you sich doin's riles me, they does."

"Yes," said a tow-headed youth about eighteen years of age, "and I've heerd some awful stories about their 'nitiation ceremonies. Do you know," he continued, lowering his voice, "that they mixes a horrid mess of blood, brains, and livers, with bats, toads, serpents, and other horrid reptiles, in a great black iron pot, and they make a fire under it, and when it's bilin' they go hoppin' and dancin' about it yellin' and singin', —

> "'Round about the caldron go;
> In the pizened entrails throw,
> Adder's fork and blind worm's sting,
> Lizard's leg and owlet's wing;
> Double, double, toil and trouble;
> Fire burn, and caldron bubble.'

They sing that and other diabolical songs that no respectable pussen ever heerd. One on 'em who stopped here over night a bit ago, and called himself Longshanks, whispered it to me in the dark, as we sat on the stoop a-drinkin' toddy. I tell you my hair stood on end, and I was so skeered I didn't sleep a wink all night."

"That reminds me," said a lanky, purple-nosed individual, who looked like a 'longshoreman, "that I actially see one on 'em myself, — a tall, cross-eyed villain with gold specs, and dressed in black from head to foot, like Belzebub, — I see him with my own eyes, kill a snake."

"And the same fellow," said the farmer, "offered my boys a cent apiece for frogs; said he liked 'em fried; but that was a blind, you know. I told the boys they had better have no dealin's with him, for Satan's money burns the fingers. I tell you what, it's my opinion that the lawabidin', God-fearin' people ought to turn out and burn their cussed place down to the ground."

"And tar and feather the hull crew," said the 'longshoreman.

"I wouldn't harm the women-folks," said the red-faced young man, "though I do believe they're nothing better nor witches, for I met one on 'em myself, a lean, yaller-haired critter, one day, in the woods a-gathering catnip and other yerbs to bile in the black pot. I made tracks from that place mighty quick, I did."

"There's a fat old fellow who seems to be the head devil," said the tow-headed bumpkin. "One evening about sundown I see him a-sittin' in the garden porin' over a book; so I crep' up along the fence, very quiet-like, and what do you think? He was a-readin' out loud, and it was a lingo nobody couldn't understand, — regular necromancy talk it was. I crawled away faster than I went. Why, look! There's one of the blood-thirsty varmints outside a-swallerin' oysters. I've seen him more nor onst when I've been a-passin' by the place. He's ginerally talkin' to the yaller-haired woman. Jimini! How he does put 'em down! You'd think he hadn't eat for a week."

Peewit now became the unconscious focus of many eyes.

"Let's call him up and pump him," said the 'longshoreman.

"It's mighty little you'll get out of him," answered the farmer; "for evil-doers aren't accustomed to blab their secrets to everybody."

Peewit had now finished the oysters, and was staring around, at a loss what next to do with himself.

" A man can't do nothin' unless he tries," answered the
'longshoreman; and then, going up to Peewit, he said,
by way of introducing himself politely, —

" Stranger, what'll yer drink? "

" Soda-water, thank you," replied Peewit, who really
felt very thirsty.

" That's a good un," said the other. " A man asks yer
what yer'll drink, and yer say ' soda-water.' There aint
no Maine law in Jersey. Will yer take rum or whiskey? "

Now Peewit of course knew that strong drink was a
tabooed article among Harmonians; but then, was he,
strictly speaking, any longer a member of the society?
There was room for doubt on this point; but there was
no doubt whatever that the mishaps of the morning
.weighed heavy on his spirits, while the oysters laid heavy
on his stomach. He had often heard the doctor say,
that a desperate disease required a desperate remedy,
and what case could be more so than his? He felt that
both physically and mentally he needed some stimulant.
A single glass, instead of doing him harm, would do him
good, and who would ever know that he had taken it?

" Well, I don't care if I do take a glass of rum," were
the words with which he accepted the polite invitation of
'longshoreman.

The two then entered the saloon, walked up to the bar,
and drank the liquor, having of course complied with the
customary preliminary ceremony of striking the glasses
together and saying, " Here's luck."

Peewit who had not tasted anything stronger than cat-
nip-tea since he became a Harmonian, smacked his lips

18

with satisfaction as he felt the fiery liquid going down his throat.

The red-faced young man, who had recoiled as the dreaded Harmonian passed, now said to the former in a whisper, —

"That's the way to work him. They're sworn to secrecy, you know."

"Nothin's wus," said the farmer, "than to eat cold isters without drinking. My rule is, a pint of liquor to a pint of isters. Let's liquor ag'in. Hot Jamaicy all round."

"Make it a stiffener," said the 'longshoreman, in an undertone to the bar-tender.

Il n'y a que le premier pas qui coute. (Would that this applied to tight boots!) Peewit swallowed the stiffener with even less compunctions of conscience than the first glass, although it brought the tears to his eyes. Then, thinking that courtesy required him to make some acknowledgment, he begged to have the honor of treating the company, — an honor that was willingly accorded him.

" You are a stranger in these ere parts I should guess?" said the former.

" No," answered Peewit; " I am from the phalanstery."

" Indeed!" said the 'longshoreman, with affected surprise. " You have a gay time up there, don't you? "

" I wish we had," replied Peewit.

" That's a good un," rejoined the other. " Now tell us how many you keep."

" How many what?"

" Why, women-folks of course."

" Three," answered Peewit, who did not suppose that

the question could have reference solely to his own connubial arrangement. " Only three at present, but I expect there will be hundreds more before the summer is over."

The inquisitors exchanged glances of unfeigned astonishment and disgust at the awful turpitude of Mr. Peewit.

" No wonder the fellow looks played out," said the 'longshoreman to the farmer.

" He's wus," whispered the latter, " nor the king of the Cannibal Islands that Parson Knox tells us about, for that pagan only has ninety-nine."

" I'd like to spend a month or so there, just to expose 'em," said the red-faced young man.

" What becomes of all the young uns?" asked the farmer.

" What young ones?" answered Peewit. " We have no young ones."

" He is on his guard," whispered the 'longshoreman. "Bar-tender, drinks all round ; Jarsey lightnin'."

One — two — three — four more drinks were taken. The farmer then returned to the charge.

" Do you mean to tell us," said he, " that no children result from your miscellaneous arrangement?"

" None of us have had any, excepting the doctor," replied Pewitt ; " and he has buried all but one."

" Buried 'em alive?" asked the tow-headed boy, turning pale.

" Yes," answered the reckless Peewit, who was rapidly getting fuddled, and did not clearly comprehend the question. " Yes, we're all buried alive in that infernal hole."

"Oh! the bloody wretches!" exclaimed all in chorus. "Let's lynch the fellow — skin him alive — pitch him in the pond."

"Softly, boys, softly," said the farmer. "Keep still. I'll manage it. Come, friend, come along with us a little way, and we'll give you a big drink," he continued, giving Peewit a shake, for that gentleman was becoming somewhat oblivious, his eyes being half closed, and his chin resting on his breast as if he had no strength in the muscles of his neck. "Come along with us."

"Nuff said, ole fell'r," answered Peewit. "Who's afraid? (Hiccup.) Lead on — I'm wish yer — for you're a jolly ole boy! — Ha! ha! ha! Reminds me of ole times — 'fore Strongsham got me. What a fool I wash! but ish all right now. (Hiccup.)

> "' For we won't go home till mornin',
>   Till daylight dosh appear.'

Ha! ha! Goojoke — goodjoke."

In this manner, laughing, singing, and talking nonsense, the most unlucky of Harmonians was inveigled, staggering towards an adjacent pond. On arriving at the brink, he was suddenly seized by eight strong arms (for, like the assassins of Cæsar, all these ministers of justice wished to have a hand in the deed), and, while actually calling it a "goodjoke," tossed into the water.

"Take that, you bigamous Turk," cried the 'longshoreman.

"This is what we call the water-cure," said the farmer.

As the water was only about five feet deep, Peewit now

came spluttering to the surface, and, puffing and blowing, scrambled ashore.

" Duck him ag'in — duck him ag'in," shouted his quondam friends, seizing him as before, and throwing him in again, with shouts of laughter mingled with execrations and epithets more forcible than polite.

Peewit scrambled out a second time, and a third time was tossed in.

" That will cool you off, you infamous Mormon!" cried one of his tormentors, as soon as his head emerged once more. " You must need it with all your women."

" Wo-wo-women!" blubbered the half-drowned victim, standing up to his neck in the water; " why they wo-wo-won't let me co-come within ten feet of my own wife."

" Tell that to the marines," the 'longshoreman called out. " You can't git off by lyin' now; it's too late."

" Oh! Oh! I've had enough; let me go!" cried the shivering sufferer, in piteous accents.

" You aint had enough to wash away your sins," cried the farmer.

As Peewit persisted in standing in the water, for he did not dare to come out again, the four indignant citizens amused themselves by pelting him for some time with mud, and finally walked away, filled with the proud consciousness of having performed a most just and praiseworthy exploit. The red-faced young man, however, seemed to be seized with a slight feeling of commiseration for the luckless victim of perfidy, and, on leaving, deposited a bottle of brandy on the ground for his benefit.

Leaving the drenched and partially sobered Peewit to make his way to dry land, we will take a glance at the course of events at Harmony Hall.

18*

A bottle of hartshorn in the hands of Dr. Goodenough had recalled Mrs. Strongitharm to consciousness. Loud were her lamentations over the remains of Jack, and bitter her objurgations against his executioner. The two pieces of the defunct quadruped were gathered together, and, by her directions, placed in a macaroni box and solemnly interred. She seemed to grieve unaffectedly for the loss of her pet, showing that even the strongest of the strong-minded possess much of the woman ; but, after the first outburst of her regret was over, she said little. Those who knew her, however, pitied Peewit.

That gentleman's absence was remarked at dinner.

"It is strange," said the doctor, "for he is usually so punctual at meal-times."

The rest of the company, however, did not think that under the circumstances it was very surprising.

Supper came, but no Peewit.

"I hope nothing can have happened to him," said Miss Griffin.

"Probably only fled from the wrath to come," said Lovell.

Mrs. Strongitharm gave the speaker a withering glance.

At last a familiar voice was heard outside singing, then an unsteady step in the hall; the door opened, and the absentee staggered in, — hatless, coatless, covered with mud from head to foot, and dripping wet. ·Swinging an empty bottle in his hand, he sang in drunken glee as he tottered forward, —

> "'Oh! Bowery gals, won't you come out to-night,
> Won't you come out to-night,
> Won't you come out to-night?
> Oh! Bowery gals, won't you come out to-night,
> And dansh by the light of the moon?'"

" Merciful Heavens ! " exclaimed Miss Griffin. " What is the matter with Joseph ? "

" He is drunk," said Professor Malpest.

The doctor looked up perfectly aghast with astonishment. He seemed riveted to his chair ; and, although his mouth was wide open, he did not utter a word.

Mrs. Strongitharm sat stern and impassable, with her eyes fixed on the recreant Harmonian.

" Where's Lishabet ? " said the latter, staggering towards the table. " Where's Lishabet ? Come, ole gal, dansh wi' me ; polky, schottish, anything ; come along, —

> " ' For we won't go home till mornin',
> Till daylight dosh appear.' "

Mr. Peewit now got hold of a chair and made a ludicrous attempt to dance a jig with it ; but the performance ended with a break-down, for he fell heavily upon the floor, knocking off two of his partner's legs.

" This is a sorrowful sight," said the doctor.

" Oh, it is heart-rending ! " answered Miss Griffin, hiding her face in her handkerchief.

Professor Malpest stuffed his napkin into his mouth, and seemed to be undergoing a fearful internal struggle to suppress the manifestation of his emotions.

The expression of concentrated wrath and disgust visible in the eyes of Mrs. Strongitharm would have petrified the gay Peewit, if his vision had not been obfuscated by liquor.

Charity whispered something to Leander, who rose, and, taking him by the arm, said, —

" Peewit, my dear fellow, you had better go to bed. Come with me."

"Whof for?" answered Peewit, who was still sitting on the floor amidst the ruins of the chair. "Whof for gotobed?"

"Because you are intoxicated."

"I intoshicate! That's a good un. Ha! ha! ha!" answered the hilarious gentleman, with a silly simper.

"What have you been drinking, sir?" asked Mrs. Strongitharm, sternly.

"Drinkin'! I drinkin'! Do I look as hif been drinkin'?" replied Peewit, with a stupid leer. "If drunk — mush be ze oyshters — oyshters did it."

"Oysters!" cried the doctor. "Has brother Joseph been tempted to eat oysters, — oysters, which contain the living principle? Has the sin of gluttony found its way into Harmony Hall? Is the apple turned to an oyster?"

"Yesh," said Peewit; "four doshen raw."

"Raw? then he eat 'em alive!" exclaimed the doctor, with a look of dismay.

Professor Malpost showed the whites of his eyes, and then going up to Peewit caught the almost helpless Harmonian by the legs, while Lovell took him by the arms, and, lifting him from the floor, they carried him up to bed, in spite of his kicking and struggling, and the continued reiteration of his assertion that he wouldn't go home till morning.

The next day, when Peewit opened his eyes, the awful form of Mrs. Strongitharm loomed up before him, standing by his bedside. The unhappy Utopian instantly buried his head under the quilt.

"You may well hide your face in shame," said she, "after your atrocity of the morning, and disgracing yourself in the evening. But I shall waste no words on you.

I shall no longer sully my good name by alliance with such an incorrigible profligate. The copartnership between us is dissolved."

Peewit looked up with an expression of hope.

" It will be useless for you to implore," continued the termagant; " my decision is irrevocable. Henceforth, you can follow your own path to perdition. I leave you to your reflections." And so saying, the incensed dame, with a look of withering scorn at the recreant and very much relieved Peewit, swept out of the room.

He breathed more freely.

" Thank God, it is over !" he said. Then he tried to go to sleep again, but could not; for he felt sick at the stomach and had a raging headache. But the feelings of deep contrition and repentance, that he had experienced on awakening, had been singularly modified by the happy turn that had been given to his case by Mrs. Strongitharm.

He had been turning uneasily on his pillow for some time, when he heard a light tap at his door. ·Miss Griffin entered.

" Joseph," said she, " you do not appear well. I am sorry for you, and have brought you a piece of toast and a cup of catnip tea."

" She is a cherub," said Peewit to himself; and then, in the exuberance of his gratitude, he extended both arms, and with the tea in one hand and the toast in the other, repeated, in a husky voice, Scott's beautiful lines, —

> " ' O woman! in our hours of ease
> Uncertain, coy, and hard to please;
> When pain and anguish wring the brow,
> A ministering angel, thou.'

"O Miss Minerva, how different you are from Mrs. Strongitharm!"

"Woman," answered Miss Griffin, "was not created to exist for self; her nature is too deep; her sympathies too cosmopolitan. She has a mission to fulfil on earth, — a mission of love.'

"*She* don't seem to think so," replied Peewit, sipping the tea and nibbling at the toast.

"She? She is not a true woman," answered Miss Minerva.

"She is an ogre," exclaimed Peewit; but, could his sight have penetrated the door, his tongue would have cloven to the roof of his mouth, for the outraged object of his vituperation stood listening behind it.

"She is a half man, like her dress," said Miss Griffin. "No wonder she has driven you to desperation. She is too masculine, Joseph, to appreciate the delicacy of your nature."

"She is feminine enough to understand yours, you hussy!" cried Mrs. Strongitharm, bursting into the room. "You coarse, impudent female, to come here debauching my partner! And what have *you* to say for yourself, sir? You drunken brute! you weak-spirited shadow of a man!" she continued, turning fiercely towards Peewit, who shrunk to the farther side of the bed, and barricaded himself behind a fortification of bolsters and pillows. However he must have been still somewhat reckless from his recent carouse, for he answered her with unwonted temerity, —

"Madam, your apartment is at the other end of the house."

"He dares to answer me!" screamed Mrs. Strongitharm. "He dares to answer me! This is your work, you yellow-haired siren! you green-eyed monster! But my name is not Elizabeth Strongitharm or you shall repent of it;" and with that she seized Miss Griffin by the hair with one hand, while with the other she wrenched off her elegant jockey hat. But the blood of all the Griffins was up, and with her nails the furious maiden scratched the face of her assailant, and tore her lace collar to shreds. The shrieks and screams of the ladies now rang through the building, chairs and tables were overturned, while ribbons and hair flew in all directions.

Peewit jumped out of bed, spilling the hot tea over his bare legs, which made him howl with pain, and endeavored to thrust a bolster between the amazons, but, as he did so, the Griffin's claws, in scratching about wildly, came in contact with his cheeks, leaving five blood-stained lines, while the fist of the Strongitharm, directed at the head of her adversary, landed upon his interposed nose, causing the blood to fairly spout.

The awful commotion alarmed the whole household, and everybody came rushing to the scene of battle.

The doctor arrived first, puffing and blowing, and almost out of breath with the exertion of hurrying upstairs.

The combat ceased at his presence.

"Why—why—why!" he exclaimed; "what's this?—what's this? Discord in Harmony Hall! I am astonished —astonished! Have you forgotten the precepts of St. Augustine? *Ira furor est.* What's the matter? What's the matter?"

Both the ladies began vociferating at once, and the epithets of "Hussy," "Strumpet," "Shameful woman," "Abandoned female," "Vile creature," "Hateful thing," and other choice expressions of feminine wrath were freely bandied about, until the two women were actually on the point of recommencing the row, when the doctor seized Mrs. Strongitharm in his arms, while Mr. Lovell did the same to Miss Griffin. The irate and highly excited ladies were then forcibly borne to their respective rooms, where the doctor advised them to spend the rest of the day in silent reflection, and, by way of balm to their wounded feelings, sent each of them a copy of "Hervey's Meditations" and a bottle of Mrs. Winslow's Soothing Syrup.

Professor Malpest had peeped in during the scrimmage, but, thinking from appearances that a sort of free fight was in progress, fled to the cupola, where he locked himself in and stayed till dinner-time.

The doctor had been sorely troubled by the riotous and disgraceful conduct of Peewit on the preceding evening, and the additional vexation of spirit caused by the ignominious wrangle between the ladies almost threw him into a fever. It was clear to his mind that Peewit, the fallen Peewit, was the primary cause of all the disturbance ; but it was not in his nature to inflict cruel or unusual punishments (excepting in the form of long discourses) ; in fact, any penalty inflicted on the culprit would have been felt more severely by the tender-hearted old doctor than by the sinner himself. Yet would it be safe to permit such a disorderly and abandoned character to continue with his flock, without taking some means to check his vicious propensities, and prevent his example from infecting others? In his perplexity he walked up and down his study, with his hands behind his back, shaking his head, and anon muttering passages from Aristotle and Marcus Aurelius. The dinner hour found him still undecided.

Peewit did not come down to the table, but remained in his room. The excitement of the morning broil had driven away his headache; but he was ashamed to show his face.

The dinner that day was a mournful meal. The doctor did not utter a word, and the rest of the party, out of respect, and partly because their feelings also oppressed them, remained silent. Hardly anything was eaten, for, with the exception of Professor Malpest, no one had any appetite.

When the cloth was removed, the doctor slowly and solemnly rose, raised his spectacles to his forehead, and proceeded to address the company, looking (as Lovell afterwards said) like a Lord Chancellor holding a High Court of Justice over the dinner-table.

"My dear brethren," said he, "look at me, and behold the calmness, the serenity that is derived from overcoming the evil passions of the heart. As St. Augustine tells us, 'Quod partes iræ atque libidinis tam vitiose moventer, ut eas necesse sit frenis sapientiæ cohiberi;' we must subject our anger and our lust to the bridle of wisdom.

"The petty trials and privations incident to our short probation on earth cannot disturb my equanimity. I mention this, not for the sake of personal glorification, but because, although in youth my appetites were strong, my humble efforts to keep down the spirit of self-indulgence have at last been crowned with success; which is a practical proof that this happy condition can be obtained by those who earnestly strive for it."

"If they live long enough," said Leander, *sotto voce*.

"If we give way to one debasing passion," continued
19

the doctor, "others will rise up to torment us; love is attended by jealousy; jealousy by hatred; hatred by envy, malice, and all uncharitableness; and we are liable at any moment to become lost in anger, for ' ira furor brevis est,' as Piccolomineus says.

"When the rules and regulations of this establishment were drawn up, no provision was made for such scandalous and calamitous occurrences as have shocked us during the last twenty-four hours. Such doings could not be foreseen. I supposed that the potent voice of reason would ever be found sufficient to sway the weak or the unworthy in this peaceful abode; but, alas! our error is now manifest, and it is with infinite pain that I acknowledge, what is patent to us all, that some members of this society have shown themselves still tainted with the leaven of the world. Brother Joseph Peewit must be held responsible as the chief author of the disgrace that has befallen us. He stands convicted, by his own confession, of having eaten live oysters; and, as one crime infallibly leads to another, his gluttony (to use a mild term) was followed by the imbibation of strong drink, whereby he became helplessly inebriated; and, as if with a deliberate intention to drive us all to despair, he followed up the revel of yesterday, as we all know too well, by this morning exciting a dreadful disturbance among some of the female members of the society. I consider him an exceedingly dangerous person, and would like to have your opinions as to what is the best course to pursue under these distressing circumstances."

"My opinion," said Professor Malpest, "is this: since he has been guilty of intemperance in food and drink, let him be put on a diet of bread and water for one week. Since he has created trouble among the ladies, let him be prohibited from speaking to them during his probation. This would satisfy the requirements of strict justice."

Mrs. Strongitharm and Miss Griffin now both began talking at once, as loud and as fast as they could; but Mrs. Strongitharm having the more powerful organ, she shut up her rival, or, to speak more correctly, succeeded in making herself heard in spite of her.

" Leave him to me," said she; " I'll manage him,— I'll bring him to reason."

" *You* bring him to reason!" screamed Miss Griffin. " It is you who have driven him to despair."

" Better leave him to himself," said Lovell; " his head-ache will be a stronger argument than any other."

After a protracted and animated discussion, the council broke up without having come to any definite conclusion.

The doctor retired to his study, and soon afterwards sent for Peewit, who obeyed the summons with the air of a criminal going to execution. What passed at the interview, we unfortunately have not been able to ascertain; but the door was ajar, and Miss Griffin, who happened to pass by two or three times, heard the doctor quoting Greek and Latin to Peewit, who was sitting on a stool, with his hands on his knees, which were close together, like an Egyptian statue,— the image of resignation. At the expiration of an hour, Peewit emerged looking very weary, and carrying in one hand a vial of spirits of camphor, and, in the other, the " Regeneration of Man." He threw the book under a table, and then directed his steps to the grove at the end of the garden, tossing the vial of camphor over the fence on his way, and sat down on a bench, with his hands in his pockets, in the position of the rake in Hogarth's picture of the "Morning after the Marriage." Miss Griffin soon joined him, and they were observed, for a long time, in close and earnest conversation.

After the departure of Peewit, Professor Malpest entered the doctor's study, and, apparently choking with suppressed emotion, declared that he was almost overcome with grief at the scandalous and deplorable events that had transpired.

"Such," said he, "is the consequence of admitting persons into the society whose minds are not sufficiently matured by years to comprehend and follow up the exalted doctrines of Harmonianism. The sooner all such disreputable characters were got rid of, the better it would be for those who remained."

He did not refer particularly to brother Joseph; there were others whose presence he feared would be even more disastrous to the younger sisters, unless means were taken to counteract the effect of their manœuvres. Women are so completely the creatures of impulse, that, when the promptings of nature begin to be felt, the presence of a man — a man whose passions are subordinate to his reason — is required as a monitor and guide. He then reminded the doctor that the month which had been granted to Miss Charity before giving her adhesion to her father's most admirable plan for her welfare had now passed.

"It is up to-day, dear brother," said the doctor; "and I will immediately send for my daughter, and you shall be affianced."

"I fear, sir," answered the professor, "you will find that a malign influence has been exercised over her young mind by one who has no claim upon her."

"What do you mean? Whom do you refer to?"

"I refer, sir, to one who has forced himself upon us unasked; who has never read one line of your immortal works, and is incapable of understanding them like a true Harmonian; to one still tainted with the leaven of the world, and who continues amongst us with no other intention than to instil the subtle poison of passion, with which he is himself affected, into the heart of your daughter. I refer to that witless reprobate, Leander Lovell."

"Can such depravity be possible?" said the doctor; "and that, too, after I have clearly explained to him the nature and consequences of that infirmity, together with the remedies prescribed by the greatest philosophers of ancient times. I am astonished."

"Behold, sir, the confirmation of my words," said the professor, pointing to Charity and Leander, who were strolling through the garden hand in hand.   •

"It is incredible, incredible. I can hardly believe the evidence of my senses," said the doctor, going to the window and calling to the lovers, whom he ordered somewhat peremptorily to come to him at once.

"You may need to exert all your firmness, sir," said the professor, "for it is possible that she may even prove wanting in filial obedience."

Charity and Leander entered the study.

"My child," said the doctor, taking his daughter by the hand, "the month that you very properly asked, for the purpose of meditating upon the new duties that are about to devolve upon you, has now elapsed, and I have

19*

called you to me to name the day when you will be united to the man of my choice."

"Papa," said Charity, imploringly, "do not ask me to marry that person."

"Why not, my dear?"

"Because I am utterly indifferent to him."

"That is all the better," answered the doctor; "you will thus be enabled to fulfil the duties imposed upon you by your sex, solely from a sense of obedience to the divine command to — ; but I need not explain this now."

"If I became his wife, I should hate him. I hate him now."

"Hate!" said the doctor. "How can such a sentiment have found its way into Harmony Hall? You should strive to overcome such feelings. But you cannot do it alone; your mind is too weak; you require the aid of a stronger will. Let me hear no more nonsense from you, my child; for in a fortnight from to-day, I intend that you shall marry brother Nicholas, the most upright and conscientious of men."

"I cannot do it, I cannot do it, father," answered Charity, weeping; "for I not only feel a repugnance against him, but —" she hesitated, cast down her eyes, and colored deeply — "I love another."

"You love, carnally speaking," cried the doctor; "and when you know that it is contrary to my precepts. Thus does one fault lead to another."

"Such," said Professor Malpest, "is the inevitable result of contact with the worldly-minded. If permitted to continue, there is no knowing what lamentable consequences might ensue."

Leander, who had maintained a respectful silence while the doctor was speaking, could contain his suppressed wrath no longer.

" You despicable sycophant! " said he, with clenched fists, approaching the professor, who shrank trembling behind the doctor's chair, " if you dare to utter one syllable against her, or against me, I shall fell you to the earth."

He doubtless meant " the floor," but that is immaterial. His voice attracted the attention of the doctor, who had thus far seemed oblivious to his presence.

" You are the cause of all this trouble," said the old man. " It is you who have called forth in my daughter the sinful affections of the flesh, in direct contravention to the rules and regulations of this establishment, made and provided ; culminating in sedition, privy conspiracy, and rebellion against the will of her parent, thereby violating the fifth commandment. You are a disgrace to the society, sir, and I desire you to contaminate us no longer by your presence."

" Enough, sir," answered Lovell. " Since you are blind to your own interests and to those of your family, and are so utterly unjust to me, I should consider it a degradation to remain longer with you. I shall go at once, but hope before long to return with proofs of the dishonesty of that contemptible, calculating parasite, who is living at your expense, and deceiving you by his hypocrisy."

" Do you presume to traduce brother Nicholas? " cried the doctor, his voice husky with rage. " To defame my best friend before my face? This is adding insult to injury. You are an infamous scoundrel, sir, an infamous scoundrel!" And so saying, the old gentleman, who was livid with passion, seized Lovell roughly by the coat-collar; Charity threw her arms around her father's neck, while Professor Malpest, for safety, jumped on top of the table, upsetting the inkstand over a MS. of the doctor's, and scattering pens, papers, pamphlets, and wafers, in miscellaneous confusion over the floor.

"Discord in Harmony Hall! I am astonished," exclaimed Mrs. Strongitharm coming in, taking Lovell in her arms, and putting him unresistingly out of the room.

"It was enough to excite St. Anthony," said the doctor, dropping exhausted into his chair; "but I was hasty. I acknowledge my fault. *Ira furor est;* but it is over now. Let the young man depart in peace. Charity, my child, behold how your unreasonable self-will has brought my gray hairs to shame. Well may you shed tears. Retire now to your room, and meditate in sorrow over the effects of your obstinacy. Reason and reflection may show you the error of your ways."

Lovell packed his valise in a few minutes, and was about leaving the house, when Charity tapped him on the shoulder.

"Leander," said she, "how can you desert me so thoughtlessly, merely because your pride has been wounded? What will become of me with no one here to counteract that man's influence over my father?"

"I cannot remain without a loss of self-respect," answered Lovell, "and we would gain nothing by my doing so. I have with me copies of papers (that I have made secretly) which I think contain evidence of Malpest's dishonest trickery. If I succeed in verifying my suspicions, I shall return and expose him. In the mean time if anything important should occur, — you know what I mean, — write to me."

Lovell had proceeded but a few steps from the house when he heard the voice of the doctor, and, turning, saw the old gentleman hastening after him.

"My young friend," said he, "I was hasty with you awhile ago ; I confess my fault, and ask you to excuse it. It is well for you to go, but let us part in peace and good will."

"My dear sir," answered Lovell, "it is not in your nature to do anything that could give me the slightest ill feeling towards you ; but as to that black hearted vil—"

"Stop, my boy — stop ; there, give me your hand ; farewell."

So they parted.

When Leander had gone about a quarter of a mile he again heard his name called. This time it was Peewit.

"Well, Joe," said he, "come to bid me good-by ? "

"She's an angel ! " exclaimed Peewit, who was almost out of breath from running.

"She is certainly as angelic as a woman can be."

"I knew you could appreciate the beautiful. You are a man of taste," replied Peewit, grasping Leander by the hand. "And how gentle and considerate she is ! there is nothing strong-minded about *her*."

"But still she is not wanting in capacity," replied Lovell.

"Wits ! As to wits, I wish I had half so much. Think how well she can write ! "

"I presume she can," answered Leander, "though I have never yet had the pleasure of receiving any letters from Miss Charity."

"Charity! What Charity? Ah! Miss Goodenough. Oh! yes! Why I was talking about Minerva — my Minerva."

"Minerva? Miss Griffin? Oh! Ah! I understand. Why, Joe! are you in love with that angular female?"

"I adore her," replied Peewit. "She is the apple of my eye. I admire every separate freckle on her face. Did you ever see such a figure?"

"Can't say I ever did."

"Such beautiful yellow hair; such languishing gray eyes; so soft a voice; such a —"

"Now, Joe, please stop, I do indeed believe she is a most estimable lady, but —"

"But!" interrupted Peewit. "How can you put in any 'buts'? She is perfection itself. You never saw her equal."

"I cannot agree with you there, no matter how exalted may be my opinion of her."

"You have no judgment — no judgment," replied Peewit, letting go of the hand he had till then held in his own. "But there is no accounting for tastes; 'tastibus non est disputandibus,' as the long-winded doctor would say. Truly love is blind."

"I don't want to be personal, but must say, that it seems to me you are singularly wanting in discernment," said Lovell, rather tartly.

"I would not exchange my perceptive faculties for yours," answered Peewit, with spirit; "particularly if I had to exchange ladies also."

The two gentlemen continued to spat with each other until they were on the point of seriously quarrelling about the beauty of their lady-loves, like two gallant knights of old, when the contention was happily put an end to by the opportune appearance of the Rev. Mr. Knox.

" Ah! my good friend," said he, addressing Peewit, "I am happy to meet you. Your appointment with me will be kept, I hope? "

" We shall be punctual, sir, if eight o'clock is a con‐ venient hour to you."

" Perfectly. Adieu," said the minister going in the direction of Harmony Hall.

" What does this mean? " asked Lovell.

" Why, the truth is," replied Peewit, coloring slightly, " that Mrs. Strongitharm divorced herself this morning, in the same free and easy way that she took me, so that now I am at liberty — *I am at* LIBERTY, Lenny."

" And mean to remain so, I presume, from your joyous‐ ness? "

" I am going to marry her this very evening."

" Marry Mrs. Strongitharm?"

" No — no — no — my Minerva. I'm going to marry my Minerva, and I want you to give the bride away."

" It seems to me that Dr. Goodenough is a more proper person to do that."

" Chut! " said Peewit, lowering his voice. " Not so loud. The ogre might hear us. Oh, you don't know what a romantic, sentimental creature she is! "

" The ogre? "

" No — no — my Minerva. Chut! It's an elopement. She's going to meet me by moonlight alone ; and I've arranged it all with the Rev. Hieronymus, who thinks — but no matter what he thinks ; " and here the hilarious Peewit in the exuberance of his spirits gave Leander a poke in the ribs. " After the ceremony at the church we take the stage-coach to Communipaw, and go thence by the horse-car to Jersey City, where we will spend the honey-moon."

CHAPTER X.

The Rev. Hieronymus Knox takes the Bull by the Horns.

AFTER the stirring scenes of the last chapter it will be a relief to the reader's mind to turn to the worthy pastor of All Saints, and to learn how it happened that he was going in the direction of Harmony Hall when his fortunate mediation averted the threatened knightly tilt between Messrs. Lovell and Peewit.

His interview with the last-named gentleman on the preceding day had given him food for much serious thought. The stories that had reached his ears of the daily and nightly abominations at the phalanstery had sorely troubled his mind. He gave little heed to the reported horrors that had so excited the countrymen at the tavern, and brought poor Peewit to grief; these he regarded simply as vulgar exaggerations, though where there was so much smoke he thought there must be some fire ; and in fact so much was given in the form of positive averments, that the most incredulous could not have doubted that the home of the New Utopians was little better than a brothel of abandoned men and women, desperate characters, presided over by a licentious, hoary-headed old libertine named Goodenough, — an artful and determined emissary of the Evil One.

He knew that legal proceedings, or, in default thereof, more summary processes for the abolition of this public nuisance were under serious consideration by some of the members of his congregation, the women — especially those with marriageable daughters — being particularly exasperated, and urging the men on ; but violent measures found little favor with the minister of the gospel of peace. Yet this was not owing to any timidity in his temperament, for he had not hesitated in the line of self-imposed duty to risk his life among the savages of the South Sea until failing health had obliged him to return to civilization. He had ever found persuasion more efficacious than force, and, although the whited sepulchre whose walls it was proposed to raze was almost within the shadow of his church, he strongly discountenanced all illegal measures. Did not his enforced return, he thought to himself, seem like a special interposition of Providence? Might he not be the preordained agent of the Almighty to enter boldly into that fortress of Satan, and rescue its hapless inmates from his grasp? His interview with Peewit gave him encouragement. Since there was one repentant sinner, might there not be others whom a few timely words would reclaim from their fallen state?

The good man passed a sleepless night, cogitating over the matter ; and the next morning announced to his wife that he had determined to proceed that very afternoon to the stronghold of Belial, and beard the lion in his den. The poor woman, who was of a nervous, apprehensive temperament, and who had seen her husband's dwelling surrounded by hundreds of howling, painted savages, thirsting for his blood, and who fondly hoped that such perils were over forever, was almost paralyzed with terror at his temerity. She entreated, she implored him to give up the rash project.

No considerations of personal safety could have induced

the dauntless missionary to swerve a hair's breadth from
what he considered the path of duty ; but the voice of his
wife was ever potent with him ; her tears he could seldom
withstand ; and it is very possible his resolution would
have been shaken, had it not been for the arrival of some
female neighbors, who were loud in approbation of their
pastor's self-sacrificing intention. It was currently reported, they said, that the arch-rake Goodenough possessed not less than seven wives ; another of the inmates
of the place was known by his own confession to have
three, and he had unblushingly boasted that he expected
several hundred more. What became of all the children?
None had ever been seen about the premises. Here the
ladies exchanged significant glances with each other, and
shook their heads. Such doings were not to be put up
with. No woman was safe while such libidinous wretches
existed in their midst. They should be extirpated root and
branch. It was a wonder the Lord did not smite them
with thunder and lightning. They almost drove the
minister's wife into hysterics ; but his resolution was only
strengthened by what he heard. It was in vain that she
hung upon his arm, and begged him, with tears in her
eyes, not to trust himself in such a dangerous place ; or,
if he persisted in going, let him at least arm himself for
the struggle with the kitchen carving-knife, and take a
posse of citizens for protection.

"My dear," said Mr. Knox, kindly but firmly, "you
know that for righteousness' sake I have incurred perils
by land, and perils by water, perils from savage beasts
and still more savage men, and think you I would shrink
now from a new, even though greater, danger? I shall
go, cost what it may, and go alone ; armed only with my

sermon on the 'Wages of Sin,' with which I converted
Mumbo-Jumbo, Goree Maori, and so many other heathen,
and, with the Good Book for a shield, I shall unfold to
those benighted and hardened sinners of the new Gomor-
rah the great truths of revealed religion, unless my voice
be arrested by the hand of Death. My will is at the
bottom of my trunk. Farewell!"

It was with fearful forebodings that his timorous,
trembling wife saw the hardy champion of the Gospel
sally forth on his hazardous expedition. He was on his
way to Harmony Hall when he met Lovell and Peewit,
as we related in the preceding chapter.

When he reached the gate, he found Charity leaning
against it, gazing up the road, watching the fast receding
form of Leander. Miss Griffin was by her side.

"Truly," said the Rev. Mr. Knox to himself, looking
at Charity; "truly Satan works with beautiful tools. She
is weeping. Perhaps she, also, is repentant."

"Madam," said he aloud, "are you one of the inmates
of this establishment?"

"I am, sir," answered Charity.

"And do you never think of your artless and innocent
childhood, your happy past, before you had been taught
the deceit and wickedness of the world? Do you not
regret the life you lead here?"

"Indeed I do, sir. I regret it bitterly."

"There is hope yet," said the reverend gentleman, "and
— pardon my inquisitiveness; my motives are good — are
you one of those who are — who are — connected with
Dr. Goodenough?"

"Yes, sir," answered Charity; "I have no one here to
protect me, no one to love, but him."

The Rev. Mr. Knox shook his head sadly, and said to himself, " So young, so innocent-looking, and yet so depraved! It is truly lamentable."

" And you, madam," said he, turning to Miss Griffin; " I presume you also are one of the unfortunates?"

" Alas! sir," answered Miss Minerva, " what woman is not unfortunate! It is her lot in life to be so."

" It is her own fault if she do not raise herself when fallen."

" Ah! sir, she should not be chided while society exists as at present constituted."

" Have you no desire to change your present condition?"

Miss Minerva blushed deeply, fixed her eyes on a buttercup, simpered, and answered with some confusion of manner, —

" Woman must yield to her destiny, sir. She was not created to exist alone; and I shall not shrink from the performance of any of the functions imposed upon me by my sex."

" I suppose that neither of you unhappy ones has passed through the ceremony of marriage?"

" Not yet," replied Miss Griffin, without raising her eyes.

" Why, unhappy?" said Charity. " Marriage is now a hateful word to me."

The minister looked aghast. " What brazen effrontery!" he said to himself. " Truly, I am at the gates of a new Sodom. But why skirmish at the outposts, when, perhaps, the main work is accessible?" So without another word he abruptly left the young ladies, and, marching boldly up to the front door, rang the bell.

It happened that Mrs. Strongitharm was at that

20*

moment passing through the hall, and she opened the door to the visitor. Her appearance confirmed the unfavorable impression that had already been made on his mind, for her face was blotched with the marks of Miss Griffin's nails, — induitable signs, as he interpreted them, of excessive and long-continued debauchery, while he inferred from her gay bloomer dress that she was the favorite sultana of the harem, — the true scarlet lady of this modern Babylon.

"I am the sectarian clergyman of Foufouville," said he, on being ushered into the presence of Dr. Goodenough, "and have considered it a duty I owed to my parishioners, to the whole community, and to myself, to call upon you."

"I am delighted to see you, sir," answered the doctor, rising and extending his hand, which, however, Mr. Knox avoided touching.

"I labored for many years as a missionary among the Feejee islanders," said he; "but never in all my experience among those untutored savages did I hear of such enormities as have been reported to me as being committed by the people over whom you preside. Intemperance, concupiscence, excesses in short, of every kind, are among the charges that have been brought against you. I trust, for the sake of human nature, that they have been greatly overdrawn, and have desired to make a personal investigation before deciding upon what ulterior measures to adopt for the abolition of this crying social evil."

The doctor, who naturally supposed that allusion was made to the occurrences related in the last chapter, and which were still the burden of his thoughts, answered as follows, in a tone which would have indicated only sorrow and vexation of spirit to any one whose mind was not preoccupied with a false impression, but which appeared to the clergyman only an additional evidence of hardened depravity.

"We must plead guilty to the charge, sir, but I did not suppose that what took place within these walls was known beyond them."

"It is known, sir," answered Mr. Knox, "and has excited merited reprobation and indignation throughout the community ; and I have considered it an obligation incumbent on me, in consequence of my calling, to make an effort — with the divine assistance — for your reformation. I am pained and surprised that an aged man like yourself, whose white hairs denote that he should be preparing for a better world, should countenance such misdoings."

"I think, my dear sir, that you are laboring under a slight misapprehension," replied the doctor. "It is true that, as the founder of this society, it is perhaps just that I should be held in a measure responsible for the conduct of the individuals composing it, and, whenever they have shown symptoms of desiring to go astray, I have striven hard to overcome the promptings of the flesh with the voice of reason. I acknowledge with regret that my efforts have been but partially successful, and the irregularities that have lately marked the conduct of some of our unworthy members have sorely tried my patience ; however, I am happy to be able to inform you that the chief cause of our trouble has this day quitted the establishment, while the one whose riotous proceedings have doubtless been the immediate occasion of your visit appears to be sincerely penitent."

The Rev. Mr. Knox sharply scrutinized the countenance of Dr. Goodenough; but he could detect no indications of guile or deceit there.

"Your remarks embarrass me, sir," said he. "I perceive that there must have been exaggerations, perhaps actual fabrications, in the current rumors. Still I find it difficult to reconcile your language with what I have seen and heard with my own eyes and ears. I met a young woman at the gate, very fair to look upon, — in a physical point of view, — whom I took the liberty of questioning, and who openly confessed her affection for you, whom she looked up to as her protector."

"My daughter, of course," said Dr. Goodenough; "and I will mention that, had it not been for some untoward circumstances, I should have called upon you this day to ask your good offices in the marriage ceremony two weeks hence, when she is to be united to my co-laborer in the cause of humanity, Professor Malpest."

"I am completely nonplussed," said Mr. Knox. "Have you any objection, sir, to inform me definitely of the objects of your society?"

"On the contrary, sir, I wish them made known to the whole world," replied the doctor. "Here are five hundred copies of our circular, together with our rules and regulations. I will be glad if you will distribute them. We endeavor to live up to them, as closely as our infirm natures will permit; but flesh is weak, and you should not be surprised at the appearance of an occasional backslider."

The doctrines of the Harmonians and their stoical rules of life did not meet with entire approval from the sectarian clergyman; but they were so radically different, in fact, so directly opposed to what he had been led to expect, that he could not forbear smiling.

" I regard all men as brothers," said the doctor ; " but most of them are dwelling in darkness, and, what you have been striving to accomplish for the Feejees, I am endeavoring to do for all mankind."

" My dear sir," said the pastor of All Saints, " I must ask your pardon for the unjust suspicions that induced me to intrude upon you. But it is well I came, for truly the good people hereabouts are laboring under a strange delusion ; they have been singularly misinformed. There is much that is commendable, and nothing that is positively objectionable, in the principles of your society. But — stop — I find nothing about any profession of faith. May I take the liberty of asking your views on this subject, — the most important of all, — for you know what the blessed apostle says, ' Many shall be called, but few chosen.' "

" That, sir," said the doctor, " is the cardinal point of my belief."

" Then, my dear friend, you are a true sectarian," cried the minister, passing at once from the extreme of mistrust to the extreme of confidence, and, in the revulsion of his feelings, grasping the doctor cordially with both hands. " The sectarian is the only true church."

Here there ensued a long discussion between the Rev. Mr. Knox and Dr. Goodenough, on certain theological doctrines ; a discussion, the manuscript report of which, now lying on the table before us, covers no less than twenty-five pages of foolscap. After long deliberation, we have decided to omit it, partly because, unlike Foufou-ites in general, we have a strong aversion to religious polemics, and partly because to give it would serve

no other purpose than to amuse the profane. We will
only state that, after arguing till a late hour, the dispute
became quite acrimonious, and each was more firmly convinced than before that his own was the only orthodox
faith. The pastor of All Saints vehemently maintained
that none but sectarians could be saved, while the doctor
was equally positive that the only road to salvation lay
through Harmony Hall. The upholder of sectarianism re-
cited the ninety-nine articles of his creed, and, in support of
them, "piled Pelion upon Ossa," that is to say, Moses and
all the prophets on the evangelists and Maccabees, citing
chapters, verses, and half verses, in a manner which sometimes seemed like an imitation of Swift's famous "top-
knot come down." The doctor met him with argument
for argument, and prophecy for prophecy. St. Peter
was pitted against St. Paul; St. Matthew against St.
Mark; the Kings against the Judges; Jeremiah against
Job. St. Origen and St. Augustine were brought up as
bottle-holders, to support their principals, and all the
ancient philosophers dragged in as witnesses. The doctor quoted whole pages of Greek and Latin, while the
parson spouted Hebrew, and once, in the excitement of
the moment, Feejee. As their voices waxed louder and
louder, the favorable opinion they had formed of each
other grew smaller and smaller, till at last these two
worthy and Christian gentlemen appeared actually on the
point of coming to blows, when Professor Malpest happily
put an end to the wrangle, by entering the room and
announcing that supper was ready.

The doctor, who, though his spirits were greatly per-
turbed, was utterly incapable of harboring malice, cordially invited his visitor to partake of his hospitality; but

the conscientious missionary, who had dined more than once with the King of the Cannibal Islands, positively shrank from sitting at the same table with a brother man who held such very erroneous and heretical opinions as the founder of Harmonianism, whom he now believed more firmly than ever was doomed to eternal hell-fire and damnation. He excused himself with courtesy, however, and left the house to keep his appointment at the church, which, in the heat of discussion, he had entirely forgotten to mention to Dr. Goodenough.

CHAPTER XI.

Some original Letters now first published; together with a few Extracts from our Newspaper Files.

Thus far the interesting and invaluable journal of Miss Griffin has served us as a guide, in following the fortunes of the Harmonians. It was the skeleton — to use a favorite though frightful anatomical simile — on which, with the assistance of other authorities, it was easy to build up the body of our work. But now the charming ennuyée leaves us, and we can no longer depend upon a daily record of the sayings and doings at Harmony Hall to give us an uninterrupted narrative. Were we to attempt, under these circumstances, to continue the historical form, our story would be constantly broken by hiati, — a sort of kangaroo method of proceeding, — jumping from one event to another. We shall, therefore, adopt the more simple and satisfactory plan of publishing our original authorities; leaving it to the imaginative reader to draw his own conclusions, and to fill up the intervals as best he may.

The following letter, although signed by Mr. P., appears to be in the handwriting of his wife, formerly Miss Griffin, —

JOSEPH PEEWIT, ESQ., TO MRS. ELIZABETH STRONGITHARM.

"JERSEY CITY, May 23d, 1850.

" MADAM, — Since you happily released me from the

hateful copartnership that existed between us, I have formed a matrimonial alliance, according to the forms prescribed by the *church* (for a connection unsanctified by those rites I regard as *sinful*), with one who can appreciate the depth of my nature.

" My wife unites with me, in begging you to accept the assurance of our distinguished consideration.

" J. PEEWIT."

We find the following marriage notice in several papers of the month of May, —

" On the 22d inst., by the Rev. Hieronymus Knox, rector of All Saints, Foufouville, Mr. Joseph Peewit to Miss Serena Minerva Griffin. No cards."

In the Jersey City " Palladium" of a later date, the following appears, under the head of " City Items," —

" SINGULAR OCCURRENCE. — Yesterday afternoon about five o'clock, as the usual crowd was pouring from the ferry-boat, a masculine-looking woman, in bloomer costume, suddenly made a rush at an inoffensive-looking man, crying, ' The wretch! I've got him.' The gentleman, on catching sight of the furious female, dropped his carpet-bag and umbrella, and sought safety in flight. The bloomer caught him by one of his coat-tails, but, by a desperate effort, he succeeded in breaking away from her grasp, leaving the torn remnant in her hands. He then ran rapidly up the street, hotly pursued by the woman. Our reporter, who happened providentially to be on the spot in search of an item, impelled by a sense

21

of duty to the public, followed after; together with a crowd of men, boys, and dogs, who joined in the chase, shouting, hooting, yelling, and barking; frightening respectable citizens; startling the police; stampeding a drove of cattle, to the astonishment and indignation of the drovers; and scattering a flock of geese in all directions. One goose flew clear across the river and alighted on top of the mainmast of a clipper, greatly alarming an ancient mariner in an adjoining canal-boat, who feared it was an albatross. Another soared into the blue empyrean till it was lost to sight, and has not yet come down. The owner is about to sue the city for damages. Pursued and pursuers rushed up A Street into B Street; through B Street to C Avenue; and down C Avenue, without halting, to Belgrave Square. They ran twice around the square, like Hector and Achilles around the walls of Troy, then down D Street and into a blind alley, where the ' fox who had lost his tail' (as some one unfeelingly called the skirtless unfortunate) endeavored to escape, by jumping over fences and cutting across back yards; but his impetuous huntress followed hard after, taking the fences in gallant style, with the roaring rabble at her heels. Finally, after doubling once or twice, the poor fellow took refuge in the Communipaw Oyster House (where it seems he lives), shutting and bolting the door in the face of his pursuer.

" A second female now popped her head out of one of the upper windows, and began abusing the outsider in unmeasured terms. Her vituperation was returned with interest; both parties being encouraged by the crowd, with shouts and laughter and cries of, ' Go it, ole gal!' ' Give it to her!' ' Lam her ag'in!' etc.

" Finally, the lady in the window seized a pitcher of

water, and soused it over the head of the lady in the street. At last policeman A. No. 1 came up, and escorted the irate bloomer to the station house."

FROM THE SAME, OF THE NEXT DAY.

" Although we decline any responsibility for statements made by our reporters, we give publicity to the following, in justice to the aggrieved party.

" ' *To the Editor of the J. C. Palladium:*

" ' Sir,—Your grossly exaggerated account of a trans-action between private parties, with which the public is in no way concerned, would excite in me only indigna-tion, were it not for the poltroonery shown in thus traducing an unprotected female ; and I hereby warn you that I shall cowhide your reporter (who was the greatest goose of all) the first time I meet him.

" ' ELIZABETH STRONGITHARM.' "

FROM THE SAME, OF THE SAME DAY.

" LOST. — Near the Canal-Street Ferry, a black leather carpet-bag and blue cotton umbrella, containing a soiled shirt and a pair of socks. Any person leaving the above at the Communipaw Oyster House, will receive the thanks of the owner and no questions asked."

FROM THE SAME, OF A LATER DATE.

" *COURT OF PETTY SESSIONS, JEFFRIES J.*

" *The People* vs. *Joseph Peewit.* —The defendant in this case was charged with bigamy, in having on, or about the 22d of May, espoused a Miss Serena Minerva Griffin, although he had a wife still living. The prosecution having failed to furnish legal proof of the first marriage, the case was dismissed with a warning from the judge to the defendant, that it was only because he had not been actually married to the complainant, that he had escaped involving himself in a serious difficulty. Peewit, who promised never to offend again, seemed quite astonished at getting off. The decision was received with acclamations by the spectators,— a manifestation that was promptly suppressed by the presiding magistrate, with that stern sense of judicial decorum that has ever characterized the American bench.

For the people, the district attorney. For the defendant, Messrs. Sharpe & Kean.

MISS GOODENOUGH TO MR. LEANDER LOVELL.

"H. H., May 25th.

" My own Leander, — Oh, how lonesome it is here without you! and then such dreadful goings-on, I can't bear to tell you. That good-for-nothing Mr. Peewit has run away with poor Miss Griffin.   How can women be inveigled into doing such things? As soon as Mrs. Strongitharm found it out, she started after them, and I presume will not return.

"This morning John Long and Mary Short gave warning. They are to be married on Thursday, and then set up in the public line. Papa sent for John, and gave him a long lecture. I happened to be in Miss Griffin's room overhead when they were talking; but I won't repeat everything that papa said; in fact I did not quite understand it all, not even all that which was in English.

John said he wasn't a chicken ; though what he meant by it I don't know, unless that he wouldn't be hen-pecked.

"Mary has just brought me your letter enclosed in an envelope addressed to her. How happy I am that you promise to write every day! Yet have I cause for uneasiness, for you know the two weeks are up on the 4th of June, and that dreadful day is drawing near; but I rely upon you. Please don't have anything more to do with that hateful Mr. Longshanks, who wrote you that unfeeling letter. Break off your partnership with him. What is the use of business? We only want two or three thousand a year to live on, and you can make that easily enough in some other way. Adieu.

"Ever your own
"CHERRY."

FROM THE SAME TO THE SAME.

" Thursday.

"John and Mary are married and gone. They had a dreadful scene in the morning, for Bridget, the cook, told him Mary had been receiving letters every day from New York ; so he suspected all sorts of naughty things, and became furiously jealous, and threatened to kill her and then commit suicide ; but I pacified him by telling him the letters were for me, and then he dropped on his knees and begged Mary's pardon, and kissed her hands, and wanted to kiss me too, for he was almost beside himself, and laughed although tears were in his eyes, and the cook cried and I cried ; so that altogether we had quite a time. By-the-by, Professor Malpest was surprised at so many letters coming for Mary, and this morning, as ill luck would have it, he happened to come in just as she

21*

was handing me your last, and gave me such a look, and I felt the color come and go to my cheeks, and I know he suspected something. Now that she is gone, enclose your missives to Bridget O'Brien. I will tell her to hand them to me unperceived. O Lenny! it is painful to me to deceive my father in this way; but what can I do? Is it a woman's duty to sacrifice the happiness of her life to a parent's unreasonableness? Why do you write such short notes? I don't think that 'business,' hateful 'business,' is a valid excuse. Am I not of more importance in your eyes than 'business'?"

.*"Your C."*

FROM THE SAME TO THE SAME.

"Saturday.

"I have not received a line since Mary Short left, three days ago. O Lenny! this is not kind. When Bridget told me this morning she had nothing for me, I shut myself up in my room and had a good cry. Minerva (poor thing!) always said that men were unfeeling creatures; and I believe she was right. Now that so few are left here, this great house seems like a 'banquet hall deserted,' and as the professor has papa entirely to himself, his influence over him seems to increase every day. Papa has positively determined that — you know what — shall take place on the 4th, which is only a week from to-day. I shudder, Lenny, but trust in you. Can you believe it, but this morning he actually spoke to me harshly, and called me 'pig-headed,' because I begged at least for a postponement? A certain person persecutes me from morning till night with his odious attentions. O Lenny! do not keep me any longer in suspense. Write immediately on receipt of this.   "C."

FROM THE SAME TO THE SAME.

"Sunday.

" Why do you keep me in this dreadful state of suspense? It is eighty-nine hours and a half (89½) since I received your last note. This is cruel. Papa's infatuation for you know who grows upon him, and he is now almost unkind in his manner towards me. I feel as if there was no one in the world who loved me, but you, — and you, too, seem to have deserted me. Your neglect is very, very painful to me. Truly, as Minerva said, — woman's lot is an unhappy one.

" If you don't write to me soon, I don't know what I shall do. " C. G."

FROM THE SAME TO THE SAME.

"Wednesday.

" DEAREST LEANDER, — Your cruel silence is more than I can bear. Oh! it gives rise to such dreadful suspicions! I cannot bear to dwell upon them. *He* tells me it is clear you have found some other Cherry, and your continued neglect seems to verify his words. I feel as if my heart would break. " C."

FROM THE SAME TO THE SAME.

"June 2d.

" SIR, — It is now a week since you have deigned to write to me. This *atrocious* conduct proves too clearly that you have ceased to care for me. Some other and fairer form has usurped my place in your volatile heart. You are unworthy of the love of a true woman; but, thank Heaven! my eyes have been opened in time, before my feelings had become too deeply engaged; and now, sir, your indifference is only equalled by mine, and I hereby release you from an engagement that could only be conducive to unhappiness, since mutual affection is wanting."

"Charity Goodenough.

" O Leander! I did not expect this from you."

LEANDER LOVELL, ESQ., TO RICHARD LONGSHANKS, ESQ.

"Hotel of the Metropolis.

"Half-past 11 o'clock, A. M., June 3d.

" Dear Dick, — Quit all business and come to me *immediately.* This is urgent and most important. Although I have written regularly once a day and sometimes twice, she has failed to receive my letters for at least a week. The postmaster of the city told me it could not be the fault of his department; so I have telegraphed to the postmaster-general at Washington. There is a dark mystery somewhere. If that villain is at the bottom of it, he shall find that he has roused the slumbering lion, who will prove a thorn in his side, which will make him drink the cup of bitterness to the very dregs.

" Richard, my friend, she has broken off our engagement, and I am miserable, for I have loved her. Oh, how I have loved her! and this evidence of the lightness of her character seems only to increase my passion. With that fickle sex it is ' Out of·sight, out of mind;' but no, she was right. Had she not just cause to suppose I had ceased to love? I am incensed at myself for having blamed her. To-morrow is the day, — the fatal day fixed by her father. There is no time to lose. We must take decided measures. Richard Longshanks, give up all and come to the hotel without delay, on receipt of this. If I fail to obtain her there will be no joy for me henceforth in life.   " In haste.

                                                        " L. L."

RICHARD LONGSHANKS, ESQ., TO LEANDER LOVELL, ESQ.

                                                        "1 o'clock.

" DEAR LEN, — Your note reached me about an hour ago, just as I was sitting down to lunch at Gudgeon's (by the way, that's the place for mock-turtle). There is no hurry, since the marriage is not to take place till to-morrow, and we can drive down there in a couple of hours.

" I will dine with you at six o'clock, and we will discuss the matter calmly over our wine and cigars.

                                                        " R. L.

" P. S. — I would like to try you at chess again this evening."

MISS GOODENOUGH TO MR. LEANDER LOVELL.

                                                        " June 3d.

" MY OWN DEAREST LENNY, — Come to me at once — the whole secret is out. Oh, how hasty I was ! — how I have wronged you ! To think of that vile thing, Bridget, giving your letters to Professor Malpest as fast as she received them. Oh, the wicked, good-for-nothing traitress ! — and then to think of the duplicity of that dark villain of a professor, to keep telling me that since you did not write to me it was evident you had ceased to love me — and your dear letters in his coat-pocket all the time. Why did I listen to him? How could I believe you false? I am so overcome that I hardly know what I write. I dread to tell you the rest, and yet I must.

"Believing (credulous that I was) the insinuations of that perfidious man, that you were not true to me, that you had found some other Cherry more attractive than my poor self, I weakly yielded to the solicitations, or rather the commands, of my father; and, supposing our engagement to be at an end, and feeling by turns indignant or utterly prostrated in spirit (wretched girl that I am!) I reluctantly consented to marry that false, unprincipled deceiver. He wanted the ceremony to take place immediately, but I insisted on postponing it until the day previously decided on by papa, which gives me thirty-six hours' grace from this time, — for six o'clock to-morrow afternoon is the appointed hour.

"When Bridget perceived my grief at my impending calamity, she attributed it entirely to my not receiving the letters (for she did not know of my — Ugh! I shudder to think of it), and she stole up to my room, where I was almost crying my eyes out, and confessed what she had done. I reproached her bitterly for her double-dealing, and asked her how she could do such a thing; and then she began to sob, and hung down her head, and said my trouble was nothing to hers; and then she gave mysterious hints, and went on in a very strange manner; but I could not make out what she was driving at, for the only intelligible thing she said was, 'Sure, miss, I niver dhramed you would take it so harred.' As soon as she left me, I went straight to the professor and demanded the letters. He at first prevaricated about them; but when I informed him that Bridget had told me all, he turned pale and actually seemed to grow weak in the knees, which proves that even the greatest of criminals can be ashamed of his wicked deeds. Then he said he had burnt them; but this proved to be a deliberate false-hood, for immediately afterwards he showed them all to my father, who became violently excited against me, and said they were a physiological proof that I ought to be married without delay.

"The professor afterwards had a grand scene with Biddy. I suppose he was reproving her for informing against him; but she is a girl of spirit, and answered him back, but I did not hear what she said.

"Lenny, come to me *instantly*, or I shall do something desperate.

"Your own, own
"CHERRY.

"P. S. — Bear in mind that I don't know a word of what was in your letters, excepting what papa told me, and that was nothing.

"I shall watch for you all day long, to-morrow.

"Was there ever in the wide world such an unlucky girl as I am? — engaged to two at once!"

MESSRS. SHARPE & KEAN TO LEANDER LOVELL, ESQ.

"WALL STREET, June 3d, 1850.

"DEAR SIR, — We have the pleasure of informing you that the investigations, instituted under your instructions of the 23d ult., have resulted most happily; for we have obtained indubitable evidence that Malpest has defrauded Dr. Goodenough out of sums of sufficient magnitude to insure his conviction of grand larceny.

"On comparing the copies of his vouchers, furnished us by you, with the books of Messrs. Grubb & Co., general provision dealers, it was found that either the figures in his receipts had been altered, or, what is more probable, that the entire originals were forgeries, — that firm not having received the sums alleged as having been receipted for. To specify, we subjoin a copy from the entries in the ledger of sales to the said Malpest, as fiscal agent for the Society of Harmonians, which, compared with the vouchers, shows a difference in his favor of 225 $\frac{48}{100}$ dollars."

[Here follow the items from the ledger of Grubb & Co.]

" An examination of the books of Messrs. Weevil Bros., flour merchants, Kane & Co., sugar dealers, and Rice & Curry, wholesale grocers, revealed similar, though more extensive, frauds.

" We have also put ourselves in communication with Palladio Styles, Esq., the architect, and, from the developments already come to light, have reason to believe that the peculations of Malpest will be found to have commenced with the very foundation of the benevolent institution of Dr. Goodenough.

" The proper course for you to pursue is, to confer with the District Attorney, who will issue a warrant for the arrest of the guilty party.

" In regard to Dr. Goodenough, we regret to say that we do not think the facts, as presented to us, in relation to that gentleman, are quite sufficient to prove him to be *non compos mentis*, and consequently we cannot conscientiously advise you to apply for a writ *de lunatico inquirendo*.

" If you have reason to believe that the young lady is restrained of her liberty against her will, and she is of age, the matter can be judicially investigated under the *habeas corpus* act.

" Respectfully, your obedient servants,

"SHARPE & KEAN."

22

CHAPTER XII.

In which the Virtuous are rewarded, and the Wicked punished.

On the 4th day of June, 1850, two cavaliers were seen ascending a hill. It was a lovely afternoon. The tender buds, incipient leaves, were sprouting forth on the branches of all the trees, harbingers of the dense foliage of summer; nature's soft carpet (in some places in grain), beautifully variegated with daisies, buttercups, and other floral ornaments, covered with its soft verdure the face of the landscape, while birds of varied plumage were heard carolling their epithalamiums in the boughs overhead, or seen bringing dry twigs, with which to build the nuptial couch. Did the scene of our story lay in Arcadia, in the early age of Iron and Innocence, we should add that lambs were skipping on every hill-side, shepherds, with blue silk ribbons in their hats (if it was a stage Arcadia), piping their impassioned strains to beautiful shepherd-esses, in red rosettes, and the sparkling waters, trickling from the dissolving snows of Taygetus flowing in bubbling brooks and purling streams to swell the volume of the classic Alpheus, while the king of birds perched on top of Acro-Corinthus was looking down from his eyrie in search of something to eat. But, alas, for romance! The incident of which we are speaking occurred in this prosaic nineteenth century, in the sterile State of New Jersey. So, instead of Strephons and Chloes, the sturdy farmer was seen

ploughing his weary way through eighteen inches of sand
and mud (for he was a sub-soiler, though not a free-soil-
er), anon scowling and swearing at his raw-boned Rosi-
nante, anon smiling serenely as his mental vision took in
future acres of cabbages; while his homely housewife,
with bare arms and frock tucked up to her waist, displaying her many-colored balmoral, was busy in the dairy
making Dutch cheese. The shrill voice of chanticleer,
crowing defiance to his haughty rivals, was echoed in all
directions, while the feathered inmates of his harem
cackled joyously over new-laid eggs, feeling as happy as
a poet who had just been delivered of a new idea, a lay
of love, which might perhaps develop itself into a full-
grown volume, and eventually bring him golden eggs —
unless killed by the cold hand of criticism. From a
neighboring marsh, the frog, degenerate descendant of
the antediluvian labyrinthodon, croaked an accompani-
ment to legions of crows, who were flying northward and
cawing hoarsely in their flight. All nature seemed to be
singing a song of welcome at the coming of summer, the
scale of the unmusical gamut being crowned by the steam
whistle of Old Buck, the locomotive of the Camden and
Amboy Railroad, which gave a series of shrieks that
would have startled the American eagle, if that game
bird could be alarmed by empty noise.

We used the term " cavaliers " in a metaphorical sense,
for our two heroes were not on horseback, but were driving in a buggy. The mud with which their vehicle and
their persons were liberally bespattered, and the jaded
appearance of their steed, showed that they had come a
considerable distance. In fact they had driven from
New York. The superficial observer might have mistaken

them for a couple of itinerant fortune-seekers, for, in the front part of the wagon, there was a hand-organ, while a pedlar's pack was strapped behind the seat; but he who scrutinized them more closely would have seen in the refined features and delicate hands of the younger traveller the tokens of gentle blood, while the air and manner of the older of the two, who seemed fond of handling and jingling the silver coins in his pocket, showed the true man of the world, — that is to say, the world of Wall Street.

"Whip him up, Dick! make him go!" cried the younger, impatiently. "It seems to me we crawl."

"Crawl!" answered the other. "Why, we've been crawling fifteen miles an hour, since leaving the ferry. There is no hurry, Lenny, my boy, for it is not yet four o'clock."

"Ha! there it is," exclaimed the one addressed as Lenny, on reaching the top of a hill, pointing to a large building in the vale below. "Those walls contain all that I prize on earth. Perhaps at this moment she is waiting for me, and could see the dust that we would raise, if there was any. Poor Cherry, she has no sister Anne to keep her company! Even Biddy, the cook, is false. But her Leander is true. As to that scoundrel — may my right arm be with—"

"Now Lenny Lovell, just keep cool," said Dick, whom the intelligent reader has of course recognized as Mr. Longshanks, and who now sprang from the wagon, tied the horse to a tree, and a nose-bag of oats to his head.

"Cool!" answered Lovell, "I am perfectly cool, and if I catch the fellow I'll thrash him within an inch of his life, — the contemptible miscreant! Do hurry up. You move like a snail. I want to be off."

" Listen to me," replied Longshanks, lighting a cigar. " If you enter the premises you will be certain to kick up a rumpus, for, disguised as you may be, your voice will betray you, the young lady will scream, perhaps she'll faint, or you will pitch into Malpest, and all will be up. Old Goodenough will take the alarm, and make her marry the fellow instanter."

" She would not do it."

" Perhaps not; but I never like to trust to luck. The better plan is for me to assume the pack (for the doctor is the only one who knows me), and go on a reconnoissance. If possible I shall obtain an interview with the fair one, and arrange the programme for your meeting. By the way, I hope you've made arrangements with a parson?"

" Yes," answered Lovell, " and Peewit, at his particular request, is to give the bride away. I did the same for him, and one good turn deserves another."

" It was Peewit, not the Griffin, you should have given away."

" Is this a time to joke? I agree to your project, but insist on going with you."

" If you will do it," replied Longshanks, " take the hand-organ, my gay and gallant troubadour; but I charge you not to follow me into the house. I will return and let you know what is to be done. Then I shall go to the village, where the sheriff is to meet me, and while you are borne in the buggy on the wings of love, I shall spring the trap. Give me your love-letter; it requires no answer, I believe; and help me on with these things."

22*

"How heavy this confounded hand-organ is!" said Lovell, as they started for Harmony Hall. "It will twist my shoulders off."

"This plaguy pack almost breaks my back," answered Longshanks, trudging along with difficulty under his burden.

While our two paladins were tramping towards Harmony Hall, Dr. Goodenough was sitting in his study reading some letters just received by mail. Among them was the following from Prof. Gummp.

PROF. GUMMP, OF LEIPSIC, TO DR. JONATHAN GOODENOUGH.

"RESPECTED FRIEND, — Accept my congratulations on the triumphant success of your most worthy enterprise. The great American people have conferred new obligations on the rest of mankind.

"I am sorry to say that my translation of that elevated work, the New Utopia, does not seem to be appreciated by the German intellect, and its publication has subjected me to a pecuniary loss. It is too profound in thought, and its sentiments are too lofty for the materialistic mind of the present day; but the time will come when its superlative merits will be understood, — a time when practical realism shall give place to speculative idealism, when man, no longer anthropopathical, shall contemplate the metaphysical harmonics of the soul, and, ceasing to ingurgitate the biological philosophy of the present, shall reject amphibological physianthropics and exist in his sphere according to the preordained universal laws of androgynal asthetics.   "Your brother in Progress,

"GUMMP."

Professor Malpest was in his room, dyeing and frizzling his hair, cleaning his false teeth, washing his face with cream, pulling out superfluous hairs with a tweezer, and dressing himself in the customary costume of a bridegroom.'

In the kitchen, Biddy the cook was scrubbing the floor and muttering to herself as she worked. "Sure and what does he mane by a sittlement?" said she. "Be jabers, there is only one sittlement will contint the daughter of Pathrick O'Brien. And what for did he want to sind me off to the city this day? I misthrust there's some diviltry up, ochone! But 'it's an ill wind that blows nobody no good!' If it's me young mistress he's a-decavin' too, by the howly Virrgin! but it's to the ould docther himsilf I'll confess —I will."

Her meditations were interrupted by the discordant strains of the most out-of-tune hand-organ ever ground in public. Biddy was not in the best of humors, and the jarring sounds grated disagreeably on her nerves.

"Be off with you," she cried, going to the door, — "be off with you, with your ould dog Thray; sure we've throubles enough of our own without listening to those of a baste."

"Don't speak so harshly to the poor man," said Charity, who was sitting in her window, as she tossed a shilling to Bridget. "Give him this trifle, and if you don't like his music, tell him he need not play any more."

Biddy threw the money at the organ-grinder, and noticed as she again ordered him away that he was most shabbily dressed, had a large black patch over one eye, and his slouched hat drawn down over the other as if he were ashamed to show his face ; in fact, little of it could be seen excepting a beard and mustache that would have done honor to the most ferocious of bandits.

The musician picked up the silver coin, and, kissing it, put it in his pocket. He stopped turning his forlorn instrument, but instead of going away sat down on a stump, being apparently very much fatigued.

The cook resumed her work and her soliloquy,

"He'll make it right, will he indade?" said she, "when sure it's only the praste himself can do that same. Bridget O'Brien was never born to be a cookin' and scrubbin' all her life like me poor ould mother in Mullygatawny. Why should I be slavin' down here while Miss Charity — but no harrum to her, for she's a swate young crater — sits a mopin' and a mopin' upstairs doing nothing at all at all. Aint me father's daughter as good as she and perhaps a dale betther?"

Her reflections were again interrupted. This time it was by a peddler. If Joseph's coat of many colors had been worn by all his descendants, and been patched and repatched by successive generations down to the present time, it could not have looked worse than the garment which had fallen to the lot of that peddler, and his whole costume was in keeping with it; he looked, in short, like a living embodiment of "Old Clo." By a strange coincidence he also had a black patch over one eye, and the lower part of his face was concealed by a muffler, as if he were suffering from the toothache.

"Any pins, needles, thimbles, scissors, thread?" said he, deliberately walking in and setting his pack down on the kitchen floor.

"Go long wid yez," said Biddy; "I don't want nothing to do with you, nor any of your tribe."

"Here are some beautiful rings, breastpins, bracelets; smuggled in," continued the persistent peddler with a wink. "Got to sell 'em to reduce stock. Have 'em cheap."

"I tell yez I don't want nothing," said Biddy ; but her eyes betrayed her tongue, for she seemed unable to raise them from an enormous pinchbeck brooch containing twenty-seven pieces of different-colored glass.

" This is an elegant jewel," said the peddler, holding up the glittering bauble, — "the latest style, quite the fashion, all the rage, just like the one Queen Victoria wore at her coronation."

" Sure and it *is* a beauty," said Biddy ; " but how can I buy it when I haven't niver a cint of money? "

" No money?" replied the peddler. " Well, then, suppose I tell you a way of getting this matchless, magnificent, superb, superfine work of art without paying a penny? "

" It's a-jokin' ye are," said Biddy, as her eyes sparkled.

" No, I mean what I say. Are there not other ladies in the house? "

" None but Miss Cherry, — a swate gurrl as ever lived ; but she won't come down, for she's got the megrims like, and kapes herself shut up in her room all the day long a-sobbin' and a-cryin' as if her heart would break — poor thing ! I suspicion there's a young man summus about, and he's played her false, for they are decavin' critters are the men forninst us women-folks."

The peddler held the brooch up to the window so that the bits of glass sparkled and flashed in the sunlight.

" Possibly," said he, " your young mistress may be induced to purchase some of my valuable wares ; so just listen to me. If you will take this wax flower to her, and ask her to examine it well, she may buy it; but, mark! don't show it to anybody else; and mind! tell her that a peddler is here with letter-paper and envelopes. Do that, and this gorgeous jewel, which formed part of the loot of Delhi, where it was the principal ornament in the famous peacock's throne of Aurungzebee, who captured it in battle from Genghis Khan, who stole it from the Emperor of China, — this unique gem shall be *yours.*"

Biddy did not wait to be bidden a second time, but, snatching the wax flower, she bounced out of the kitchen, her hoops in her heedlessness catching in her pail, upsetting it and spilling the dirty water over the floor, completely saturating the unlucky peddler, who happened to be sitting within a foot of it. She ran upstairs and into Miss Charity's room without knocking, for, in her eagerness to possess the showy prize, she did not think of the dignity and politeness which should ever be found in the descendants of Brian-Boru.

Charity was sitting by her window, watching and weeping, for the wedding day, so joyfully anticipated by most young maidens, brought no visions of happiness to her.

"Why does that grizzly organ-grinder sit staring at me from the stump with his hideous one eye?" she said to herself. "He has doubtless his sorrows, poor man; but what are they to mine, alas! Perhaps even he is capable of love; perhaps there are those who have loved him. He is again kissing the mite I gave him. Why did I not send him more?"

"Ah! miss," exclaimed Bridget; "there's such a nice-spoken gintleman downstairs, with such beautiful things to sell, and a black patch over his eye."

"I want nothing that *he* can give," answered Charity. "If he is hungry, offer him food."

"He asked me to show you this jewel of a flower, miss. You might fancy it, for it's a rare plant."

"I care no longer for flowers, nor for anything. Leave me."

"And he has leather-paper and invilopes, mum," said Biddy, who would not be rebuffed.

Charity had mechanically glanced at the flower. Suddenly she started.

"*It is — it is — an oleander.* O LEANDER!" she cried, clasping her hands together. Then (for even the most artless of women are more or less *rusé*) she thought of the perfidious cook, and said with assumed calmness, —

"This is my favorite flower. I will look over the man's stock. Perhaps I will take some letter-paper."

Miss Charity descended into the kitchen, her face suffused with smiles and blushes ; but, on seeing the peddler, she turned pale and started back. She had expected to meet Lovell. Mr. Longshanks she did not recognize, for she had seen him only once before, and that was in the evening.

"The original of this rare flower is not far off, miss, and here are pins and needles — (my name is Longshanks)," — said he, speaking alternately aloud, or in a whisper, according as what he said was meant for the ears of Miss Charity or of Biddy.

"Here," said he, "are wax figures of all kinds. Here's Gen'l Washington (that's him sitting on the stump), and a bust of Napoleon (all mustaches and whiskers), and Julius Cæsar (with a hand-organ) ; and here are fine-tooth combs (we've got a carriage), all ivory, and coarse ones, real tortoise-shell, — no mock-turtle here, — (but it's only a buggy), and jews-harps, penny-whistles, pictures of Cupid (what shall I tell him), and here are envelopes too, and letter-paper."

As he spoke, he ran his finger over the edge of a package of envelopes, causing them to diverge so that the young lady saw her name written on one of them.

" Won't you buy them (and meet him on top of the hill) ? "

" Yes, yes," answered Charity. " How much are they? "

" How much ! Let me think. (At what hour ?) I usually get five or six shillings for them. Suppose we say five and a half ? Does that suit you? *Five and a half!* "

" Yes, — I agree to it, —*five and a half,*" said Miss Charity, taking the package and handing a dollar bill to Longshanks.

" Five and a half (on top of the hill)," said he, giving the young lady a dollar in small change, and handling Biddy the brooch of Genghis Khan.

Professor Malpest now came into the kitchen, dressed to perfection, and, giving a sharp look at the peddler, ordered him to leave.

" I'll have no swindling tramps in my house," said he ; " off with you."

Longshanks having satisfactorily finished his negotiation, prepared to obey, when the professor, encouraged by his apparent meekness, rudely pushed him by the shoulders to accelerate his exit. Like a flash the false peddler turned and struck him a stunning blow with his fist, between the eyes that fairly made him reel, following it up with a left-hander on the nose, that caused the blood to spirt out over his white waistcoat, and to trickle over his spotless cravat and well-starched shirt-bosom. Charity screamed, Biddy yelled " bloody murther," and the recipient of the castigation, clapping his hands over his face, fled from the kitchen. The doctor, disturbed by the outcry, came hurrying in to see what was the matter ; but the instant Longshanks caught sight of him he dropped his pack, scattering its contents around in miscellaneous confusion, and, darting out of the door, ran up the road as fast as he could go. He could not have run faster had the doctor been pursuing him with a legion of Greeks and Romans. The organ-grinder, impatient to receive intelligence of his beloved, followed hard after him, leaving his instrument in the middle of the road. Longshanks did not stop until, quite out of breath, he reached the top of the hill. When Leander at last caught up with him, he was so full of laughter that it was five minutes before the impatient lover could get an intelligible word out of him as to the result of his adventure. While they were throwing off the toggery that concealed their ordinary habiliments, he told Leander of the arrangement made with Charity.

In the mean time Professor Malpest, with battered visage and soiled garments, slunk crestfallen to his room, astounded at the impudence and audacity of a beggarly peddler.

The doctor led Charity into his study, and, after a long and learned preamble, which we will not inflict on the reader, informed her that the clergyman would soon arrive to unite her in the holy bonds of matrimony, to that exemplary and upright man, brother Nicholas Malpest, and he hoped that she was quite prepared for the ceremony. Miss Charity, with a dissimulation of which

23

no one would have supposed her capable, had she not given such a striking and lamentable proof of it on this occasion, answered that she " would consent to be married that night."

Her father, joyous at this evidence of filial obedience, pressed her to his heart. Her tears flowed fast ; and we regard these evidences of sorrow as having been highly creditable to her, for they were doubtless caused by some compunctions of conscience at the deceit of which she was guilty towards her parent. Is there not a lesson in this to old and young? We are not much given to moralizing, — it is tedious to the author and a bore to the reader, — but we will observe here, that this conduct of Charity Goodenough proves that in misfortune evil thoughts will come to us in spite of ourselves, thoughts of which in happiness we never would have deemed ourselves capable. What virtue is there in apparent goodness which has never been tried? The false may be as fair to look upon as the real ; it is only when weighed in the balance that it is found wanting. We do not mean to insinuate by this that our heroine was less perfect than young ladies in general. Artless maiden, openly engaged to the man of your choice, chide not poor Cherry for misconduct, of which you yourself would doubtless have been guilty, had you been subjected to the same temptation. Good young man, shake not your head and say you " would not want such a deceitful girl." Suppose you were in the place of Leander Lovell. Ah! that would make a difference, — would it not? Prim mother of a family, solemn *pater familias*, you will have read this book in vain if — but enough ; not wanting the reader to skip that which it gives us trouble to write, we will sermonize no more.

On leaving her father, Charity hied to her room, hastily wrote some lines on a sheet of paper, and, putting a few articles of apparel in her satchel, stole softly downstairs, passed out of the house by the back door, and, escaping through the garden, met her anxious and impatient lover at the appointed trysting-place. They were soon speeding at a rapid rate towards the altar of Hymen.

At six o'clock, the Rev. Hieronymus Knox made his appearance at Harmony Hall; and at the same time Professor Malpest emerged from his room, wearing an expression of complete satisfaction, and apparently much in love — with himself, notwithstanding the piece of court-plaster on his nose. The professor, the doctor, and the minister entered the reception room. But the bride, where was she? The doctor was about to go in search of her, when the sound of approaching footsteps was heard; the door was thrown wide open by Biddy, and Richard Longshanks, Esq., whom the professor instantly recognized as the quondam peddler, walked into the room accompanied by two constables.

" I have a warrant for the arrest of this man," said he, laying his hand on the shoulder of the professor, who turned pale from the terror of conscious guilt.

" What for — what — what for? " he asked, with quivering lips.

" For forgery," answered Longshanks. " For forging the names of Grubb & Co., Weevil Bros., Rice & Curry, Palladio Styles, and others, to certain false receipts, and thus defrauding Dr. Goodenough out of considerable sums of money."

" What can this mean? " asked the doctor.

" It means, sir," replied Longshanks, " that this thieving knave has inveigled you into this Foufouville folly in order to rob you at his leisure ; and, by obtaining the hand of your daughter, to eventually get possession of all your property."

" It cannot be possible," said the doctor. " Brother Nicholas guilty of dishonesty ! It is all an error."

Malpest, who had partially recovered his presence of mind, turned to Longshanks, and, in a low tone of voice, proposed to compromise the matter, offering him money, and adding, " As to the girl, she can go."

" Despicable scoundrel ! do you judge others by yourself ? " answered Longshanks. " You cannot bribe me."

" Bribe !" exclaimed the doctor. " Can it be true? I am dumfounded."

Then suddenly seized with indignation, he grabbed Malpest by the collar, and shook him as a cat would shake a mouse. The miserable wretch, who in his encounter with the peddler had shown himself a still greater coward even than scoundrel, dropped on his knees and begged piteously for mercy.

" Drag him away ! drag him away ! off with him !" cried the doctor. " Will wonders never cease? What will happen next? I am overwhelmed."

A constable now stepped forward with his handcuffs, and was about to fix them on Malpest's wrists, when Biddy, who had stood peeping at the proceedings through the half-open door, rushed in, exclaiming, —

" Ah ! the doubly decavin' villain, but he's cotched in his own trap, he is, by the howly St. Patrick. But ye'll

not take him away at all, at all, till he's made an honest
woman of me."

"What do you mean, what do you mean, Biddy?" inquired Longshanks.

"And what do I mane, is it? Sure what I mane is
that I'm a'most three months gone already; bad luck to
him!"

"Hey! what! has he got you in the fam—" cried
Longshanks, tossing his hat up to the ceiling, dancing
about with frantic delight, and giving way to transports
of laughter.

"Nicholas guilty of concupiscence! I am horrified,"
said the doctor, sinking back in his chair, as if utterly
deprived of strength by the dreadful and unexpected intelligence.

"Bridegroom, what say you to this new charge?"
asked Longshanks.

"Let me off! let me off! I'll make it all right. I'll do
anything."

"It isn't I that will thrust him for that same," said
Biddy.

"I am sick at heart," said the doctor. "This vile
business must be settled. Infamous wretch! if you will
marry that woman, whom you have deceived, I will not
prosecute you, — you shall keep your ill-gotten gains;
otherwise, the law must take its course."

"Anything — anything," answered Malpest.

"Stand up then," said the Rev. Hieronymus Knox.

The weak-kneed rascal scrambled trembling to his feet,
and, maintaining himself with difficulty on his legs, was
married to Biddy, the cook.

23*

When the ceremony was over, the doctor could no longer control his rage and exasperation.

"D—n you, you infernal emissary of Satan!" he cried, swearing for the first and only time in his life; "get out of my sight, and never let me see your face again."

By way of emphasis to his order, he gave Malpest a vigorous kick behind, which sent him howling out of the room like a whipped cur. He immediately made his exit from the house, and when last seen was hurrying up the road, with Biddy — who feared her husband would escape her — in full chase, her red hair streaming in the wind, and glowing in the setting sun as if it were on fire. Longshanks and the constables, recollecting that their warrant was still unexecuted, followed after.

"Sir, you need repose. I will go. Adieu," said the Rev. Mr. Knox, taking his departure.

The doctor, when the excitement under which he was laboring had somewhat subsided, resolved to seek consolation in the society of his daughter. He went up to her room, and knocked at the door, once, twice, thrice; but, receiving no response, he entered. Her unfinished embroidery stood in its accustomed corner, her clothing was strewn about in disorder, and on her work-table he observed a note addressed to himself. He opened it and read as follows, —

"June 4.

"DEAR, DEAR PAPA, — In a few hours I shall be the wife of the noblest and truest of men, — my own Leander. Pardon me for my wicked deception; my feelings are stronger than my will.

"Ever your own

"CHERRY."

Dr. Goodenough was alone in Harmony Hall.

.   .   .   .

.   .   .   .

.   .   .   .

.   .   .   .

We had the honor of becoming acquainted with Dr. Goodenough about a year after the occurrence of the events that we have recorded in this narrative. He was then residing in the city with his daughter and son-in-law, Mr. and Mrs. Lovell. Most of his time was spent in preparing a new edition of his works (which his publisher, with singular blindness to his own interests, declined to bring out) ; for, notwithstanding his disastrous experience at Harmony Hall, he still continued to cherish his theories of reform. But his ideas would seem to have undergone some modification, for he acknowledged that the time had not yet come for their practical development. "Human beings," he said, "must first cease to be anthropopathical, and the mind of man attain a higher sphere of organization." In the evenings it was his greatest delight to take his little grandson, Jonathan G. Lovell, in his arms, and dance him on his knee.

We are happy to say that he eventually regained possession of the real estate appertaining to the former phalanstery ; but his property was, nevertheless, much diminished by the embezzlements of Malpest.

The old gentleman never liked to talk about his experiment at Harmony Hall, and it was seldom alluded to in his presence. The few months passed there appeared also to have left a painful impression on the mind of Mrs. Lovell ;. but it was otherwise with her husband, who always spoke of his Harmonian experience as a mere frolic. He long wore on his watch-chain a silver shilling, — a cherished memento of that period. He was exceedingly liberal to organ-grinders, whom he seemed to regard with a sort of fellow-feeling, until they became an intolerable nuisance, gathering around his house like mice about a Dutch cheese. Mr. Longshanks, his partner in business, was a constant visitor at his hospitable mansion. He appeared to have a strange weakness for peddlers, having been known, on one occasion, to buy out the whole stock in trade of an itinerant vender of small notions, at his own price, much to his astonishment, and distribute the miscellaneous assortment among some fortunate beggars who happened to be standing by.

Joseph Peewit, Esq., when we last heard of him, was residing near Jersey City (where he kept a fancy store), with his small but rapidly increasing family. His wife, much to his chagrin, threw the MS. of her invaluable lecture, on the Co-relation of the Sexes, into the fire, before the honeymoon was over. Posterity will thank us for the few fragments we have preserved of that remarkable production. After her marriage she withdrew entirely from the world of letters, refusing even the position of Secretary to the Literary Society of Communipaw.

Mrs. Strongitharm soon consoled herself for the loss of the fickle Peewit, and took another partner. He professed to be a spiritualist; and certainly a most violent spirit seemed to have gotten possession of him, for he gave Mrs. S. a Roland for all her Olivers by making her head the medium of constant knocks.

As to Malpest, the doctor, according to his promise, refused to appear against him; but he was, nevertheless, tried, and convicted of forgery, and sentenced to ten years' imprisonment. During his incarceration he was occasionally visited by reformers, and others, — mostly of the female sex; for many persons regarded him as the victim of misplaced confidence, and more than one was heard to hurl anathemas on the head of Dr. Goodenough, who was regarded as the author of his ruin. He was, however, averse to receiving visitors, seeming to shrink from contact with his kind. The most persistent caller, and the one whose coming seemed to cause him the greatest annoyance, was a coarse, flashily-dressed woman, with a hideous, cross-eyed infant in her arms, who always heralded her advent by a large piece of pasteboard, which bore the following superscription in letters nearly a quarter of an inch long, —

"MRS. PROFESSOR MALPEST,
"Née O'BRIEN."

We regret to say that he was pardoned by the governor after about a year's imprisonment.

CHAPTER XIII.

An Account of the Philosopher Fou-fou.

WE have completed our history of the decline and fall of Harmonianism. But Harmonianism was but a branch of the banyan-tree of Foufouism, — the most wide-spread of all isms, — and we doubt not that we will be gratifying a natural curiosity in the reader, if we now give some account of the founder of the fraternity of Foufouites.

The means of doing so are happily at our command, for among the posthumous papers of the late lamented Dr. Goodenough, there was found a MS. translation of a very rare and curious Chinese work on Fou-fou, not a single copy of which has yet made its way into any of the public libraries of America or.Europe.

We subjoin this unique and interesting specimen of celestial literature without presuming to make editorial changes, with the exception of dotting an occasional *i*, for the doctor was notoriously negligent in his chirography.

FOU-FOU, — A TALE OF CHINA.

Translated into Latin from the original Chinese of LY-ING, by Ignatius Hook, a Jesuit missionary, and done into English with notes by DR. J. GOODENOUGH.

In the 77th year of the reign of the great Fi-fo-fum, Khan of the Celestial Flowery Kingdom, Brother to the

Sun and Moon, Lord of Heaven and Earth, and of the Seven Umbrellas, that is to say 2,222 years before the birth of Confucius,[1] there dwelt in the village of Yangts-chankiangkong[2] a retired rice-merchant, by the name of Bum. Now this Bum, who was a man of portly dimensions, had amassed a large fortune by selling spoiled rice for good, and, being the richest man in Yangtschankiang-kong, was much puffed up with self-conceit, and was greatly respected by all his neighbors,[3] who stuck out their tongues and scratched their right ears[4] whenever he passed. He was a man of low extraction, who in early life had made a living by keeping a corner tea-store. He laid the foundation of his fortune during the great rebellion of the Southern provinces, when he contracted with the government to supply the army with one million catties of rice, and one hundred thousand taels of cattle. So bad was the quality of the food supplied by Bum, that when they were attacked by those terrible opium-eaters, the long haired Kanchew[5] Tartars, they had not strength to run away, and every one of them had his pigtail cut off two inches below his ears,[6] thereby incapacitating him from ever again serving the Khan as a soldier. So, in spite of, or rather perhaps in consequence of, the misfortunes of his

---

[1] This is clearly a chronological error, probably the fault of some transcriber, for as Confucius flourished in the sixth century B.C., it would place the reign of Fi-fo-fum some years anterior to the Deluge.

[2] The name of this town does not appear on any of the modern maps of China; but they are notoriously defective.

[3] How little human nature has changed!

[4] To this day a mark of respect in Thibet. — *See Travels of Huc in Tartary.*

[5] Now called Manchoos; probably from the singular historical circumstance here related.

[6] Doubtless a circumlocutory method of expressing decapitation.

country, Bum waxed wealthy and grew in the esteem of his fellow-citizens. His business increased; he had agents in different provinces, and hundreds of boats for the transportation of his produce. They are called Bum boats to this day. So Bum, having become a man of wealth and consequence, removed from his miserable bamboo dwelling in the environs of Yangtschankiangkong, and built himself a sumptuous mansion of porcelain and lacker ware in the very centre of the town. Of course he cut off all his former friends and acquaintances.

It had long been the wish of Bum to have an heir to his name and his wealth; but the divine Buddh, doubtless incensed at the wicked manner in which he had acquired his riches, long denied him this happiness. It was in vain that he erected a water prayer-mill [7] that turned off one thousand prayers an hour; it was in vain that he laid on the altar of Buddh rich offerings of fat pigs, boiled fish, and gallons of hot Sam-shoo wine; [8] it was in vain that he shut himself up in the joss-house and performed the three hundred and thirty-three genuflections, and nine hundred and ninety-nine prostrations, touching the big toe of the idol with his nose at each prostration; the god could be neither bribed nor cajoled into acceding to his wishes. At last, after twenty-five years of marriage, Mrs. Bum, who was the finest-looking woman in China, for she weighed nearly three hundred pounds, was seized with one of the four hundred and forty-four mala-

---

[7] Prayer mills are still common in the Lama convents, and private houses of Tartary. Some of them are turned by the foot, like a knife-grinder's machine, and the industrious owner can go on with his handiwork while his machine is praying for him. — *See Travels of Huc in China and Tartary.*

[8] It is still customary in China to offer food and drink to the gods, — a practice that is encouraged by the priests.

dies of the body, and obliged to take to her bed. Dr.
Quak was at once called in, and, in one month under his
management, the poor woman was brought to the point of
death, being reduced to mere skin and bones. But she
eventually recovered, and in less than a year, to the astonishment of everybody, crowned the hopes of her husband by giving birth to a son.

In the excess of his joy Bum gave a grand feast to all
his friends and relations. There were birds'-nests soup,
bon-bon stew, fried rat, sugar-cane worms, shrimp patties,
salted eggs, sea-weed jelly, red-billed magpies, peacock's
brains, mandarin ducks, boiled blubber, fish tripes, sharks'
fins, sea-slugs, water snakes, dromedary's hump, fried
frogs, kabobs, Bohea tea, Sam-shoo wine piping hot, and
sweetmeats of every imaginable kind; in short, all the
delicacies known to the culinary art of China, whether in
or out of season. All the guests stuffed themselves until
they were sick,[9] and as to Bum, he ate so much, and drank
so much, and laughed so much, that he went off in a fit of
apoplexy. His relations of course went into the deepest
mourning, dressing themselves in white[10] from head to
foot, and letting the hair of their heads grow until it
reached a length of nearly a quarter of an inch.[11]

The little Peepee — for so the baby was named — was
nursed with the greatest care. When he became old
enough to begin his education a giver of wisdom was pro-
cured for him, who kept him see-sawing backwards and

[9] This is not strange, for it has always been considered polite in China
for the host to press his guests to eat, and the height of ill-breeding on the
part of the latter to refuse anything offered. — *See Sirr, five years in China.*

[10] The mourning color in China; and how much more respectful to the
Ruler of all things than black!

[11] To this day the greatest compliment that can be paid to the deceased.

forwards from morning till night, repeating letters of the
alphabet, or passages from the forty-four books of instruc-
tion. At six years of age he knew six letters; at ten he
knew, by heart, quite a number of verses from the four
sacred books; and at fifteen he had made some progress
in the five classics. All the ladies of the village who had
daughters about his own age were amazed at his wonderful precocity. He was fond of displaying his learning
before his youthful companions, and cared nothing for
their silly amusements. When one would propose a
game of bones, he would answer with a verse from the book
of Ho; when challenged to play at hop-scotch, he would
turn up his nose and walk away with an air of disdain.
In consequence of these peculiar ways he was nick-named
Fou-fou, which, in very ancient Chinese, is supposed to
have meant " transcendental wisdom."

Now it happened that next door to the widow Bum
there lived an old lady, by the name of Mah, whose husband had also been an army contractor. He had agreed
to furnish every man with a blue silk umbrella, but, being
a covetous person, he had sent them, instead, miserable
cotton parasols, wholly ineffectual in protecting the sol-
diers from the sun and rain. The inconvenience suffered
from the heat was partly remedied by their fans;[12] but
they had no protection against the dampness, and consequently all caught cold. This accident, however, turned
out fortunately, for the whole host set up a simultaneous
coughing, which so alarmed the insurgent Tartars,—who
supposed that an army of not less than a million of men
was advancing against them,—that they immediately

[12] Every man, woman, and child carries a fan, which seems more indispensable to a Chinese than a pocket-knife to a Yankee. — *Forbes.*

turned their camels' heads towards the West, and never stopped, in their flight, until they reached the top of the Himalaya mountains.[13] When the mighty Fi-fo-fum heard how shamefully his army had been swindled, his rage was so great that he would have plucked his beard out by the roots, if he had had any, and he at once sent High Commissioner Hang to investigate the charges of peculation that had been brought against Mah. The contractor was arrested, and, the charges against him being fully proven, he was sentenced to forfeit all his ill-gotten gains into the public treasury, to be hauled over the coals on a gridiron, to receive one thousand strokes of a bamboo, to be flayed alive, to be hanged, drawn and quartered, and to have his ancestors for fifteen generations degraded;[14] but the latter part of the sentence was a superfluous piece of justice, for Mah was not known to have any ancestors.

Mah, having obtained a private interview with Hang, not only succeeded in persuading that official of his innocence, but actually induced him to declare that the contractor, having been the means of delivering the country from the Tartars, was an eminently patriotic citizen. The sentence of the Court against him was, accordingly, abrogated by the Commissioner. As an evidence of the cost of legal proceedings in those days, it was remarked that Mah, although finally declared innocent, was shorn of nearly four-fifths of his property. The wealth of Hang was greatly increased about the same

[13] This important incident in the history of the Central Flowery Kingdom is not mentioned by any other author.

[14] To degrade a man's ancestors from the rank they enjoyed in life, is one of the most dreaded punishments in Chinese criminal law. — *Sirr.*

time. For his services in this transaction the emperor presented him with a peacock's feather, — the highest honor to which a subject could aspire.[15] Mah, who still remained in comfortable circumstances, lived, contentedly, for several years, highly esteemed by all, and at last died of the gout, leaving a disconsolate widow, and a daughter, named, Ah-me.

This young lady, who was a few years younger than Fou-fou, was one of the most beautiful of her sex. Her complexion was the color of a ripe olive; her eyes were small, black, languishing, and more oblique than any other eyes in China; her feet were about the size and shape of her fist when doubled up; she had no calves to her legs,[16] was flat-breasted, and straight-waisted, — in short, she was a perfect beauty. As she grew up to womanhood she naturally attracted the attention of all the beaux in the neighborhood, and several soon became suitors for her hand; for, in those days of innocence, the young people themselves regulated their matrimonial affairs, instead of leaving them to their parents, as is the custom at present.

One day the beautiful Ah-me entered her mother's boudoir of gilt bamboo.

"Mamma," said she, "I am the most embarrassed girl in China; I have received four offers. First came the haughty Hi-tun, the eldest son of the mandarin Poo-poo; then, that ferocious soldier, Bang Wang, who has often

---

[15] In modern times a present of three peacock's feathers is one of the most signal marks of imperial favor. — *Notes on China.*

[16] This is the natural consequence of contracting the feet in childhood, and is a defect found in all women whose feet have been thus disfigured.— *Davis. View of China.*

told us how many Tartars he killed in the last campaign ; next, that rollicking young gentleman, Jak, master of the fire-crackers on the revenue junk, Hi-poop ; and lastly came that exceedingly wise and studious youth, Fou-fou."

"Who has the most cash?"[17] inquired the judicious Mah.

"Hi-tun," answered Ah-me, "possesses the tablets of one thousand seven hundred ancestors ;[18] he is the most perfect master of the ceremonies in Yangtschankiang-kong ; no one can handle the chop-sticks so gracefully as he ; not one keeps his pig-tail so nicely oiled ; his nails are six inches, and his nose an inch and a half long ; but then he has not got much cash, and he is too proud to work. Bang Wang expects, some day, to be a mandarin of the blue button ; but he has nothing, at present, as he himself acknowledges, excepting his valor, and his tom-tom. Jak, who is tired of life on the ocean wave, as he says, and wants to come to anchor, has only his pay, and his rations. Fou-fou is immensely rich."

"Then, of course, you accepted him," said Mah.

"I rejected the whole of them," answered Ah-me.

"Silly girl, what have you done!" exclaimed Mah.

Lest the conduct of Ah-me seem strange, it must be stated that the handsome Si-si kept a retail tea-store directly opposite the residence of Madam Mah. In personal appearance he was a model of Chinese elegance ;

---

[17] A copper coin worth about one-eighth of a cent. It has a square hole in the centre for convenience in stringing.

[18] Every wealthy Chinese gentleman keeps an apartment called the "Hall of Ancestors," in which are ranged the tablets of his deceased progenitors.

24*

for he was nearly five feet and a half high, his complexion was yellow, his pig-tail long, and his nose short, his forehead low, and his cheek-bones high, his ears large, and his eyes small, his fingers thin, and his legs thick, his lips straight, and his eyes oblique, his cheeks sunken, and his stomach protuberant. The gentle Si-si had never told his love, but let concealment, like a thief in a candle, consume his substance, while his passion burned all the more fiercely; but his heaving breast and languishing glances betrayed his emotions, which were answered by a responsive flutter in the heart of Ah-me.

The effect of the young lady's cruelty to her suitors was heartrending. The haughty Hi-tun, out of pure spite, married his washerwoman's daughter, and was, in consequence, discarded by all his family. When last heard from they were making a living by taking in plain washing,—Hi-tun doing the ironing.

Bang Wang attempted to commit hari-kari,[19] but only succeeded in ripping open his yellow silk gown. His after fate is unknown.

Jak was said to have drowned his sorrows in the bowl. Certain it is that he was seen cruising around the canals, for many years, always jolly, and, according to rumor, with a wife in every port excepting Yangtschankiang-kong.

As to Fou-fou he resolved to put an end to his grief by putting an end to his life; so, one dark night, he deliberately threw himself into the canal; but the water was exceedingly cold, and whether this cooled his pas-

---

[19] This singular custom is now confined to Japan.

sion, or whether he was afraid of freezing to death, — a method of shaking off this mortal coil he had not contemplated, — certain it is, that, on rising to the surface and finding himself directly under the stern of the Hipoop, he at once seized hold of the rudder and there clung. The man at the wheel finding the vessel would not obey her helm, or rather that her helm would not obey him, naturally imagined that the junk was bewitched, and falling on his face, in abject terror, vowed to all the gods that if the Evil Spirit were taken away he would present the priests of Buddh with one-half the curry he had stolen the day before (he promised the whole, but mentally intended only to give half). Jak, coming up and learning the difficulty, called him an ignorant land-lubber, and gave him a kick that sent him through the gangway head-foremost into a hogshead of molasses.

" Shiver my timbers!" said he, " but I'll make her work."

He then gave the wheel a jerk; it turned half round and immediately sprang back, for Fou-fou was holding on to the rudder with one hand, and with the other grasping the tail of the carved dragon on the stern of the vessel. Jak made two more attempts to turn the wheel, but with the same result, and being now convinced that Sheitan was at the bottom of the matter, — that is to say, of the junk, — he dropped on his marrow-bones and began to stutter a confused medley of phrases from all the prayers to Buddh that he had heard from time to time in his cruises, — it being the first evidence of piety he had given since he followed the canals. The junk, left to herself, soon drifted plump against the bank, and

Fou-fou, having waded ashore, endeavored to sneak home unperceived. The Hi-poop remained quietly alongside the bank until daybreak, by which time — as evil spirits prowl about only at night — her rudder was found to be clear, and she proceeded on.her way, with a fair wind, at the rate of a mile an hour, both Jak and the land-lubber forgetting their terror-stricken vows.

The next day the adventure of Fou-fou was known all over the town, for his action had been seen by one of the guardians of darkness.[20] He became the laughing-stock of everybody; but, as his thoughts were wandering in the sublime regions of transcendental metaphysics, he passed by the scoffers disdainfully, not stooping to reply to their ribaldry.

In a week the beautiful Ah-me married the gentle Si-si, and that is the last we hear of her.

Fou-fou, being now completely disgusted with the world, shut himself up in his house for twenty-five years, giving himself up entirely to the study of philosophy. Having attained the age of nearly fifty years, and his beard reaching down to his waist, he at last emerged from his seclusion and announced to his wondering · townsmen that he had found the true key to human'happiness.

"The permanent principles of Nature," said he, "are three: the active principle, or spirit; the passive principle, or matter; and the neutral principle, or mathematical laws of justice and harmony. The nature of man was co-ordinate with this division, and contained: 1. His physical nature, adapted to the passive principle, or matter; 2. His moral nature, adapted to the active princi-

---

[20] Night watchmen.

ple, or spirit; and, 3. His intellectual nature, adapted to the neutral principle of law and justice. In order to construct, synthetically, a true harmonic sphere out of this methodical analysis of the principles of man's physical, moral, and mental nature, individually and collectively, with regard to general society and universal unity, we must follow the theory of the four movements, and mixing up the cabalistic, or emulative impulse, with unityism, or harmonizing aspiration, till they form a cosmological equilibrium, we obtain, as a solution, that all property and women should be held in common." *

The utterance of these subversive, levelling, revolutionary, and atrocious doctrines, raised a terrible commotion in Yangtschankiangkong, especially among the bonzes, who possessed most of the property of the place. The bonzes excited the women, and the women excited their husbands; so, in the midst of a general hue-and-cry Foufou was arrested, and brought before the old mandarin, Poo-poo, on the charge of heresy and rebellion.

" Prisoner," said Poo-poo; " what have you to say in answer to this charge?"

"There are two phases of incoherence," answered Foufou, " containing each seven social periods; two phases of combination containing each nine social periods. As soon as society shall have reached the thirty-second, which is the apogee of harmony, the pivotal or anti-harmonic age of the race will begin, the Aurora Borealis will be converted into a boreal crown, and the soul of man cease to be vertiginated by the viripotency of woman. This is axiopistical."

---

* For a modern plagiarism of this speech, see the New American Cyclopædia, under the heading FOU. — *Note by the author.*

"Can't you speak Chinese?" said Poo-poo.

"The human race will perish," continued Fou-fou; "but, by a series of bicomposite transmigrations, be transmogrified into the seventh sphere."

"Take him away! take him away!" cried Poo-poo; "he is nothing but a crack-brained visionary, and can do no harm."

But the bonzes were not to be cheated of their prey, nor was the resentment of the women allayed; so an appeal was taken, and the case brought before High Commissioner Hang. Hang instantly decided that the criminal should have his head shaved, be put in the pillory for three days, be chopped into mince-meat, and that his doctrines should be applied to himself as far as possible. The merciful Fi-fo-fum[21] remitted all but the latter part of this sentence, and as the population of the province was estimated at 3,000,000, and its assessed wealth was 10,000,000,000 cash, the portion belonging to each inhabitant, according to the theory of Fou-fou, was 3,333⅓. It was accordingly directed that this sum be paid to him, deducting the dues of the court; and, as these amounted to exactly 3,333, he received, on his discharge, just one-third of a cash, and his property was confiscated for distribution among the rest of the people. The sentence was highly applauded in Yangtschankiangkong, though in the end it gave rise to great dissatisfaction, from the fact that not a single cash that had belonged to the estate of Fou-fou actually found its way into the pockets of the people. For the extraordinary wisdom displayed in the decision of this case, Hang was raised, by the

---

[21] The emperor must have been quite aged at this period.

Khan, to the position of Minister of Eternal Equity. Fou-fou bought a cracker with his one-third of a cash, and, being convinced that no man is a prophet in his own country, resolved to emigrate from Yangtschankiangkong. He started the next morning, following the course of the So-long canal. About 12 o'clock he met a couple of ox-drivers named Gee-wo and Go-long, who were taking a mid-day rest from their labors. They told him they were very poor men, who worked hard for a mere pittance in order to support their wives and families. Their employer was the proprietor of the adjoining tavern of the Five Felicities; he had always paid them their wages regularly, and they had never been discontented with their lot, even though it was not an easy one. Fou-fou told them that their contentment showed their ignorance and folly; and then he unfolded his views to them at length. They comprehended very little of what he said, excepting that they were entitled to a portion of their master's property, which seemed to them quite reasonable; and, when the philosopher promised them a good dinner, if they would join him, they at once abandoned their oxen in order to follow him. He took them to the tavern of the Five Felicities, and ordered a feast for three. The superintendent of the chest[22] gave the necessary directions to the governor of the kettle,[23] and in a short time the steward of the table[24] placed the food before the three hungry men. When they had finished Fou-fou started to leave with them without paying; but Gin-sling, the landlord, stopped them, and demanded his money. Fou-fou

---

[22] The landlord. [23] The cook. [24] The waiter.

began to explain his philosophy, and endeavored to convince him that since he and his companions were entirely penniless he owed them, in strict equity, much more than a beggarly meal. Gin-sling could not see the matter in that light; and, accordingly, the three philosophers were arrested, and taken before a Dispenser of Justice named Meen-fun, followed by the parents, wives, children, and other relations of Gee-wo and Go-long, who were loud in their imprecations against Fou-fou, for having got the ox-drivers in trouble. Meen-fun, with that eye for poetical justice for which the Chinese have ever been famous, ordered, as a preliminary punishment, that a powerful purge be administered to each of the culprits; and — [Here there is a lacuna in the MS. of Dr. G.]

Late in the afternoon Fou-fou arrived in front of a joss-house.[25] A number of ragged, suspicious-looking men were prowling around it, and he at once began to harangue them on the uselessness of joss-houses, and the absurdity of the doctrines taught in them. "They support in idleness," said he, "hundreds of good-for-nothing priests, who should be tilling the soil, and adding to the productiveness of the land, and who pretend that their teachings are the inspirations of Buddh, whereas, they are nothing but the fabrications of a few crafty or visionary men to take advantage of the credulity and superstition of the mass of the people. They call themselves the priests of perfect reason, and yet no two of them interpret the doctrines of Buddhism alike, and they keep the people in a perpetual state of distraction by their dissensions." He spoke for more than an hour, and supposed

[25] A place of worship.

he had made a great impression on his hearers ; but the moment he finished, one of the men said, —

"That is a nice gown the fellow has on ; let's take it."

"We should first cut his throat," said another, "so that he may not inform against us."

"Good ! good !" cried the rest of the wretches ; and, immediately seizing the philosopher, they were on the point of putting their murderous design in execution, when the great gong of the pagoda sounded the signal for the sunset prostrations. Instantly the robbers fell flat on their faces, with their noses buried in the dust, and Fou-fou, taking advantage of the circumstance, leaped over their prostrate bodies, and fled for safety to the joss-house. The chief priest, a venerable, long-bearded bonze, named Hum-drum, took him by the hand, chin-chinned[26] him three times, and thus addressed him,—

"Stranger, I have heard thy discourse, and witnessed thy mishap, which would have ended in thy robbery and murder, if thy assailants had not feared to incur the wrath of Buddh had they failed to perform the nine prostrations at the appointed hour. Thus do desperate and blood-thirsty men, who cannot be controlled by the fear of human laws, tremble before the terrors of a future punishment. Let this be a lesson to thee to rail no more against institutions that have saved thee from pillage and death. Thou canst rest with us this night, for we are enjoined to be charitable, even to those that despitefully use us.

"Eat, drink, and sleep, and to-morrow go thy way in peace." . . . .

. . . .

[26] The Chinese method of salutation.

25

The next day Fou-fou reached the city of Nintschang-yangtscheufu, the metropolis of the province of Yán-kee. It was in vain that he sought admittance to the public houses, for his clothes were, by this time, so travel-stained and soiled that he was regarded as a suspicious character. The Inspector of the Books,[27] at the hotel of the Three Perfections, told him there was no room for such unprofitable-looking customers; while the Guardian of the Portals,[28] at the House of Social Relations, threat-ened to kick him away if he did not leave quietly; con-sequently, he had no chance to repeat the exploit he had performed at the inn of the Five Felicities. So, having nothing else to do, he took his stand on the steps of the principal pagoda, and began to harangue the multitude; but, as every one was absorbed in the worship of a graven image of silver, called the "almighty dollar," very few persons stopped to listen to him, and those few merely laughed at him, for a moment, and then passed on. Now the Yan-kees were a practical people, and the last in all China among whom he would have been likely to find followers; but it happened that Chew-yung, a penniless opium-eater, accompanied by a drunken vaga-bond, named Rum-punch, were among those who heard him propound his theory of the distribution of property, and they were struck with the propriety of the proposi-tion, and immediately enrolled themselves among his disciples. The beggars of the city also gathered around him, attracted by the promising nature of his tenets, so that he soon found himself at the head of quite a numer-ous body of malcontents.. A revolution might have been the result, but the ensuing night being very cold, and his

---

[27] The clerk, or book-keeper.   [28] The porter.

followers, observing that he was clad in a warm, woollen gown, while they had almost nothing to cover their nakedness, made a second application of his doctrines to himself, and, stripping him of his last garment, divided it among themselves. In the morning the philosopher, Fou-fou, was found frozen to death.

After the demise of Fou-fou, his followers spread themselves over the empire; but their leader being gone, they no longer formed a homogeneous body; but, while adding to their numbers, split themselves into different sects (similar to the manner in which the learned tell us that some minute animals increase — by division[20]), each sect holding some tenet, or tenets, different from the others. These subdivisions repeated the process, and as the original type, according to natural philosophers, may, by natural selection, branch off into species and genera, which, in course of time, differ widely from each other, and from the parent stock, some hardly retaining a single characteristic of this latter, so the Foufouites, as they have spread over the earth, and been subjected to varying influences, have gradually become divided into an innumerable number of lodges, each one of which maintains some principles that are scouted by the others, while individuals are found who do not believe in one single precept promulgated by the founder of the order.

[20] Called, in modern scientific nomenclature, "Multiplication by Division." I would respectfully suggest to the Academy of Sciences, the more appropriate term of "The Logarithmic Method of Reproduction," since, by the division of the monads, other monads are subtracted from them.

CHAPTER XIV.

CONCLUSION.

The chapters of our book having reached the unlucky number of thirteen, we feel bound, as a true Foufouite, in justice to our publisher and ourself, to write a fourteenth in order to avert the misfortune notoriously attendant on the former figure. What Foufouite would make the 13th at table? Who would want to work 13 hours a day?. Who would pay 13 dollars for what he could get for less? Who would want to travel by a train that only went 13 miles an hour? How many more juries would disagree if they consisted of 13 instead of 12? What school-boy would want the multiplication table extended to 13? Who does not remember being whipped in his 13th year? What boy of 13 does not wish he was nearer the age of stove-pipe hats? What girl of that age does not look forward longingly to long frocks and beaux? What mother does not begin to feel anxious for her daughter when she reaches that age? What poor man would want 13 children? Who (unless a woman) would have 13 hats? Who could fall in love with a girl who had only 13 teeth? Who would want to wait 13 years for a wife, notwithstanding Jacob waited 14? What girl (with proper ideas) would look at a man with only 1300 a year? What wife would let her husband smoke 13 cigars after dinner? How many have been ruined by holding 13 cards? Who would take 13% for his money if he could get 14? Who would invest in a petroleum company that promised only 13%? What auctioneer stops at 13 if he can get 13 and a " aff"? Who would give 13 cents for a shilling if he could help it? What poet since the days of Byron (the most unhappy of men) has put 13 ideas into 13 lines? Who would want the toothache for 13 days? Who would boil an egg 13 minutes? Who would cut a pie in 13 pieces? Who would voluntarily listen to a sermon that extended to 13thly?

Having shown what a very unlucky number 13 is, we . could give an equally convincing demonstration of the folly of beginning anything on Friday ; but as this is generally acknowledged, we will forbear.

Dr. Goodenough has long since passed away, and the Society of Harmonians ceased to exist, but Foufouism still flourishes throughout the world among all nations. It is upheld by all classes and conditions of men and women, its insignia decorating the plebeian as well as the aristocrat, the ignorant and the learned, the poor and the rich. Gibbon considered the whole history of the Roman Empire too much for one man to undertake, and in this account of the decline and fall of Harmonianism we have confined our attention to a mere phase of Foufouism, leaving an immense field unexplored for future gleaners. We have purposely forborne from comments, believing it to be the duty of the historian to relate facts rather than to give opinions, and leaving it to the judicious reader to draw his own conclusions. We have not conformed to the usual practice of other great writers of putting the authority for each transaction in notes at the foot of the pages, partly because we wished to be original, and partly in order that the reader's attention might not be perpetually distracted from the important events narrated in the text.

Foufouism still exists, but in consequence perhaps of the discredit thrown on the order by the failure of the phalanstery, there are many weak-kneed brethren who not only shrink from avowing, but actually deny their connection with it. Hating gammon, nonsense, and hypocrisy, we, who have written this book, do not hesitate to acknowledge, openly, that we belong to the fraternity; and as there should be nothing secret in our society we shall now make known a few of the signs by which the public may recognize a Foufouite at a glance.

When a man, whether in speaking or writing, uses long words where short ones are better, it is *primâ facie* evidence that he is a candidate for admission into the society.

When you find an author using mystical "transcendental" language from which the thought (if there is any) can only be evolved by patient study, or the use of a dictionary, — and nineteen times out of twenty it is not worth the trouble, — you can rest assured that he is a Foufouite of the first water, and that his admirers likewise belong to the brotherhood. We have noticed, in the course of much miscellaneous reading, that whenever a writer has an idea that is really worth recording, he invariably takes pains to express it in the clearest language that his faculties can command.

Dunsbyism (if we may coin a word from Mr. Dickens) of any kind is an indubitable sign.

So also is affectation.

When you find a man sacrificing comfort to vain show you can set him down as one of our Grand Masters.

When you find a native citizen of the United States — a true-born Yankee — aping foreign manners, dress, or forms of speech, you may confidently point your finger and say, " There goes a Foufouite."

All those who prefer what is foreign to what is domestic, not because it is better (which it is too often), but because it is foreign, are claimed by us.

Any American who makes a parade of heraldic signs and devices (no matter how justly entitled to them according to the laws of heraldry) must have imbibed our principles.

In short, any native American, who is not also a true American, is a Foufouite.

All women, who talk politics or political economy, we hail as sisters.

Those who are called strong-minded hold a high place in our order.

All snobs are Foufouites, although all Foufouites are not, necessarily, snobs.

Many of the F. F. V.s also belong to the O. F.s.

Among the insignia of the order are flashy habiliments, mock jewelry, or even much of the real article, and the hat cocked over one eye. Self-conceit is the most infallible sign of all.

Foufouites flock to mock auctions; they support astrologers, mediums, seventh daughters, and people whose "sands of life have nearly run out;" they relieve importers from all sorts of worthless foreign rubbish; they rail at democratic institutions; they invest in lotteries (in Wall Street, as well as elsewhere); lose their money in gambling hells; squander it in rum-shops, and keep up the price of Greek and Latin dictionaries.

Notwithstanding that our, order includes; among its members, people of every station and condition of life, from kings upon their thrones, down to beggars in the streets, it is extremely rigid in its rules of admission, and no elevation of rank, no amount of wealth, will secure this privilege, unless the party has given proof of adherence to our principles. What those principles are, we do not feel at liberty to state; in fact, like the doctrines of Buddh, they are so numerous that probably no one individual knows the whole of them; for it should be borne in mind that Foufouism is older than freemasonry, and that every generation of men gives birth to some new principle, the adoption of which carries with it the appellation of Foufouite.

The moving words in which the historian of the Decline and Fall describes the completion of his great work are doubtless familiar to the reader; but it is necessary to have been in a similar position in order to fully appreciate them.

It is in the seclusion of our study — which is also our bedroom (and we will add our children's nursery) — that we are writing these last lines of the last page of our book. In parting with it we feel like parting with a familiar friend, for it has been our daily companion during nearly three long winter months; still, as the publisher tells us it may possibly pay, the poignancy of our regret at having finished it is somewhat alleviated.

The accomplishment of our laborious task has been attended by many drawbacks. Only future commentators will know the amount of research involved, by the ex-

treme difficulty they will have in hunting up our authorities. • We have perseveringly prosecuted our labors in
spite of constant interruption from our children, surrounded by the ruins of their Christmas toys, and our
attention constantly distracted by the gambols and noise
of their pets, a cat, two kittens, and three puppy-dogs.

Our son, six years of age, the heir to our name (would
we could add fortune), is climbing up on our shoulders,
and our little daughter is sitting on our knee. Having
just pinched their ears to keep them quiet, ours are the
only dry eyes amongst us. In this affecting manner we
take our leave of the reader, consoled by the reflection
that, while the life of the historian must be short and precarious, his book may long survive on the shelves of
second-hand book stores, and be of service to future generations of trunkmakers and hatters.

THE END.

NEW BOOKS
And New Editions Recently Published by
CARLETON, Publisher,
NEW YORK.

N.B.—The Publishers, upon receipt of the price in advance, will send any of the following Books by mail, postage free, to any part of the United States. This convenient and very safe mode may be adopted when the neighboring Book sellers are not supplied with the desired work. State name and address in full.

Victor Hugo.

LES MISÉRABLES.—The celebrated novel. One large 8vo volume, paper covers, $2.00 ; . . . cloth bound, $2.50

LES MISÉRABLES.—In the Spanish language. Fine 8vo. edition, two vols., paper covers, $4.00 ; . . cloth bound, $5.00

JARGAL.—A new novel. Illustrated. . 12mo. cloth, $1.75

THE LIFE OF VICTOR HUGO.—By himself. . 8vo. cloth, $1.75

Miss Muloch.

JOHN HALIFAX.—A novel. With illustration. 12mo. cloth, $1.75

A LIFE FOR A LIFE.— . do. do. $1.75

Charlotte Bronte (Currer Bell).

JANE EYRE.—A novel. With illustration. 12mo. cloth, $1.75

THE PROFESSOR.— do. . do. . do. .$1.75

SHIRLEY.— . do. . do. . do. $1.75

VILLETTE.— . do. . do. . do. $1.75

Hand-Books of Society.

THE HABITS OF GOOD SOCIETY ;. with thoughts, hints, and anecdotes, concerning nice points of taste, good manners, and the art of making oneself agreeable. The most entertaining work of the kind. .. . . 12mo. cloth, $1.75

THE ART OF CONVERSATION.—With directions for self-culture. A sensible and instructive work, that ought to be in the hands of every one who wishes to be either an agreeable talker or listener. . . . . 12mo. cloth, $1.50

THE ART OF AMUSING.—Graceful arts, games, tricks, and charades, intended to amuse everybody. With suggestions for private theatricals, tableaux, parlor and family amusements. Nearly 150 illustrative pictures. . 12mo. cloth, $2.00

Robinson Crusoe.

A handsome illustrated edition, complete. 12mo. cloth, $1.50

Mrs. Mary J. Holmes' Works.

'LENA RIVERS.—	. . .	A novel.	12mo. cloth,	$1.50
DARKNESS AND DAYLIGHT.—	.	do.	. do. .	$1.50
TEMPEST AND SUNSHINE.—	.	do.	. do. .	$1.50
MARIAN GREY.—	. . .	do.	. do. .	$1.50
MEADOW BROOK.—	. . .	do.	. do. .	$1.50
ENGLISH ORPHANS.—	. .	do.	. do. .	$1.50
DORA DEANE.—	. . .	do.	. do. .	$1.50
COUSIN MAUDE.—	. . .	do.	. do. .	$1.50
HOMESTEAD ON THE HILLSIDE.—		do.	. do. .	$1.50
HUGH WORTHINGTON.—	. .	do.	. do. .	$1.50
THE CAMERON PRIDE.—	. .	do.	. do. ..	$1.50
ROSE MATHER.—*Just Published.*		do.	. do. .	$1.50

Miss Augusta J. Evans.

BEULAH.—A novel of great power.			12mo. cloth,	$1.75
MACARIA.—	do.	do. . .	do. .	$1.75
ST. ELMO.—	do.	do. *Just Published.*	do. .	$2.00

By the Author of "Rutledge."

RUTLEDGE.—A deeply interesting novel.		12mo. cloth,	$1.75
THE SUTHERLANDS.—	do. . .	do. .	$1.75
FRANK WARRINGTON.—	do. . .	do. .	$1.75
ST. PHILIP'S.—	do. . .	do. .	$1.75
LOUIE'S LAST TERM AT ST. MARY'S.—	.	do. .	$1.75
ROUNDHEARTS AND OTHER STORIES.—For children.		do. .	$1.75
A ROSARY FOR LENT.—Devotional Readings.		do. .	$1.75

Captain Mayne Reid's Works—Illustrated.

THE SCALP HUNTERS.—		A romance.	12mo. cloth,	$1.75
THE RIFLE RANGERS.—	.	do.	. do. .	$1.75
THE TIGER HUNTER.—	.	do.	. do. .	$1.75
OSCEOLA, THE SEMINOLE.—	.	do.	. do. .	$1.75
THE WAR TRAIL.—	. .	do. ·	. do	. $1.75
THE HUNTER'S FEAST.—	.	do.	. do. .	$1.75
RANGERS AND REGULATORS.—		do.	. do. .	$1.75
THE WHITE CHIEF.—	. .	do.	. do. .	$1.75
THE QUADROON.—	. .	do.	. do. .	$1.75
THE WILD HUNTRESS.—	.	do.	. do. .	$1.75
THE WOOD RANGERS.—	.	do.	. do. .	$1.75
WILD LIFE.—	. . .	do.	. do. .	$1.75
THE MAROON.— .	. .	do.	. do. .-	$1.75
LOST LEONORE.—	. .	do.	. do. .	$1.75
THE HEADLESS HORSEMAN.—	.	do. .	. do. .	$1.75
THE WHITE GAUNTLET.—	*Just Published.*		do. .	$1.75